HTML
PROGRAMMER'S REFERENCE

HTML

PROGRAMMER'S REFERENCE

Thomas A. Powell and Dan Whitworth

Osborne/**McGraw-Hill**

Berkeley ▪ New York ▪ St. Louis ▪ San Francisco
Auckland ▪ Bogotá ▪ Hamburg ▪ London
Madrid ▪ Mexico City ▪ Milan ▪ Montreal
New Delhi ▪ Panama City ▪ Paris ▪ São Paulo
Singapore ▪ Sydney ▪ Tokyo ▪ Toronto

Osborne/**McGraw-Hill**
2600 Tenth Street
Berkeley, California 94710
U.S.A.

For information on translations or book distributors outside the U.S.A., or to
arrange bulk purchase discounts for sales promotions, premiums, or
fund-raisers, please contact Osborne/**McGraw-Hill** at the above address.

HTML Programmer's Reference

Publisher   Brandon A. Nordin
Editor-in-Chief   Scott Rogers
Acquisitions Editor   Megg Bonar
Project Editor   Emily Rader
Technical Editor   Bob Mullen
Copy Editors   Claire Splan, Andy Carroll
Proofreaders   Linda Medoff, Paul Medoff
Indexer   David Heiret
Computer Designer   Jean Butterfield
Illustrator   Brian Wells

34567890 DOC DOC 90198765432109

ISBN 0-07-882559-8

About the Authors...

Thomas A. Powell is the author of Osborne's *HTML: The Complete Reference*. His firm, Powell Internet Consulting, designs Web sites for large corporate clients. He is the developer of the Web Publishing Program at the University of California, San Diego, Extension.

Dan Whitworth provides editorial, writing, and HTML services for Powell Internet Consulting and its clients.

CONTENTS @ A GLANCE

CONTENTS

3   Special Characters   297

4   Color Reference   333

5   Reading a Document Type Definition . . . 341

INTRODUCTION

HTML is the core technology of the Web. Web pages rely on this markup language for structure and, unfortunately, often for presentation as well. There is a constant struggle between what HTML was designed to do and the needs of the people who use the technology. HTML has changed dramatically since its inception, and other technologies have been developed to complement its core facilities. Today HTML has many nuances and complexities that are unknown to all but those who study the specifications very carefully. This book describes the core elements of the HTML 4 specification, as well as many common elements introduced by Netscape, Microsoft, and WebTV that today's Web designers should find useful.

Chapter 1
General HTML

The Hypertext Markup Language (HTML) is a structured markup language used to create Web pages. A markup language like HTML is simply a collection of text codes, called *elements*, that are used to indicate the structure and format of a document. A user agent, usually a Web browser, interprets the meaning of these codes and renders a Web page appropriately.

HTML Elements

Elements in HTML consist of alphanumeric tokens within angle brackets, such as **<B>**, **<HTML>**, **<IMG>**, and **<H1>**.

Most elements consist of paired tags: a start tag and an end tag. The start tag is simply a symbol for the element, surrounded by angle brackets. The symbol for bold text is **B** and its start tag is **<B>**. An end tag is identical to a start tag except that the symbol is preceded by a forward slash: **</B>**. An element's instruction applies to whatever content is contained between its start and end tags:

`<B>`This text is bold`</B>` but this text is not.

Some elements, called *empty elements*, do not require an end tag because they do not enclose content. One example is the break element **
, which indicates a line break. Other elements do not require an end tag because the end of the content they affect can be inferred from surrounding elements. An example is the list item element **<HR>, which indicates a horizontal rule that occupies a line all its own. For some elements, such as the paragraph element **<P>**, an end tag is optional.

NOTE: Many people, including other HTML book authors, refer to all markup structures in HTML as tags. While this may be common parlance, the word "tag" refers only to the character sequences, such as **<B>** or **</B>**, that make up an element. The word "element" corresponds to the tags and the content they enclose. The distinction is not that important for most document authors, and most people will understand the use of the word "tag" at all times. However, "element" is the correct expression except when referring to the actual markup characters themselves.

HTML specifications define the type of content an element can enclose, or its *content model*. This can include other elements, text, a mixture of elements and text, or nothing at all. For example, the **<HEAD>** element provides general information about an HTML document. Its content model only allows it to contain a small number of related elements, such as **<TITLE>** and **<META>**. The content model for the bold element **<B>** allows it to enclose text and some elements, such as the one for italic **<I>**, but not others like **<HEAD>**. The content model of the break element **
** is *empty* because it encloses no content. Content models define the relationships that are possible between elements and content in valid HTML documents.

An HTML start tag can sometimes contain attributes that modify the element's meaning. Attributes within a tag's brackets must be separated from the element's name by at least one space. Some attributes are self-explanatory and indicate an effect simply by their name. An example is adding the **COMPACT** attribute to the ordered list element: **<OL COMPACT>**. Other attributes indicate an effect by assigning a value to their name. **<OL TYPE="I">** assigns the bullet type of an ordered list to uppercase roman numerals. An element may contain multiple attributes if those attributes are separated by at least one space, as in **<OL COMPACT TYPE="I">**.

A complete HTML element is defined by a start tag, an end tag (where applicable), possible attributes, and a content model. The diagram in Figure 1-1 shows an overview of the syntax of a typical HTML element.

HTML Rules

HTML is a well-specified language with rules that should be followed. Many documents that you find on the Internet may not follow these rules, but this does not mean that these rules are not important—just that they are not strictly enforced by all browsers. This has lead to somewhat sloppy coding styles. Following the rules is suggested, because while browsers should not

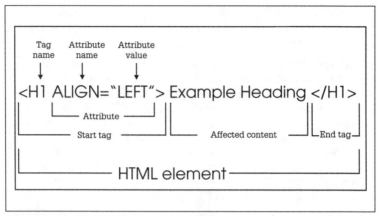

Figure 1-1.   HTML element example

misinterpret correct HTML, they may certainly misinterpret sloppy or proprietary HTML.

- **HTML documents are structured documents.** HTML is defined precisely using a document type definition, or DTD (defined later in this chapter under "Document Types"), written using SGML (Standard Generalized Markup Language). The DTD formally defines the structure of HTML documents. It defines what elements a document can contain, their possible relationships to one another inside a document, and their possible attributes and values. In the structural sense, an HTML document is a collection of items like paragraphs, lists, boldfaced entries, links, and so on. If the elements in an HTML document are well structured and agree with the formal definition, the document is said to be valid.

- **Element names are not case sensitive.** An element like **<hTml>** is equivalent to **<html>** or **<HTML>**. Element case does not matter to a browser. However, writing elements consistently in upper- or lowercase makes HTML documents easier to understand and maintain. Convention suggests that uppercase is the preferred practice.

- **Attribute names are not case sensitive.** **<HR NOSHADE>** is equivalent to **<HR noshade>** or **<HR NoShade>**. As with elements, consistent use of case improves legibility, and uppercase is preferred. Certain attribute names, particularly those for script event handling, are often put in lowercase or mixed case: **<B onClick="alert('Test')">** or **<B onclick="alert" ('Test')">**. While attribute names are not case sensitive, there are still conventions that should be followed.

- **Attribute values may be case sensitive.** The value of an attribute may be case sensitive, especially if it refers to a file. The filename in **<IMG SRC="filename.gif">** may not be the same as the filename in **<IMG SRC="FILENAME.GIF">**; it depends on whether or not case matters to the operating system of the server containing the file. For example, in the UNIX environment, filenames are case sensitive. Always specify a filename exactly as it has been saved, and consider using a consistent lowercase naming scheme that does not include special characters or spaces.

- **Element names cannot contain spaces.** Browsers treat the first space encountered inside an element as the end of an element's name and the beginning of its attributes. **<I M G>** does not mean **<IMG>**, the image element. It means **<I>**, the italic element, with two undefined attributes **M** and **G**.

- **Attribute values may contain spaces or special characters only if the value is enclosed by quotes.** Some attributes require a known value, usually a string like **LEFT**, **RIGHT**, or **CENTER**. These values do not require surrounding quotes unless they contain embedded spaces. Whether an attribute is user-defined or can contain only a specified value, it does not require quotes unless spaces or special characters occur within the value. For example, the values for the **SRC** and **ALT** attributes in the following element contain no spaces and therefore require no quotes.

```
<IMG SRC=dog.gif ALT=Rover>
```

Changing the value for the **ALT** attribute to My dog Rover introduces spaces into the value, and quotes must be added.

```
<IMG SRC=dog.gif ALT="My dog Rover">
```

Omitting quotes in the previous example assigns "My" to the **ALT** attribute and causes "dog" and "Rover" to be treated as two undefined attributes. Surrounding a value with quotes has no negative consequences if they are not required. For stylistic reasons, it is better to quote everything, because values might change. Values that contain any characters other than alphanumeric characters (a–z, A–Z, 0–9), dash (-), or period (.) must be quoted. Be careful with "special characters."

- **Browsers ignore space characters in HTML content.** Browsers will collapse any sequence of spaces, tabs, and returns in an HTML document into a single space character. These characters convey no formatting information unless they occur inside a special preformatting element like **<PRE>**, which preserves their meaning. Extra spacing can be used liberally within an HTML document to make it more legible to HTML authors.

- **HTML documents may contain comments.** HTML supports comments that are not displayed within a browser window. Comments are denoted by a start value of **<!--** and an end value of **-->**. Comments can be many lines long. For example,

```
<!--

          Document Name: My HTML Document
          Creation Date: 6/5/98

          (c) 1998 Big Company, Inc.
-->
```

  is a valid comment. Be careful not to put spaces among the dashes and exclamation point in the comment. Comments may also include HTML elements; however, older browsers may have problems with commented markup.

- **Elements should be nested and not crossed.** Elements often contain other elements inside the document section they enclose. Any element that starts within a section enclosed by another must also end there. An element's tag pairs should be nested within one another and their end tags should not cross, as shown here:

```
<B><I>Correct</I></B>

<B><I>Not correct</I></B>
```

- **Browsers ignore unknown elements.** Browsers ignore elements they do not understand, but they do attempt to interpret any content enclosed by an unknown element. If a browser does not understand the **<STORY>** element in **<STORY>**The Moon and Sixpence**</STORY>**, it ignores it. It does, however, render the words "The Moon and Sixpence" as normal text.

- **Browsers ignore unknown attributes.** Browsers ignore any attributes they do not understand. Technically, the imaginary

CLOWN attribute in the following example is well-formed HTML. Unless a browser happens to understand it, however, it is ignored.

```
<IMG CLOWN="BOZO" SRC="bozo.gif">
```

Browser Issues

In practice, the final arbiter of an HTML document's correctness is the browser used to view it. Browsers rarely enforce formally defined HTML, but liberally interpret what they treat as acceptable. They make guesses about unusual constructs and attempt to render whatever they receive. Because permissiveness varies from browser to browser, and even between different versions of the same browser, simply testing pages in a browser does not ensure portability of documents. This is one of the most challenging aspects of authoring an HTML document.

Standards should eventually help deal with browser issues, but for now they do not necessarily guarantee an acceptable document from a user's point of view. Authoring HTML to a recognized DTD and using a program called a *validator*, which checks that written code meets the specification, helps to ensure that documents are open to the widest possible audience. Most end users, however, do not concern themselves with such specifics, but draw their beliefs about appropriate code from how their browsers render that code. Even if a validator states that a document is correct, things may not work in a browser due to bugs in the software or a lack of standards compliance by the browser. It is always a good idea to test documents under an assortment of browsers, including Microsoft Internet Explorer, Netscape Navigator, WebTV, and even Lynx. They should also be tested on multiple platforms like Windows and Macintosh, when available. Understanding and following a formal HTML definition takes time and practice. However, the benefits to cross-platform rendering and document maintenance make it worthwhile. This is essential for large corporations with many documents. Fortunately, the path toward writing well-formed HTML documents does not require an initial understanding of the language's nuances. Well-formed documents share a common, easily comprehended document structure. Like peeling an onion, understanding this makes it easier to understand the nuances of HTML later, all the way down to the character level.

HTML Syntax

All well-written HTML documents share a common structure, as shown in Figure 1-2. An HTML document begins with a **<!DOCTYPE>** declaration indicating the version of HTML used by the document. Following this, the **<HTML>** element encloses the actual document. It contains two primary sections: the head and the body, enclosed respectively by the **<HEAD>** and **<BODY>** elements. The *head* contains identifying and other meta-information about the document. It always contains the document's title, enclosed by the **<TITLE>** element. The *body* contains the actual document content.

Document Types

HTML follows the SGML notation for defining structured documents. From SGML, HTML inherits the requirement that all documents begin with a **<!DOCTYPE>** declaration. In an HTML context, this identifies the HTML "dialect" used in a document by referring to an external *document type definition,* or *DTD.* A DTD defines the actual elements, attributes, and element relationships that are valid in the document. The **<!DOCTYPE>** declaration

```
<!DOCTYPE HTML PUBLIC "html version">
<HTML>
<HEAD>
<TITLE>Document Title</TITLE>
    ...Other supplementary information goes here...
</HEAD>
<BODY>
    ...Marked-up text goes here...
</BODY>
</HTML>
```

Figure 1-2.   HTML document template

allows validation software to identify the HTML DTD being followed in a document and verify that the document is syntactically correct. Any HTML construct not defined in the document's DTD should not occur. The **<!DOCTYPE>** declaration for the strict version of HTML 4 is shown here:

```
<!DOCTYPE HTML PUBLIC "-//W3C//DTD HTML 4.0//EN">
```

The HTML document template suggests always using a **<!DOCTYPE>** declaration. In some cases this may not be practical. Including a DTD declaration conveys the intention to follow it. It is better to omit a **<!DOCTYPE>** declaration than to include one that will not be followed. (For a more detailed discussion of DTDs, see Chapter 5.)

The <HTML> Element

The **<HTML>** element delimits the beginning and the end of an HTML document. It contains only the **<HEAD>** element and the **<BODY>** element. The HTML document template shown previously in Figure 1-2 displays the typical use of the **<HTML>** element as a container for all other elements in a document. The **<HEAD>** element is optional; the HTML 4 DTD does not require its use, nor do popular browsers. However, including it structures a document more clearly by separating the content of the document from the information that is used to describe the content.

NOTE: Chapter 2 contains detailed discussions of all of the HTML elements.

The <HEAD> Element

The **<HEAD>** element encloses a document section that contains identification and supplementary information about the document. Browsers do not generally display this information directly, though the effects of this information, particularly of scripts and style sheets, may be very obvious. Including the **<HEAD>** element in a document is not technically necessary, because its boundaries can always be inferred. Nevertheless, it should always be included for document style and legibility. In the HTML 4 DTD, the elements allowed within the **<HEAD>** element include **<BASE>**, **<ISINDEX>**, **<LINK>**, **<META>**, **<OBJECT>**, **<SCRIPT>**, **<STYLE>**, and **<TITLE>**. These are described in the following table.

Element	Description
<BASE>	Defines base URL for all relative URLs in a document
<ISINDEX>	Indicates that a document has a searchable keyword index
<LINK>	Defines relationships between a document and other documents (table of contents, style sheets, etc.)
<META>	Defines information about a document, usually for indexing
<OBJECT>	Defines an object to be included in an HTML document
<SCRIPT>	Encloses scripting language statements for client-side processing
<STYLE>	Encloses style sheet rules for a document
<TITLE>	Defines the document title (see the following section)

The <TITLE> Element

The **<TITLE>** element is the only element that must be used in every HTML document. It gives an HTML document a title by which it is known to browsers and indexing robots. Browsers display the document title while it is being viewed, generally at the top of the browser window, and they also use the title in bookmark lists. A document title may contain standard text and character entities (for example, **©**), which are briefly discussed later in this chapter. HTML markup is not permitted in a **<TITLE>** element. There should only be one **<TITLE>** element in a document, and it should always be placed in the head of the document.

The <BODY> Element

The body of an HTML document is delimited by **<BODY>** and **</BODY>**. Under the HTML 4 specification, the **<BODY>** element is optional, but should be included. There can be only one **<BODY>** element per document. Common **<BODY>** attributes include **BGCOLOR** (background color); **BACKGROUND** (background image); **TEXT** (body text color); and **LINK**, **ALINK**, and **VLINK** (colors for links, active links, and visited links).

The **<BODY>** element may contain many other HTML elements. These fall into three distinct groups: block-level elements, text-level elements, and character entities.

Block-Level Elements

Block-level elements define structural content blocks like paragraphs or lists. If a document is written carefully in a block style, it may be possible to improve its machine readability. Block-level elements include paragraphs, divisions, headings, preformatted text, lists, tables, forms, and other elements. The basic idea of a block-structured document is illustrated in Figure 1-3.

Paragraphs

Surrounding text with the **<P>** and **</P>** tags indicates that the text is a logical paragraph unit. (As discussed later in this chapter, logical elements define *what* their content is, in a structural sense, but not necessarily *how* it should be displayed.) Browsers usually place a blank line or two before the paragraph, but the exact rendering of the text depends on the browser. Text within the **<P>** element is normally rendered flush left with a ragged right margin. The **ALIGN** attribute makes it possible to specify a left, right, center, or justified alignment. The closing tag for this element is optional.

Divisions

The **<DIV>** element structures HTML documents into unique sections or divisions. Adding the **ALIGN** attribute makes it possible to align a portion of the document to the left, right, or center, and

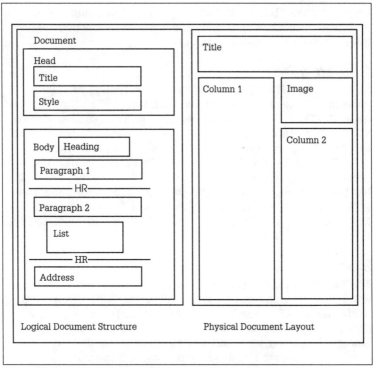

Figure 1-3. Outline of a block-structured document

under some browsers to justify the text. By default, content within the **<DIV>** element is left-aligned. Divisions are also useful when used in conjunction with style sheets or with scripts, particularly for moving regions around the screen.

Headings

The six different heading elements are used to create "headlines" in documents. These range in importance from **<H1>**, the most important, to **<H6>**, the least important. Most browsers display headings in a larger and/or bolder font than normal text. Many HTML authors think of heading elements as formatting that makes text bigger or bolder. In fact, heading elements convey logical meaning about a document's structure. Sizing and weight are relative to the importance of the heading, so **<H1>** level headings are larger than **\<H3\>** headings. Text included in heading elements is displayed on a line of its own, and visual browsers generally insert an extra line after a heading.

Centered Text

In the original HTML 2–based browsers, centering text was impossible. One of the major additions introduced by Netscape was the **\<CENTER\>** element. Later versions of HTML, such as version 3.2, adopted this element because of its widespread use. To center text or embedded objects, simply enclose the content within **\<CENTER\>** and **\</CENTER\>**. While **\<CENTER\>** appears to be a text-formatting style element, since the HTML 3.2 specification it has been defined as a block-level structuring element. Under the HTML 4 DTD, **\<CENTER\>** is an alias for **\<DIV ALIGN="center"\>**. Note that **\<DIV ALIGN="center"\>** can also cause an unwanted line feed, while **\<CENTER\>** does not.

Block Quotes

The **\<BLOCKQUOTE\>** element encloses large block quotations within a document. Enclosing text within **\<BLOCKQUOTE\>** and **\</BLOCKQUOTE\>** usually indents the blocked information. Like a paragraph element, text within the **\<BLOCKQUOTE\>** element ignores all spacing, tabs, and returns and requires the use of **\<BR\>** or other elements to modify line wrapping and spacing.

Preformatted Text

The **\<PRE\>** and **\</PRE\>** tags can be used to surround text that should not be formatted by the browser. The text enclosed within the **\<PRE\>** element retains all its spacing and returns, and does not reflow when the browser is resized. Scroll bars and horizontal scrolling are required if the lines are longer than the width of the window. The browser generally renders the preformatted text in a monospaced font, usually Courier. Limited text formatting, such as bold, italics, or links, can be used within the **\<PRE\>** tags.

Lists

There are three basic forms of lists in modern HTML: ordered lists (**\<OL\>**), unordered lists (**\<UL\>**), and definition lists (**\<DL\>**). Two other rarely used list elements, **\<MENU\>** and **\<DIR\>**, are sparsely supported and are usually treated as an unordered list. Lists are block formatting elements that define a block structure. They can be nested, and can contain other block-level structures, such as paragraphs. In all cases, the list item element **<LI>** is used to define list items, and to mark them with a bullet or a number.

Horizontal Rules

A horizontal rule, indicated by the **<HR>** element, is a block-level element that can be used to divide HTML documents into visually distinct regions. **<HR>** can have some logical meaning as a section break. Under an alternative browser, such as a speech-based browser, a horizontal rule might theoretically be interpreted as a pause. A hand-held browser with limited resolution might use it as a device to limit the text that is displayed, until it is scrolled to on the page. Commonly used **<HR>** attributes include **ALIGN**, **NOSHADE** (removes default shading effects), **SIZE** (defines rule thickness in pixels), and **WIDTH** (defines width by pixels or percentage).

Addresses

The **<ADDRESS>** element is used to surround information such as the signature of the person who created the page or the address of the organization the page is about. The HTML specification treats **<ADDRESS>** as an idiosyncratic block-level element. Like other block-level elements, it inserts a blank line before and after the block; and browsers tend to render it as italicized text. It may enclose many lines of text, formatting elements to change the font characteristics, and even images. According to the specification, it is not supposed to enclose other block-level elements such as **<UL>**. Browsers generally allow this, though, particularly with the paragraph element.

Tables

Tables represent information in a tabular way, like a spreadsheet, in rows and columns. Because many HTML documents rely less on text than their printed equivalents, Web-based tables have become an important way to structure documents. In its simplest form, a table places information inside the cells formed by dividing a rectangle into rows and columns. The syntax of tables is relatively complex and includes the ability to set individual table cell characteristics. The basic elements for creating tables are **<TABLE>**, **<TR>**, and **<TD>**; these and the rest are listed in the following. For a complete discussion, look up each of these elements in Chapter 2.

Element	Description
<TABLE>	Defines a table
<TR>	Defines table rows
<TD>	Defines table data cells
<TH>	Defines a table header
<CAPTION>	Defines a table caption
<THEAD>	Defines a table header
<TFOOT>	Defines a table footer
<TBODY>	Defines a table body
<COL>	Defines a column within a table
<COLGROUP>	Creates column groups within a table

Forms

Forms are commonly used on the Web as a way to collect comments, to allow users to order products, and to gather information about users. The **<FORM>** element and its associated elements (see the following table) allow for the creation of forms, ranging from simple text entry fields to more complex multiple-field forms. Regular HTML markup elements, including both block- and text-level elements, can be used within the **<FORM>** element.

Element	Description
<FIELDSET>	Groups related elements within the <FORM> element; may include any of the elements listed in this table
<INPUT>	Creates an input control for a form
<TEXTAREA>	Creates a multiple-line text input field contained within a form
<SELECT>	Creates a pull-down menu
<OPTION>	Specifies choices on a pull-down menu, defined by <SELECT>
<BUTTON>	Creates a clickable button associated with an <INPUT> field
<LABEL>	Creates a label associated with an <INPUT> field
<LEGEND>	Creates a caption associated with a <FIELDSET> grouping

Text-Level Elements

While block elements are used to create groups or sections in a document, they usually contain content, typically text. The text within block elements can also be formatted using text-level elements. There are two kinds of text elements in HTML: physical and logical. *Physical elements,* such as **<B>** for bold and **<I>** for italic, are used to specify how text should be rendered. *Logical elements,* such as **<STRONG>** and **<EM>**, indicate what text is, but not necessarily how it should look. While there are common renderings for logical text elements, the ambiguity of these elements and the limited knowledge of this type of document structuring have minimized their use. The rise of style sheets and the growing diversity of user agents will most likely lead to a significant increase in the use of logical elements.

Physical Character-Formatting Elements

Common HTML supports a number of elements that can be used to influence physical formatting. The elements have no meaning other than to make text render a particular way. Any other meaning is assigned by the reader. The following table shows some common physical elements.

Element	Description
<I> ... </I>	Italic
<B> ... </B>	Bold
<TT> ... </TT>	Teletype (monospaced)
<U> ... </U>	Underline
<STRIKE> ... </STRIKE>	Strikethrough
<S> ... </S>	Alternative form of strikethrough
_{...}	Subscript
^{...}	Superscript
<BIG> ... </BIG>	Bigger font (one font size bigger)
<SMALL> ... </SMALL>	Smaller font (one font size smaller)

Logical Elements

Logical elements indicate the type of content the elements enclose. The browser is then relatively free to determine the presentation of that content, although there are expected renderings for these elements that are followed by nearly all browsers. While this conforms to the design of HTML, there are issues about perception. Will a designer think "strong" or "bold"? HTML purists push for strong, since a browser for the blind could read strong text properly. For the majority of people coding Web pages, however, HTML is used as a visual language, despite its design intentions. A quick survey of sites shows that logical text elements are still relatively rare. When style sheets become more commonplace, HTML authors may want to reexamine their use of these elements. The following table illustrates the logical text-formatting elements generally supported by browsers.

Element	Description
<CITE> ... </CITE>	Citation
<CODE> ... </CODE>	Source code
<DFN> ... </DFN>	Definition
<EM> ... <EM>	Emphasis
<KBD> ... </KBD>	Keystrokes
<SAMP> ... </SAMP>	Sample (example information)
<STRONG> ... </STRONG>	Strong emphasis
<VAR> ... </VAR>	Programming variable

Breaks

Browsers usually insert blank lines between individual paragraphs, and tend to collapse empty <P> elements since they represent logical units, not physical formatting. To insert a return, the <BR> element must be used. The <BR> element is a text-level element that inserts a single carriage return or break into a document.

Links

Linking between documents, or between sections of the same document, is one of the most important aspects of HTML. Links can employ complete URLs (Uniform Resource Locators) to connect to any HTML document anywhere on the Web. They can also use "relative" links that define a path to another document on the same system as the referring document. The anchor element **<A>** is used with text or images to create clickable hyperlinks in the body of an HTML document. The **HREF** attribute defines the URL or path of the document or object being linked. (URLs are not limited to HTML documents; for a more detailed discussion of URLs, see Appendix A.)

The **<LINK>** element, which is used only in the head of an HTML document, is used to define relationships between documents (such as identifying a table of contents) or to link the document to an external style sheet.

Images

Images can be placed in HTML documents using the **<IMG>** element. The **SRC** attribute specifies the source of the image using a URL or a relative path. Typically, images included are in the GIF or JPEG format, but the choice of the image to include is only limited by what a browser may support, which could include PNG or other formats. Once an image has been included in a document, a variety of attributes can be used to modify the properties of the included object. The **ALIGN** attribute determines an image's position relative to text flow and other content. The **HEIGHT** and **WIDTH** attributes are particularly important. A browser will download an image whose dimensions are not defined in the HTML document, but setting the **HEIGHT** and **WIDTH** attributes to the image's dimensions will allow the browser to reserve space for the image and preserve page layout during download. The **HEIGHT** and **WIDTH** attributes can also be used to resize an image, but this often leads to image distortion; it is better to resize images using a graphics-manipulation program before you load them on the server. The **HSPACE** and **VSPACE** attributes create horizontal and vertical spaces, respectively, around an image. The **<IMG>** element can be placed within the **<A>** element to create graphic hyperlinks. (A nonlinked image will not display a border unless the **BORDER** attribute is set to the desired width; however, a linked image *will* display a one-pixel border by default, unless the image border is set to zero: **<IMG SRC="picture.gif" BORDER= "0">**.) The **ALT** attribute provides alternate text (**<IMG SRC= "art.jpg" ALT="This is a Degas">**) that displays while the image is loading or when a browser's image display is turned off; in some more recent browsers, **ALT** text also displays as a tool tip when the cursor passes over the image.

Images may also be used as background images for HTML documents by using the **BACKGROUND** attribute of the **<BODY>** element.

Binary Objects

Images are not directly part of HTML. Images are binary objects that are included, or pulled into, a Web page. Other binary objects—videos, animations, sound files, and programs—can be also pulled into Web pages. Initially, since there was no way to insert an object like a video into a Web page inline, the only option was to link to it. Viewers could click on the link to launch a helper application to view a movie or hear an audio clip. Browser vendors have introduced special extensions to handle these new media types, but the long-term solution is to handle all media types in a similar fashion, as plain binary objects.

Embedded Objects (Plug-ins)

While not part of the HTML 4 specification, the **<EMBED>** element is widely used to embed objects, often multimedia objects, in HTML documents. In general, the **<EMBED>** element takes an **SRC** attribute to specify the URL of the included binary object. The **HEIGHT** and **WIDTH** attributes often are used to indicate the pixel dimensions of the included object, if it is visible. To embed a short AVI (Audio Video Interleaved) format movie called welcome.avi that could be viewed by a browser video plug-in, such as Netscape's LiveVideo, we would use the following HTML fragment:

```
<EMBED SRC="welcome.avi" HEIGHT="100" WIDTH="100">
```

Beyond **HEIGHT** and **WIDTH**, common attributes include **ALIGN**, **HIDDEN**, **HSPACE**, **ID**, **PALETTE**, **PLUGINSPAGE**, **TITLE**, and **VSPACE**. Some of these attributes, such as **ALIGN**, **HSPACE**, and **VSPACE**, work just like those for the **<IMG>** element. In fact, **<EMBED>**, **<IMG>**, and other binary inclusion HTML elements all act very similarly, which leads to the introduction of a common inclusion element called **<OBJECT>**, discussed later in this chapter.

Java Applets

It is also possible to insert new media forms into a Web page using Sun Microsystems' Java technology (http://www.javasoft.com). It uses small Java programs, called *applets*. Most popular browsers now support Java. When applets are referenced in a Web page using the **<APPLET>** element, they are downloaded and run directly within a browser to provide new functionality or media forms like animation or video. The **<APPLET>** element specifies the Java applet to run by specifying a URL to a class file containing the Java byte code. To set the applet to run, set the **CODE** attribute equal to the URL of the Java class. The **CODEBASE** attribute can also be used to set a base URL reference for the **CODE** attribute. Other basic **<APPLET>** attributes include **ALIGN, HEIGHT, WIDTH, HSPACE, VSPACE,** and **ALT.** Within the **<APPLET>** and **</APPLET>** tags, the user may specify parameters or arguments to the applet using the **<PARAM>** element. Plain text may also appear between the **<APPLET>** and **</APPLET>** tags. A small example of how **<APPLET>** might be used is shown here:

```
<APPLET CODE="http://www.bigcompany.com/java/test.class"
        ALIGN="LEFT"
        HEIGHT="100"
        WIDTH="100"
        HSPACE="10"
        VSPACE="10">
<PARAM NAME="caption" value="Hello World">
</APPLET>
```

ActiveX Controls and Generic Objects

The **<OBJECT>** element is the World Wide Web Consortium–defined way to include an arbitrary object in a Web page. Microsoft's ActiveX technology was the first technology to use this HTML style. ActiveX controls are small binary components that are downloaded to a user's system and may be accessed from within the Web page. Using **<OBJECT>** with an ActiveX control requires the page author to specify the **CLASSID** value that corresponds to the object being inserted. This unique code might be something like **CLSID:99B42120-6EC7-11CF-A6C7-00AA00A47DD2.** A variety of data items must be passed to the ActiveX control via the **<PARAM>** element, which is included numerous times within the **<OBJECT>** element. The **<PARAM>** element usually has an attribute called **NAME,** which sets the name of the parameter, and an attribute called **VALUE,** which sets the value of the parameter to the control. The individual **<PARAM>** elements are used to pass information to an included object to modify its function or appearance. For example, look at the code fragment shown here, which is used to insert a simple graphical label, and notice how the **FontName** is set to "Arial" using the **<PARAM>** element.

```
<OBJECT ID="IeLabel1" WIDTH=122 HEIGHT=57
   CLASSID="CLSID:99B42120-6EC7-11CF-A6C7-00AA00A47DD2">
   <PARAM NAME="_ExtentX" VALUE="2582">
   <PARAM NAME="_ExtentY" VALUE="1207">
   <PARAM NAME="Caption" VALUE="Test Label">
   <PARAM NAME="Angle" VALUE="0">
   <PARAM NAME="Alignment" VALUE="4">
   <PARAM NAME="Mode" VALUE="1">
   <PARAM NAME="FillStyle" VALUE="0">
   <PARAM NAME="ForeColor" VALUE="#000000">
   <PARAM NAME="BackColor" VALUE="#C0C0C0">
   <PARAM NAME="FontName" VALUE="Arial">
   <PARAM NAME="FontSize" VALUE="12">
</OBJECT>
```

While ActiveX controls were initially the first binary forms to use the <OBJECT> element, in the future all binary objects, including images, will probably use this form. The W3C is attempting to standardize included binary data by adopting a generalized approach to binary data using the <OBJECT> element. The syntax of the <OBJECT> element, when used in this manner, is best generated by tools since it is so variable, as shown by the multitude of parameter values that may have to be set. The inclusion of binary forms shows the compound document style of HTML documents.

Character Entities

The last aspect of HTML documents to be discussed are the actual characters themselves. Sometimes it is necessary to put special characters within a document. These include accented letters, copyright symbols, or even the angle brackets used to enclose HTML elements. To use such characters in an HTML document, they must be "escaped" using a special code. All character codes take the form **&*code*;**, where *code* is a word or numeric code indicating the actual character you want to put on the screen. For example, the code **©** places the copyright symbol (©) in an HTML document. The character set currently supported by HTML is the ISO Latin-1 character set. Many of its characters, such as accents and special symbols, cannot be typed on all keyboards. They must be entered into HTML documents using the appropriate code. A complete list of the character entities and their browser support is presented in Chapter 3.

Chapter 2
HTML Elements

This chapter provides a complete reference of the HTML 4 specification elements and the elements commonly supported by Netscape, Internet Explorer, and WebTV. Some elements presented here may be nonstandard or depreciated, but are included because browser vendors continue to support them or they are still in common use. The standard used in this text is the final version of HTML 4 as defined on December 18, 1997, and available at http://www.w3.org/TR/REC-html40/.

Core Attributes Reference

The HTML 4 specification provides four main attributes, which are common to nearly all elements and have the same meaning for all elements. These elements are **ID**, **CLASS**, **STYLE**, and **TITLE**.

ID

This attribute specifies a unique alphanumeric identifier to be associated with an element. Naming an element is important to being able to access it with a style sheet, a link, or a scripting language. Names should be unique to a document and should be meaningful, so while **ID="x1"** is perfectly valid, **ID="Paragraph1"** might be better. Values for the **ID** attribute must begin with a letter (A–Z and a–z) and may be followed by any number of letters, digits, hyphens, and periods.

One potential problem with the **ID** attribute is that for some elements, particularly form controls and images, the **NAME** attribute already serves its function. Values for **NAME** should not collide with values for **ID**, as they share the same naming space. For example, the following would not be allowed:

```
<B ID="elementX">This is a test.</B>
<IMG NAME="elementX" SRC="image.gif">
```

There is some uncertainty about what to do to ensure backward compatibility with browsers that understand **NAME** but not **ID**. Some people suggest that the following is illegal:

```
<IMG NAME="image1" ID="image1" SRC="image.gif">
```

Since **NAME** and **ID** are naming the same item, there should be no problem; the common browsers do not have an issue with such markup. Complex scripting necessary to deal with two different names for the image, like

```
<IMG NAME="image1name" ID="image1id" SRC="image.gif">
```

is possible, but may not be necessary.

Page designers are encouraged to pick a naming strategy and use it consistently. Once elements are named, they should be easy to manipulate with a scripting language.

Like the **CLASS** attribute, the **ID** attribute is also used by style sheets for accessing a particular element.

For example, an element named **Paragraph1** can be referenced by a style rule in a document-wide style using a fragment identifier:

```
#Paragraph1    {color: blue}
```

Once an element is named using **ID**, it is also a potential destination for an anchor. In the past an **<A>** element was used to set a destination; now any element may be a destination. For example,

```
<A HREF="#firstbolditem">Go to first bold element.</B>
<B ID="firstbolditem">This is important.</B>
```

CLASS

This attribute is used to indicate the class or classes that a particular element belongs to. A class name is used by a style sheet to associate style rules to multiple elements at once. For example, it may be desirable to associate a special class name called "important" with all elements that should be rendered with a yellow background. Since class values are not unique to a particular element, **<B CLASS="important">** could be used as well as **<P CLASS="important">** in the same document. It is also possible to have multiple values for the **CLASS** attribute separated by white space; **<STRONG CLASS="important special-font">** would define two classes with the particular **<STRONG>** element. Currently, most browsers recognize only one class name for this attribute.

STYLE

This attribute specifies an inline style (as opposed to an external style sheet) associated with the element. The style information is used to determine the rendering of the affected element. Because the **STYLE** attribute allows style rules to be used directly with the element, it gives up much of the benefit of style sheets that divide the presentation of an HTML document from its structure. An example of this attribute's use is shown here:

```
<STRONG STYLE="font-family: Arial;
font-size: 18pt">Important text</STRONG>
```

TITLE

This attribute supplies advisory text for the element that may be rendered as a tool tip when the mouse is over the element. A title may also simply provide information that alerts future document maintainers to the meaning of the element and its enclosed content. In some cases, such as the **<A>** element, the **TITLE** attribute may provide additional help in bookmarking. Like the title for the document itself, **TITLE** attribute values as advisory information should be short, yet useful. For example, **<P TITLE= "paragraph1">** provides little information of value, while **<P TITLE= "HTML Programmer's Reference: Chapter 1, Paragraph 10">** provides much more detail. When combined with scripting, it may provide facilities for automatic index generation.

Language Reference

One of the main goals of the HTML 4 specification is better support for other languages besides English. The use of other languages in a Web page may require that text direction be changed from left to right or right to left. Furthermore, once supporting non-ASCII languages becomes easier, it may be more common to see documents in mixed languages. Thus, there must be a way to indicate the language in use.

LANG

This attribute indicates the language being used for the enclosed content. The language is identified using the ISO standard language abbreviation such as fr for French, en for English, and so on. RFC 1766 (ftp://ds.internic.net/rfc/rfc1766.txt) describes these codes and their format.

DIR

This attribute sets the text direction as related to the **LANG** attribute. The accepted values under the HTML 4 specification are **LTR** (left to right) and **RTL** (right to left). It should be possible to override whatever direction a user agent sets by using the **<BDO>** element. However, no browsers yet support this attribute.

Events Reference

In preparation for a more dynamic Web, the W3C (World Wide Web Consortium) has defined a set of core events that are associated with nearly every HTML element. Most of these events cover simple user interaction such as the click of a mouse button or a key being pressed. A few elements, such as form controls, have some special events associated with them, signaling that the field has received focus from the user or that the form was submitted. Last, intrinsic events like document loading and unloading are also described. The core events are summarized in the following table.

Event Attribute	Event Description	Allowed Elements Under HTML 4
onblur	Occurs when an element loses focus, meaning that the user has moved focus to another element, typically either by clicking the mouse on it or tabbing to it.	\<A>, \<AREA>, \<BUTTON>, \<INPUT>, \<LABEL>, \<SELECT>, \<TEXTAREA> Also \<APPLET>, \<AREA>, \<DIV>, \<EMBED>, \<HR>, \<IMG>, \<MARQUEE>, \<OBJECT>, \<SPAN>, \<TABLE>, \<TD>, \<TR> (Internet Explorer 4); \<BODY> (Internet Explorer 4 and Netscape 4); \<FRAMESET>, \<ILAYER>, \<LAYER> (Netscape 4)
onchange	Signals that the form control has lost user focus and its value has been modified during its last access.	\<INPUT>, \<SELECT>, \<TEXTAREA>
onclick	Indicates that the element has been clicked.	Most display elements* Also \<APPLET>, \<FONT> (Internet Explorer 4)
ondblclick	Indicates that the element has been double-clicked.	Most display elements* Also \<APPLET>, \<FONT> (Internet Explorer 4)

2

Event Attribute	Event Description	Allowed Elements Under HTML 4
onfocus	The focus event describes when an element has received focus, namely, it has been selected for manipulation or data entry.	<A>, <AREA>, <BUTTON>, <INPUT>, <LABEL>, <SELECT>, <TEXTAREA> Also <APPLET>, <DIV>, <EMBED>, <HR>, <IMG>, <MARQUEE>, <OBJECT>, <SPAN>, <TABLE>, <TD>, <TR> (Internet Explorer 4); <BODY>(window) (Netscape 4, Internet Explorer 4); <FRAMESET>, <ILAYER>, <LAYER> (Netscape 4)
onkeydown	Indicates that a key is being pressed down with focus on the element.	Most display elements* Also <APPLET>, <FONT> (Internet Explorer 4)
onkeypress	Describes the event of a key being pressed and released with focus on the element.	Most display elements* Also <APPLET>, <FONT> (Internet Explorer 4)
onkeyup	Indicates that a key is being released with focus on the element.	Most display elements* Also <APPLET>, <FONT> (Internet Explorer 4)

Event Attribute	Event Description	Allowed Elements Under HTML 4
onload	Indicates the event of a window or frame set finishing loading a document.	<BODY>, <FRAMESET> Also <APPLET>, <EMBED>, <LINK>, <SCRIPT>, <STYLE> (Internet Explorer 4); <ILAYER>, <IMG>, <LAYER> (Netscape 4, Internet Explorer 4)
onmousedown	Indicates the press of a mouse button with focus on the element.	Most display elements* Also <APPLET>, <FONT> (Internet Explorer 4)
onmousemove	Indicates that the mouse has moved while over the element.	Most display elements* Also <APPLET> and <FONT> (Internet Explorer 4)
onmouseout	Indicates that the mouse has moved away from an element.	Most display elements* Also <APPLET>, <FONT> (Internet Explorer 4); <ILAYER>, <LAYER> (Netscape 4)
onmouseover	Indicates that the mouse has moved over an element.	Most display elements* Also <APPLET>, <FONT> (Internet Explorer 4); <ILAYER>, <LAYER> (Netscape 4)
onmouseup	Indicates the release of a mouse button with focus on the element.	Most display elements* Also <APPLET>, <FONT> (Internet Explorer 4)

Event Attribute	Event Description	Allowed Elements Under HTML 4
onreset	Indicates that the form is being reset, possibly by the press of a reset button.	<FORM>
onselect	Indicates the selection of text by the user, typically by highlighting the desired text.	<INPUT>, <TEXTAREA>
onsubmit	Indicates a form submission, generally by pressing a submit button.	<FORM>
onunload	Indicates that the browser is leaving the current document and unloading it from the window or frame.	<BODY>, <FRAMESET>

*Note that, in the table, "most display elements" means all elements except **<APPLET>**, **<BASE>**, **<BASEFONT>**, **<BDO>**, **
, **<FONT>, **<FRAME>**, **<FRAMESET>**, **<HEAD>**, **<HTML>**, **<IFRAME>**, **<ISINDEX>**, **<META>**, **<PARAM>**, **<SCRIPT>**, **<STYLE>**, and **<TITLE>**.

This event model is far from complete, and it is still not fully supported by browsers. The event model should be considered a work in progress. It will certainly change as the Document Object Model (DOM) is more carefully defined. More information about the DOM can be found at http://www.w3.org/DOM/.

Extended Events

Browsers may support other events than those defined in the preliminary HTML 4 specification. Microsoft in particular has introduced a variety of events to capture more complex mouse actions like dragging, element events like the bouncing of

<MARQUEE> text, and data-binding events signaling the loading of data. (Mouse events may be bound to data in a database.) The events are described in more detail in the following table.

CAUTION: Documentation errors may exist. Microsoft currently documents events in the object model, not in the HTML reference. On inspection, some events are obviously not supported or may have been omitted. Events were tested by the author for accuracy, but for an accurate, up-to-date event model for these browsers, visit http://developer.netscape.com or http://www.microsoft.com/sitebuilder.

Event Attribute	Event Description	Associated Elements	Compatibility
onabort	Triggered by the user aborting the image load with a stop button or similar effect.	<IMG>	Netscape 3, 4; Internet Explorer 4
onafterupdate	Fires after the transfer of data from the element to a data provider, namely, a data update.	<APPLET>, <BODY>, <BUTTON>, <CAPTION>, <DIV>, <EMBED>, <IMG>, <INPUT>, <MARQUEE>, <OBJECT>, <SELECT>, <TABLE>, <TD>, <TEXTAREA>, <TR>	Internet Explorer 4
onbeforeunload	Fires just prior to a document being unloaded from a window.	<BODY>, <FRAMESET>	Internet Explorer 4

Event Attribute	Event Description	Associated Elements	Compatibility
onbeforeupdate	Triggered before the transfer of data from the element to the data provider. May be triggered explicitly or by a loss of focus or a page unload forcing a data update.	<APPLET>, <BODY>, <BUTTON>, <CAPTION>, <DIV>, <EMBED>, <HR>, <IMG>, <INPUT>, <OBJECT>, <SELECT>, <TABLE>, <TD>, <TEXTAREA>, <TR>	Internet Explorer 4
onbounce	Triggered when the bouncing contents of a marquee touch one side or another.	<MARQUEE>	Internet Explorer 4
ondataavailable	Fires when data arrives from data sources that transmit information asynchronously.	<APPLET>, <OBJECT>	Internet Explorer 4
ondataset-changed	Triggered when the initial data is made available from data source or when the data changes.	<APPLET>, <OBJECT>	Internet Explorer 4
ondataset-complete	Indicates that all the data is available from the data source.	<APPLET>, <OBJECT>	Internet Explorer 4

Event Attribute	Event Description	Associated Elements	Compatibility
ondragdrop	Triggered when the user drags an object onto the browser window to attempt to load it.	<BODY>, <FRAMESET> (window)	Netscape 4
ondragstart	Fires when the user begins to drag a highlighted selection.	<A>, <ACRONYM>, <ADDRESS>, <APPLET>, <AREA>, <B>, <BIG>, <BLOCKQUOTE>, <BODY> (document), <BUTTON>, <CAPTION>, <CENTER>, <CITE>, <CODE>, <DD>, <DEL>, <DFN>, <DIR>, <DIV>, <DL>, <DT>, <EM>, <FONT>, <FORM>, <FRAMESET> (document), <H1>, <H2>, <H3>, <H4>, <H5>, <H6>, <HR>, <I>, <IMG>, <INPUT>,	Internet Explorer 4

2

Event Attribute	Event Description	Associated Elements	Compatibility
		<KBD>, <LABEL>, <LI>, <LISTING>, <MAP>, <MARQUEE>, <MENU>, <OBJECT>, <OL>, <OPTION>, <P>, <PLAINTEXT>, <PRE>, <Q>, <S>, <SAMP>, <SELECT>, <SMALL>, <SPAN>, <STRIKE>, <STRONG>, <SUB>, <SUP>, <TABLE>, <TBODY>, <TD>, <TEXTAREA>, <TFOOT>, <TH>, <THEAD>, <TR>, <TT>, <U>, <UL>, <VAR>, <XMP>	
onerror	Fires when the loading of a document, particularly the execution of a script, causes an error. Used to trap syntax errors.	<BODY>, <FRAMESET> (window), <IMG> (<LINK>, <OBJECT>, <SCRIPT>, <STYLE>—Internet Explorer 4)	Netscape 3, 4; Internet Explorer 4

Event Attribute	Event Description	Associated Elements	Compatibility
onerrorupdate	Fires if a data transfer has been canceled by the onbeforeupdate event handler.	<A>, <APPLET>, <OBJECT>, <SELECT>, <TEXTAREA>	Internet Explorer 4
onfilterchange	Fires when a page filter changes state or finishes.	Nearly all elements	Internet Explorer 4
onfinish	Triggered when a looping marquee finishes.	<MARQUEE>	Internet Explorer 4
onhelp	Triggered when the user presses the F1 key or similar help button in the user agent.	Nearly all elements under Internet Explorer 4 only	Internet Explorer 4
onmove	Triggered when the user moves a window.	<BODY>, <FRAMESET>	Netscape 4
onreadystate-change	Similar to onload. Fires whenever the ready state for an object has changed.	<APPLET>, <BODY>, <EMBED>, <FRAME>, <FRAMESET>, <IFRAME>, <IMG>, <LINK>, <OBJECT>, <SCRIPT>, <STYLE>	Internet Explorer 4

2

Event Attribute	Event Description	Associated Elements	Compatibility
onresize	Triggered whenever an object is resized. Can only be bound to the window under Netscape as set via the <BODY> element.	<APPLET>, <BODY>, <BUTTON>, <CAPTION>, <DIV>, <EMBED>, <FRAMESET>, <HR>, <IMG>, <MARQUEE>, <OBJECT>, <SELECT>, <TABLE>, <TD>, <TEXTAREA>, <TR>	Netscape 4 (supports <BODY> only); Internet Explorer 4
onrowenter	Indicates that a bound data row has changed and new data values are available.	<APPLET>, <BODY>, <BUTTON>, <CAPTION>, <DIV>, <EMBED>, <HR>, <IMG>, <MARQUEE>, <OBJECT>, <SELECT>, <TABLE>, <TD>, <TEXTAREA>, <TR>	Internet Explorer 4
onrowexit	Fires just prior to a bound data source control changing the current row.	<APPLET>, <BODY>, <BUTTON>, <CAPTION>, <DIV>, <EMBED>, <HR>, <IMG>, <MARQUEE>, <OBJECT>, <SELECT>, <TABLE>, <TD>, <TEXTAREA>, <TR>	Internet Explorer 4

Event Attribute	Event Description	Associated Elements	Compatibility
onscroll	Fires when a scrolling element is repositioned.	<BODY>, <DIV>, <FIELDSET>, <IMG>, <MARQUEE>, <SPAN>, <TEXTAREA>	Internet Explorer 4
onselectstart	Fires when the user begins to select information by highlighting.	Nearly all elements	Internet Explorer 4
onstart	Fires when a looped marquee begins or starts over.	<MARQUEE>	Internet Explorer 4

HTML Element Reference

<!-- ... --> (Comment)

This construct is used to include text comments that will not be displayed by the browser.

Syntax

```
<!-- ... -->
```

Attributes
None.

Event Handlers
None.

Examples

```
<!-- This is an informational comment that can occur
     anywhere in an HTML document. The next example
```

```
shows how a script is "commented out" to prevent
non-script-enabled browsers from reading the script. -->
```

```
<SCRIPT>
<!--
    document.write("hello world");
// -->
</SCRIPT>
```

Compatibility
HTML 2, 3.2, 4; Netscape 1, 2, 3, 4; Internet Explorer 2, 3, 4;
and WebTV

Notes
Comments are often used to exclude content from older browsers,
particularly those that do not understand client-side scripting or
style sheets. Page developers should be careful when commenting
HTML markup. Older browsers may or may not render the enclosed
content.

<!DOCTYPE>   (Document Type Definition)

This SGML construct specifies the document type definition
corresponding to the document.

Syntax
```
<!DOCTYPE "DTD Identifier">
```

Attributes
None.

Event Handlers
None.

Example
```
<!DOCTYPE HTML PUBLIC "-//W3C//DTD HTML 4.0 Transitional//EN">
```

Compatibility
HTML 2, 3.2, 4; Netscape 1, 2, 3, 4; Internet Explorer 2, 3, 4;
and WebTV

Notes

The **<!DOCTYPE>** element should be used as the first line of all
HTML documents. Validation programs may use this construct
when determining the correctness of an HTML document. Be
certain to use the document type appropriate for the elements
used in the document.

2

<A> (Anchor)

This element indicates the portion of the document that is a
hyperlink or the named target destination for a hyperlink.

Syntax

```
<A
      ACCESSKEY="key"
      CHARSET="character code for language of linked
            resource"
      CLASS="class name(s)"
      COORDS="comma-separated list of numbers"
      DIR="LTR | RTL"
      HREF="URL"
      HREFLANG="language code"
      ID="unique alphanumeric identifier"
      LANG="language code"
      NAME="name of target location"
      REL="comma-separated list of relationship values"
      REV="comma-separated list of relationship values"
      SHAPE="DEFAULT | CIRCLE | POLY | RECT"
      STYLE="style information"
      TABINDEX="number"
      TARGET="_blank | frame-name | _parent | _self | _top"
            (transitional)
      TITLE="advisory text"
      TYPE="content type of linked data"
      onblur="script" (transitional)
      onclick="script"
      ondblclick="script"
      onfocus="script"
      onhelp="script"
      onkeydown="script"
      onkeypress="script"
```

```
onkeyup="script"
onmousedown="script"
onmousemove="script"
onmouseout="script"
onmouseover="script"
onmouseup="script">
```

Linked content

</A>

Attributes and Events Defined by Internet Explorer 4

```
DATAFLD="name of column supplying bound data"
DATASRC="ID of data source object supplying data"
LANGUAGE="JAVASCRIPT | JSCRIPT | VBS | VBSCRIPT"
METHODS="http-method"
URN="urn"
ondragstart="script"
onselectstart="script"
```

Attributes Defined by WebTV

```
NOCOLOR
SELECTED
```

Attributes

ACCESSKEY   This attribute specifies a keyboard navigation accelerator for the element. Pressing ALT or a similar key (depending on the browser and operating system) in association with the specified key selects the anchor element correlated with that key.

CHARSET   This attribute defines the character encoding of the linked resource. The value is a space- and/or comma-delimited list of character sets as defined in RFC 2045. The default value is **ISO-8859-1**.

CLASS   See "Core Attributes Reference," earlier in this chapter.

COORDS   For use with object shapes, this attribute uses a comma-separated list of numbers to define the coordinates of the object on the page.

DATAFLD   This attribute specifies the column name from that data source object that supplies the bound data. This attribute is specific to Microsoft's Data Binding in Internet Explorer 4.

DATASRC   This attribute indicates the **ID** of the data source object that supplies the data that is bound to this element. This attribute is specific to Microsoft's Data Binding in Internet Explorer 4.

DIR   See "Language Reference," earlier in this chapter.

HREF   This is the single required attribute for anchors defining a hypertext source link. It indicates the link target, either a URL or a URL fragment, that is a name preceded by a hash mark (#), which specifies an internal target location within the current document. URLs are not restricted to Web (http)-based documents. URLs may use any protocol supported by the browser. For example, file ftp and mailto work in most user agents.

HREFLANG   This attribute is used to indicate the language of the linked resource. See "Language Reference," earlier in this chapter, for information on allowed values.

ID   See "Core Attributes Reference," earlier in this chapter.

LANG   See "Language Reference," earlier in this chapter.

LANGUAGE   This attribute specifies the language the current script is written in and invokes the proper scripting engine. The default value is **JAVASCRIPT**. **JAVASCRIPT** and **JSCRIPT** represent that the scripting language is written in JavaScript. **VBS** and **VBSCRIPT** represent that the scripting language is written in VBScript. It may also be possible to use extended names, such as **JavaScript1.1**, to hide code from JavaScript-aware browsers that don't conform to a particular version of the language.

METHODS   The value of this attribute provides information about the functions that may be performed on an object. The values are generally given by the HTTP protocol when it is used, but it may, for similar reasons as for the **TITLE** attribute, be useful to include advisory information, in advance, in the link. For example, the browser may choose a different rendering of a link as a function of the methods specified; something that is searchable may get a different icon, or an outside link may render with an indication of leaving the current site. This element is not well understood nor supported, even by the defining browser, Internet Explorer 4.

NAME   This attribute is required in an anchor defining a target location within a page. A value for **NAME** is similar to a value for the **ID** core attribute and should be an alphanumeric identifier unique to the document.

NOCOLOR   Supported only by WebTV, this attribute overrides the **LINK** color set in the **BODY** element and prevents the link from changing color.

REL   For anchors containing the **HREF** attribute, this attribute specifies the relationship of the target object to the link object. The value is a comma-separated list of relationship values. The values and their semantics will be registered by some authority that may have meaning to the document author. The default relationship, if no other is given, is **void**. The **REL** attribute should be used only when the **HREF** attribute is present.

REV   This attribute specifies a reverse link, the inverse relationship of the **REL** attribute. It is useful for indicating where an object came from, such as the author or a document.

SELECTED   Supported only in WebTV, this attribute selects the anchor with a yellow highlight box.

SHAPE   This attribute is used to define a selectable region for hypertext source links associated with a figure to create an image map. The values for the attribute are **CIRCLE, DEFAULT, POLYGON**, and **RECT**. The format of the **COORDS** attribute depends on the value of **SHAPE**. For **CIRCLE**, the value is x,y,r where x and y are the pixel coordinates for the center of the circle and r is the radius value in pixels. For **RECT**, the **COORDS** attribute should be x,y,w,h. The x,y values define the upper left-hand corner of the rectangle, while w and h define the width and height, respectively. A value of **POLYGON** for **SHAPE** requires $x1,y1,x2,y2,...$ values for **COORDS**. Each of the x,y pairs define a point in the polygon, with successive points being joined by straight lines and the last point joined to the first. The value **DEFAULT** for **SHAPE** defines that the entire enclosed area, typically an image, be used.

STYLE   See "Core Attributes Reference," earlier in this chapter.

TABINDEX   This attribute uses a number to identify the object's position in the tabbing order for keyboard navigation using the TAB key.

TARGET   This attribute specifies the target window for a hypertext source link referencing frames. The information linked to will be displayed in the named window. Frames must be named to be targeted. There are, however, special name values, including **_blank**, which indicates a new window; **_parent**, which indicates the parent frame set containing the source link; **_self**, which indicates the frame containing the source link; and **_top**, which indicates the full browser window.

TITLE   See "Core Attributes Reference," earlier in this chapter.

TYPE   This attribute specifies the media type in the form of a MIME type of the link target. Generally, this is provided strictly as advisory information; however, in the future a browser may add a small icon for multimedia types. For example, a browser might add a small speaker icon when **TYPE** is set to audio/wav.

URN   See the "Notes" section for this element.

Attribute and Event Support

NETSCAPE 4   HREF, NAME, TARGET, onclick, onmouseout, and onmouseover. (CLASS, ID, LANG, and STYLE are implied.)

INTERNET EXPLORER 4   ACCESSKEY, CLASS, HREF, ID, LANG, NAME, REL, REV, STYLE, TARGET, TITLE, onblur, onclick, ondblclick, onfocus, onhelp, onkeydown, onkeypress, onkeyup, onmousedown, onmousemove, onmouseout, onmouseover, onmouseup, and all attributes and events defined by Internet Explorer 4.

WEBTV   HREF, ID, NAME, NOCOLOR, SELECTED, onclick, onmouseout, and onmouseover.

Event Handlers

See "Events Reference," earlier in this chapter.

Examples

```
<!-- anchor linking to external file -->
<A HREF="http://www.pint.com/">External Link</A>

<!-- anchor linking to file on local filesystem -->
<A HREF="file:/c:\html\index.htm">local file link</A>

<!-- anchor invoking anonymous FTP -->
<A HREF="ftp://pint.com/workshop/freestuff">Anonymous FTP
link</A>
```

```
<!-- anchor invoking FTP with password -->
<A HREF=
"ftp://joeuser:secretpassword@company.com/path/file">
FTP with password</A>

<!-- anchor invoking mail -->
<A HREF="mailto:fakeid@bigcompany.com">Send mail</A>

<!-- anchor used to define target destination within
     document -->
<A NAME="jump">Jump target</A>

<!-- anchor linking internally to previous target
     anchor -->
<A HREF="#jump">Local jump within document</A>

<!-- anchor linking externally to previous target
     anchor -->
<A HREF="http://www.company.com/document#jump">
Remote jump within document</A>
```

Compatibility

HTML 2, 3.2, 4; Netscape 1, 2, 3, 4; Internet Explorer 2, 3, 4; and WebTV

Notes

- The following are reserved browser key bindings for the two major browsers and should not be used as values to **ACCESSKEY**: **A**, **C**, **E**, **F**, **G**, **H**, **V**, left arrow, and right arrow.

- The **URN** attribute was defined in HTML 2. Although Internet Explorer 4 supports it, its use is unclear, particularly since URNs are not yet well defined.

- HTML 3.2 defines only **NAME**, **HREF**, **REL**, **REV**, and **TITLE**.

- HTML 2 defines only **NAME**, **HREF**, **METHODS**, **REL**, **REV**, **TITLE**, and **URN**.

- The **TARGET** attribute is not defined in browsers that do not support frames, such as Netscape 1–generation browsers.

- The **DIR** attribute is not yet supported by any browsers.

<ABBR> (Abbreviation)

This element allows authors to clearly indicate a sequence of characters that compose an acronym or abbreviation for a word (XML, WWW, and so on). See **<ACRONYM>**.

Syntax

```
<ABBR
    CLASS="class name(s)"
    DIR="LTR | RTL"
    ID="unique alphanumeric identifier"
    LANG="language code"
    STYLE="style information"
    TITLE="advisory text"
    onclick="script"
    ondblclick="script"
    onkeydown="script"
    onkeypress="script"
    onkeyup="script"
    onmousedown="script"
    onmousemove="script"
    onmouseout="script"
    onmouseover="script"
    onmouseup="script">

</ABBR>
```

Attributes

CLASS   See "Core Attributes Reference," earlier in this chapter.

DIR   See "Language Reference," earlier in this chapter.

ID   See "Core Attributes Reference," earlier in this chapter.

LANG   See "Language Reference," earlier in this chapter.

STYLE   See "Core Attributes Reference," earlier in this chapter.

TITLE   See "Core Attributes Reference," earlier in this chapter.

Attribute and Event Support
None.

Event Handlers
See "Events Reference," earlier in this chapter.

Examples
```
<ABBR TITLE="Dynamic Hypertext Markup Language">DHTML
</ABBR>

<ABBR LANG="fr" TITLE="World Wrestling Federation">
WWF
</ABBR>
```

Compatibility
HTML 4

Notes
<ABBR> is a new element that is not defined under HTML 2 or 3.2.
At present, no browsers appear to support the **<ABBR>** element.
<ACRONYM> serves a similar function but is only supported by
Internet Explorer 4.

<ACRONYM>   (Acronym)

This element allows authors to clearly indicate a sequence of
characters that compose an acronym or abbreviation for a word
(XML, WWW, and so on).

Syntax
```
<ACRONYM
    CLASS="class name(s)"
    DIR="LTR | RTL"
    ID="unique alphanumeric identifier"
    LANG="language code"
    STYLE="style information"
    TITLE="advisory text"
    onclick="script"
    ondblclick="script"
    onkeydown="script"
    onkeypress="script"
    onkeyup="script"
    onmousedown="script"
    onmousemove="script"
    onmouseout="script"
```

```
onmouseover="script"
onmouseup="script">
```

```
</ACRONYM>
```

Attributes and Events Defined by Internet Explorer 4

```
LANGUAGE="JAVASCRIPT | JSCRIPT | VBS | VBSCRIPT"
ondragstart="script"
onhelp="script"
onselectstart="script"
```

Attributes

CLASS   See "Core Attributes Reference," earlier in this chapter.

DIR   See "Language Reference," earlier in this chapter.

ID   See "Core Attributes Reference," earlier in this chapter.

LANG   See "Language Reference," earlier in this chapter.

LANGUAGE   This attribute specifies the language the current script is written in and invokes the proper scripting engine. The default value is **JAVASCRIPT**. **JAVASCRIPT** and **JSCRIPT** represent that the scripting language is written in JavaScript. **VBS** and **VBSCRIPT** represent that the scripting language is written in VBScript. It may also be possible to use extended names, such as **JavaScript1.1**, to hide code from JavaScript-aware browsers that don't conform to a particular version of the language.

STYLE   See "Core Attributes Reference," earlier in this chapter.

TITLE   See "Core Attributes Reference," earlier in this chapter.

Attribute and Event Support

INTERNET EXPLORER 4   All attributes.

Event Handlers

See "Events Reference," earlier in this chapter.

Examples

```
<ACRONYM TITLE="Extensible Markup Language">XML</ACRONYM>
```

```
<ACRONYM LANG="fr" TITLE="Soci&eacute;t&eacute; Nationale
de Chemins de Fer">SNCF</ACRONYM>
```

Compatibility
HTML 4; Internet Explorer 4

Notes
<ACRONYM> is a new element that is not defined under HTML 2
or 3.2. Under Internet Explorer 4, the **TITLE** attribute renders as a
tool tip that can be used to define the meaning of the acronym.

<ADDRESS> (Address)

This element marks up text indicating authorship or ownership of
information. It generally occurs at the beginning or end of a
document.

Syntax
```
<ADDRESS
    CLASS="class name(s)"
    DIR="LTR | RTL"
    ID="unique alphanumeric identifier"
    LANG="language code"
    STYLE="style information"
    TITLE="advisory text"
    onclick="script"
    ondblclick="script"
    onkeydown="script"
    onkeypress="script"
    onkeyup="script"
    onmousedown="script"
    onmousemove="script"
    onmouseout="script"
    onmouseover="script"
    onmouseup="script">

</ADDRESS>
```

Attributes and Events Defined by Internet Explorer 4
```
    LANGUAGE="JAVASCRIPT | JSCRIPT | VBS | VBSCRIPT"
    ondragstart="script"
    onhelp="script"
    onselectstart="script"
```

Attributes

CLASS   See "Core Attributes Reference," earlier in this chapter.

DIR   See "Language Reference," earlier in this chapter.

ID   See "Core Attributes Reference," earlier in this chapter.

LANG   See "Language Reference," earlier in this chapter.

LANGUAGE   This attribute specifies the language the current script is written in and invokes the proper scripting engine. The default value is **JAVASCRIPT**. **JAVASCRIPT** and **JSCRIPT** represent that the scripting language is written in JavaScript. **VBS** and **VBSCRIPT** represent that the scripting language is written in VBScript. It may also be possible to use extended names, such as **JavaScript1.1**, to hide code from JavaScript-aware browsers that don't conform to a particular version of the language.

STYLE   See "Core Attributes Reference," earlier in this chapter.

TITLE   See "Core Attributes Reference," earlier in this chapter.

Attribute and Event Support

NETSCAPE 4   CLASS, ID, LANG, and STYLE.

INTERNET EXPLORER 4   CLASS, ID, LANG, LANGUAGE, STYLE, TITLE, onclick, ondblclick, ondragstart, onhelp, onkeydown, onkeypress, onkeyup, onmousedown, onmousemove, onmouseout, onmouseover, onmouseup, and onselectstart.

WEBTV   No attributes.

Event Handlers
See "Events Reference," earlier in this chapter.

Example
```
<ADDRESS>Big Company, Inc.<BR>2105 Demo Street<BR>
San Diego, CA U.S.A.</ADDRESS>
```

Compatibility
HTML 2, 3.2, 4; Netscape 1, 2, 3, 4; Internet Explorer 2, 3, 4; and WebTV

Notes
Under HTML 2, 3.2, and WebTV there are no attributes for
<ADDRESS>.

<APPLET>   (Java Applet)

This element identifies the inclusion of a Java applet. The strict
HTML 4 definition does not include this element.

Syntax (Transitional Only)

```
<APPLET
      ALIGN="BOTTOM | LEFT | MIDDLE | RIGHT | TOP"
      ALT="alternative text"
      ARCHIVE="URL of archive file"
      CLASS="class name(s)"
      CODE="URL of Java class file"
      CODEBASE="URL for base referencing"
      HEIGHT="pixels"
      HSPACE="pixels"
      ID="unique alphanumeric identifier"
      NAME="unique name for scripting reference"
      OBJECT="filename"
      STYLE="style information"
      TITLE="advisory text"
      VSPACE="pixels"
      WIDTH="pixels">

      <PARAM> elements

      Alternative content

</APPLET>
```

Attributes and Events Defined by Internet Explorer 4

```
      ALIGN="ABSBOTTOM | ABSMIDDLE | BASELINE | BOTTOM |
            LEFT | MIDDLE | RIGHT | TEXTTOP | TOP"
      DATAFLD="name of column supplying bound data"
      DATASRC="ID of data source object supplying data"
      SRC="URL"
      onafterupdate="script"
      onbeforeupdate="script"
```

```
onblur="script"
onclick="script"
ondataavailable="script"
ondatasetchanged="script"
ondatasetcomplete="script"
ondblclick="script"
ondragstart="script"
onerrorupdate="script"
onfocus="script"
onhelp="script"
onkeydown="script"
onkeypress="script"
onkeyup="script"
onmousedown="script"
onmousemove="script"
onmouseout="script"
onmouseover="script"
onmouseup="script"
onreadystatechange="script"
onresize="script"
onrowenter="script"
onrowexit="script"
```

Attributes Defined by Netscape 4

```
ALIGN="ABSBOTTOM | ABSMIDDLE | BASELINE | CENTER |
      TEXTTOP"
MAYSCRIPT
```

Attributes

ALIGN   This attribute is used to position the applet on the page relative to content that may flow around it. The HTML 4 specification defines values of **BOTTOM**, **LEFT**, **MIDDLE**, **RIGHT**, and **TOP**, while Microsoft and Netscape may also support **ABSBOTTOM**, **ABSMIDDLE**, **BASELINE**, **CENTER**, and **TEXTTOP**.

ALT   This attribute causes a descriptive text alternative to be displayed on browsers that do not support Java. Page designers should also remember that content enclosed within the **<APPLET>** element may also be rendered as alternative text.

ARCHIVE   This attribute refers to an archived or compressed version of the applet and its associated class files, which may help reduce download time.

CLASS   See "Core Attributes Reference," earlier in this chapter.

CODE   This attribute specifies the URL of the applet's class file to be loaded and executed. Applet filenames are identified by a .class filename extension. The URL specified by **CODE** may be relative to the **CODEBASE** attribute.

CODEBASE   This attribute gives the absolute or relative URL of the directory where applets' .class files referenced by the **CODE** attribute are stored.

DATAFLD   This attribute, supported by Internet Explorer 4, specifies the column name from the data source object that supplies the bound data. This attribute may be used to specify the various <PARAM> elements passed to the Java applet.

DATASRC   Like **DATAFLD**, this attribute is used for data binding under Internet Explorer 4. It indicates the **ID** of the data source object that supplies the data that is bound to the <PARAM> elements associated with the applet.

HEIGHT   This attribute specifies the height, in pixels, that the applet needs.

HSPACE   This attribute specifies additional horizontal space, in pixels, to be reserved on either side of the applet.

ID   See "Core Attributes Reference," earlier in this chapter.

MAYSCRIPT   In the Netscape implementation, this attribute allows access to an applet by programs in a scripting language embedded in the document.

NAME   This attribute assigns a name to the applet so that it can be identified by other resources, particularly scripts.

OBJECT   This attribute specifies the URL of a serialized representation of an applet.

SRC   As defined for Internet Explorer 4, this attribute specifies a URL for an associated file for the applet. The meaning and use is unclear and not part of the HTML standard.

STYLE   See "Core Attributes Reference," earlier in this chapter.

TITLE   See "Core Attributes Reference," earlier in this chapter.

VSPACE   This attribute specifies additional vertical space, in pixels, to be reserved above and below the applet.

WIDTH   This attribute specifies in pixels the width that the applet needs.

Attribute and Event Support

NETSCAPE 4   **ALIGN**, **ALT**, **ARCHIVE**, **CODE**, **CODEBASE**, **HSPACE**, **MAYSCRIPT**, **NAME**, **VSPACE**, and **WIDTH**. (**CLASS**, **ID**, and **STYLE** are implied.)

INTERNET EXPLORER 4   **ALT**, **CLASS**, **CODE**, **CODEBASE**, **HEIGHT**, **HSPACE**, **ID**, **NAME**, **STYLE**, **TITLE**, **VSPACE**, **WIDTH**, and all attributes and events defined by Internet Explorer 4.

Event Handlers
None.

Example
```
<APPLET CODE="game.class"
        ALIGN="LEFT"
        ARCHIVE="game.zip"
        HEIGHT="250" WIDTH="350">

<PARAM NAME="DIFFICULTY" VALUE="EASY">

<B>Sorry, you need Java to play this game.</B>
</APPLET>
```

Compatibility
HTML 3.2, 4; Netscape 2, 3, 4; and Internet Explorer 3, 4

Notes

- The **<APPLET>** element replaces the original **<APP>** element. Parameter values can be passed to applets using the **<PARAM>** element in the applet's content area.

- The HTML 4 specification does not encourage the use of **<APPLET>** and prefers the use of the **<OBJECT>** element. Under the strict definition of HTML 4, this element is not defined.

- WebTV's current implementation does not support Java applets.

- Java applets were first supported under Netscape 2–level browsers and Internet Explorer 3–level browsers.

<AREA>   (Image Map Area)

<AREA> is an empty element used within the content model of the <MAP> element to implement client-side image maps. It defines a hot-spot region on the map and associates it with a hypertext link.

Syntax
```
<AREA
     ACCESSKEY="character"
     ALT="alternative text"
     CLASS="class name(s)"
     COORDS="comma-separated list of values"
     DIR="LTR | RTL"
     HREF="URL"
     ID="unique alphanumeric identifier"
     LANG="language code"
     NOHREF
     SHAPE="CIRCLE | DEFAULT | POLY | RECT"
     STYLE="style information"
     TABINDEX="number"
     TARGET="_blank | frame-name | _parent | _self |
          _top" (transitional)
     TITLE="advisory text"
     onblur="script"
     onclick="script"
     ondblclick="script"
     onfocus="script"
     onkeydown="script"
     onkeypress="script"
     onkeyup="script"
     onmousedown="script"
     onmousemove="script"
     onmouseout="script"
     onmouseover="script"
     onmouseup="script">
```

Attributes and Events Defined by Internet Explorer 4
```
     LANGUAGE="JAVASCRIPT | JSCRIPT | VBS | VBSCRIPT"
     SHAPE="CIRC | CIRCLE | POLY | POLYGON | RECT |
          RECTANGLE"
     ondragstart="script"
     onhelp="script"
     onselectstart="script"
```

Attributes Defined by Netscape 4

```
NAME="filename"
SHAPE="CIRCLE | DEFAULT | POLY | POLYGON | RECT"
```

Attributes Defined by WebTV

```
NOTAB
```

2

Attributes

ACCESSKEY   This attribute specifies a keyboard navigation accelerator for the element. Pressing ALT or a similar key in association with the specified character selects the form control correlated with that key sequence. Page designers are forewarned to avoid key sequences already bound to browsers.

ALT   This attribute contains a text string alternative to display on browsers than cannot display images.

CLASS   See "Core Attributes Reference," earlier in this chapter.

COORDS   This attribute contains a set of values specifying the coordinates of the hot-spot region. The number and meaning of the values depend upon the value specified for the **SHAPE** attribute. For a **RECT** or **RECTANGLE** shape, the **COORDS** value is two x,y pairs: **left**, **top**, **right**, and **bottom**. For a **CIRC** or **CIRCLE** shape, the **COORDS** value is x,y,r where x,y is a pair specifying the center of the circle and r is a value for the radius. For a **POLY** or **POLYGON** shape, the **COORDS** value is a set of x,y pairs for each point in the polygon: $x1,y1,x2,y2,x3,y3$ and so on.

DIR   See "Language Reference," earlier in this chapter.

HREF   This attribute specifies the hyperlink target for the area. Its value is a valid URL. Either this attribute or the **NOHREF** attribute must be present in the element.

ID   See "Core Attributes Reference," earlier in this chapter.

LANG   See "Language Reference," earlier in this chapter.

LANGUAGE   This attribute specifies the language the current script is written in and invokes the proper scripting engine. The default value is **JAVASCRIPT**. **JAVASCRIPT** and **JSCRIPT** represent that the scripting language is written in JavaScript. **VBS** and **VBSCRIPT** represent that the scripting language is written in VBScript. It may also be possible to use extended names, such as

JavaScript1.1, to hide code from JavaScript-aware browsers that don't conform to a particular version of the language.

NAME   This attribute is used to define a name for the clickable area so that it can be scripted by older browsers.

NOHREF   This attribute indicates that no hyperlink exists for the associated area. Either this attribute or the **HREF** attribute must be present in the element.

NOTAB   Supported by WebTV, this attribute keeps the element from appearing in the tabbing order.

SHAPE   This attribute defines the shape of the associated hot spot. HTML 4 defines the values **RECT**, which defines a rectangular region; **CIRCLE**, which defines a circular region; **POLY**, which defines a polygon; and **DEFAULT**, which indicates the entire region beyond any defined shapes. Many browsers, notably Internet Explorer 4, support **CIRC**, **POLYGON**, and **RECTANGLE** as valid values for **SHAPE**.

STYLE   See "Core Attributes Reference," earlier in this chapter.

TABINDEX   This attribute represents a numeric value specifying the position of the defined area in the browser tabbing order.

TARGET   This attribute specifies the target window for hyperlink referencing frames. The value is a frame name or one of several special names. A value of **_blank** indicates a new window. A value of **_parent** indicates the parent frame set containing the source link. A value of **_self** indicates the frame containing the source link. A value of **_top** indicates the full browser window.

TITLE   See "Core Attributes Reference," earlier in this chapter.

Attribute and Event Support

NETSCAPE 4   COORDS, HREF, NOHREF, SHAPE, TARGET, **onmouseout**, and **onmouseover**. (**CLASS**, **ID**, **LANG**, and **STYLE** are implied but not listed for this element in Netscape documentation.)

INTERNET EXPLORER 4   ALT, CLASS, COORDS, HREF, ID, LANG, **LANGUAGE**, **NOHREF**, **SHAPE**, **STYLE**, **TABINDEX**, **TARGET**, **TITLE**, all W3C-defined events, and all attributes and events defined by Internet Explorer 4.

WEBTV COORDS, HREF, ID, NAME, NOTAB, SHAPE, TARGET, **onmouseout,** and **onmouseover.**

Event Handlers

See "Events Reference," earlier in this chapter.

2

Example

```
<MAP NAME="primary">
  <AREA SHAPE="CIRCLE" COORDS="200,250,25"
        HREF="another.htm">
  <AREA SHAPE="DEFAULT" NOHREF>
</MAP>
```

Compatibility

HTML 3.2, 4; Netscape 1, 2, 3, 4; Internet Explorer 2, 3, 4; and WebTV

Notes

- By the HTML 3.2 and 4 specifications, the closing tag **</AREA>** is forbidden.

- The **ID, CLASS,** and **STYLE** attributes have the same meaning as the core attributes defined in the HTML 4 specification, but only Netscape and Microsoft define them.

- Netscape 1–level browsers do not understand the **TARGET** attribute as it relates to frames.

- HTML 3.2 defines only **ALT, COORDS, HREF, NOHREF,** and **SHAPE.**

<AUDIOSCOPE> (Sound Amplitude Display)

This WebTV-specific element displays an audioscope for a sound resource that displays a dynamic, graphical display of a sound's amplitude.

Syntax (Defined by WebTV)

```
<AUDIOSCOPE
      ALIGN="ABSBOTTOM | ABSMIDDLE | BASELINE | BOTTOM |
             LEFT | MIDDLE | RIGHT | TEXTTOP | TOP"
      BORDER="pixels"
      GAIN="number"
```

```
HEIGHT="pixels"
LEFTCOLOR="color name | #RRGGBB"
LEFTOFFSET="number"
MAXLEVEL="TRUE | FALSE"
RIGHTCOLOR="name | #RRGGBB"
RIGHTOFFSET="number"
WIDTH="pixels">
```

Attributes

ALIGN   This attribute positions the audioscope object on the page relative to text or other content that may flow around it.

BORDER   This attribute sets the width of the audioscope border in pixels. The default value is **1**.

GAIN   This attribute takes a numeric value, which is a multiplier for the amplitude display. The default value is **1**.

HEIGHT   This attribute sets the height of the audioscope in pixels. The default value is **80** pixels.

LEFTCOLOR   This attribute sets the color of the line displaying the left audio channel in the audioscope. Values can either be given as named colors or in the numeric *#RRGGBB* format. The default value is **#8ECE10**.

LEFTOFFSET   This attribute sets the vertical offset for the display of the left audio channel with positive and negative values relative to the center of the audioscope. The default value is **0**.

MAXLEVEL   This Boolean attribute specifies whether the audioscope should clip sound according to the specified gain. The default value is **FALSE**.

RIGHTCOLOR   This attribute sets the color of the line displaying the right audio channel in the audioscope. Values can either be given as named colors or in the numeric *#RRGGBB* format. The default value is **#8ECE10**.

RIGHTOFFSET   This attribute sets the vertical offset for the display of the right audio channel with positive and negative values relative to the center of the audioscope. The default value is **1**.

WIDTH   This attribute sets the width of the audioscope in pixels. The default width is **100** pixels.

Attribute and Event Support

WEBTV   All attributes.

Event Handlers

None.

Example

```
<AUDIOSCOPE BORDER="1" HEIGHT="16" WIDTH="240" GAIN="3"
            MAXLEVEL="FALSE">
```

Compatibility

WebTV

Notes

<AUDIOSCOPE> is supported only by WebTV.

<B>   (Bold)

This element indicates that the enclosed text should be displayed in boldface.

Syntax

```
<B
     CLASS="class name(s)"
     DIR="LTR | RTL"
     ID="unique alphanumeric identifier"
     LANG="language code"
     STYLE="style information"
     TITLE="advisory text"
     onclick="script"
     ondblclick="script"
     onkeydown="script"
     onkeypress="script"
     onkeyup="script"
     onmousedown="script"
     onmousemove="script"
     onmouseout="script"
     onmouseover="script"
     onmouseup="script">

</B>
```

Attributes and Events Defined by Internet Explorer 4

```
LANGUAGE="JAVASCRIPT | JSCRIPT | VBS | VBSCRIPT"
ondragstart="script"
onhelp="script"
onselectstart="script"
```

Attributes

CLASS   See "Core Attributes Reference," earlier in this chapter.

DIR   See "Language Reference," earlier in this chapter.

ID   See "Core Attributes Reference," earlier in this chapter.

LANG   See "Language Reference," earlier in this chapter.

LANGUAGE   This attribute specifies the language the current script is written in and invokes the proper scripting engine. The default value is **JAVASCRIPT**. **JAVASCRIPT** and **JSCRIPT** represent that the scripting language is written in JavaScript. **VBS** and **VBSCRIPT** represent that the scripting language is written in VBScript. It may also be possible to use extended names, such as **JavaScript1.1**, to hide code from JavaScript-aware browsers that don't conform to a particular version of the language.

STYLE   See "Core Attributes Reference," earlier in this chapter.

TITLE   See "Core Attributes Reference," earlier in this chapter.

Attribute and Event Support

NETSCAPE 4   **CLASS**, **ID**, **LANG**, and **STYLE** are implied but not explicitly listed for this element.

INTERNET EXPLORER 4   All W3C-defined attributes and events except **DIR**, and attributes and events defined by Internet Explorer 4.

Event Handlers

See "Events Reference," earlier in this chapter.

Example

```
This text is <B>bold</B> for emphasis.
```

Compatibility

HTML 2, 3.2, 4; Netscape 1, 2, 3; Internet Explorer 2, 3, 4; and WebTV

Notes
HTML 2 and 3.2 do not define any attributes for this element.

<BASE> (Base URL)

This element specifies the base URL to use for all relative URLs contained within a document. It occurs only in the scope of a **<HEAD>** element.

Syntax
```
<BASE
    HREF="URL"
    TARGET="_blank | frame-name | _parent | _self |
        _top" (transitional)>
```

Attributes

HREF This attribute specifies the base URL to be used throughout the document for relative URL addresses.

TARGET For documents containing frames, this attribute specifies the default target window for every link that does not have an explicit target reference. Besides named frames, several special values exist. A value of **_blank** indicates a new window. A value of **_parent** indicates the parent frame set containing the source link. A value of **_self** indicates the frame containing the source link. A value of **_top** indicates the full browser window.

Attribute and Event Support

NETSCAPE 4 **HREF** and **TARGET**.

INTERNET EXPLORER 4 **HREF** and **TARGET**.

WEBTV **HREF** and **TARGET**.

Event Handlers
None.

Examples
```
<BASE HREF="http://www.bigcompany.com/">

<BASE TARGET="_blank" HREF="http://www.bigcompany.com/">
```

Compatibility
HTML 2, 3.2, 4; Netscape 1, 2, 3, 4; Internet Explorer 2, 3, 4; and WebTV

Notes
HTML 2 and 3.2 define only the **HREF** attribute.

<BASEFONT> (Base Font)

This element establishes a default font size for a document. Font size can then be varied relative to the base font size using the <FONT> element. The <BASEFONT> element must be placed near the beginning of the body part of the page.

Syntax (Transitional Only)
```
<BASEFONT
     COLOR="color name | #RRGGBB"
     FACE="font name(s)"
     ID="unique alphanumeric identifier"
     SIZE="1-7 | +/-int">
```

Attributes Defined by Internet Explorer 4
```
     CLASS="class name(s)"
     LANG="language code"
```

Attributes

CLASS   Internet Explorer 4 documentation indicates that the **CLASS** can be set for the <BASEFONT> element; however, this is probably a mistake in the documentation.

COLOR   This attribute sets the text color using either a named color or a color specified in the hexadecimal *#RRGGBB* format.

FACE   This attribute contains a list of one or more font names. The document text in the default style is rendered in the first font face that the client's browser supports. If no font listed is installed on the local system, the browser typically defaults to the proportional or fixed width font for that system.

ID   See "Core Attributes Reference," earlier in this chapter.

LANG Internet Explorer 4 documentation also mentions use of the **LANG** attribute to indicate the language used. Meaning with this element is not well defined.

SIZE This attribute specifies the font size as either a numeric or relative value. Numeric values range from **1** to **7** with **1** being the smallest and **3** the default.

2

Attribute and Event Support

NETSCAPE 4 ID (implied) and **SIZE**.

INTERNET EXPLORER 4 All attributes.

WEBTV SIZE.

Event Handlers
None.

Example
```
<BASEFONT COLOR="#FF0000" FACE="Helvetica, Times Roman"
        SIZE="+2">
```

Compatibility
HTML 3.2, 4 (transitional); Netscape 1.1, 2, 3, 4; Internet Explorer 2, 3, 4; and WebTV

Notes

- HTML 3.2 supports the **<BASEFONT>** element and the **SIZE** attribute. HTML 4 transitional specification adds support for **COLOR** and **FACE** as well.

- The HTML 4 strict specification does not support this element.

- The font sizes indicated by numeric values are browser dependent and not absolute.

<BDO> (Bidirectional Override)

This element is used to override the current directionality of text.

Syntax

```
<BDO
    CLASS="class name(s)"
    DIR="LTR | RTL"
    ID="unique alphanumeric identifier"
    LANG="language code"
    STYLE="style information"
    TITLE="advisory text">

</BDO>
```

Attributes

CLASS   See "Core Attributes Reference," earlier in this chapter.

DIR   This attribute is required for the **<BDO>** element. It sets the text direction either to left to right (**LTR**) or right to left (**RTL**).

ID   See "Core Attributes Reference," earlier in this chapter.

LANG   See "Language Reference," earlier in this chapter.

STYLE   See "Core Attributes Reference," earlier in this chapter.

TITLE   See "Core Attributes Reference," earlier in this chapter.

Attribute and Event Support
None.

Event Handlers
None.

Example

```
<!-- Switch text direction -->
<BDO ID="switch1" DIR="RTL">This text will go right to
left if you can find a browser that supports this element.
</BDO>
```

Compatibility
HTML 4

Notes

It appears that no browsers support this element yet.

<BGSOUND> (Background Sound)

This Internet Explorer and WebTV element associates a background sound with a page.

Syntax (Defined by Internet Explorer 4)

```
<BGSOUND
        BALANCE="number"
        CLASS="class name(s)"
        ID="unique alphanumeric identifier"
        LANG="language code"
        LOOP=number
        SRC="URL of sound file"
        TITLE="advisory text"
        VOLUME="number">
```

Attributes

BALANCE   This attribute defines a number between –10,000 and +10,000 that determines how the volume will be divided between the speakers.

CLASS   See "Core Attributes Reference," earlier in this chapter.

ID   See "Core Attributes Reference," earlier in this chapter.

LANG   See "Language Reference," earlier in this chapter.

LOOP   This attribute indicates the number of times a sound is to be played and either has a numeric value or the keyword **infinite**.

SRC   This attribute specifies the URL of the sound file to be played, which must be one of the following types: .wav, .au, or .mid.

TITLE   See "Core Attributes Reference," earlier in this chapter.

VOLUME   This attribute defines a number between –10,000 and 0 that determines the loudness of a page's background sound.

Attribute and Event Support

INTERNET EXPLORER 4   All attributes.

WEBTV   LOOP and SRC.

Event Handlers

None.

Examples

```
<BGSOUND SRC="sound1.mid">
```

```
<BGSOUND SRC="sound2.au" LOOP="INFINITE">
```

Compatibility

Internet Explorer 2, 3, 4; WebTV

Notes

Similar functionality can be achieved in Netscape using the
<EMBED> element to invoke LiveAudio.

<BIG>   (Big Font)

This element indicates that the enclosed text should be displayed
in a larger font relative to the current font.

Syntax

```
<BIG
    CLASS="class name(s)"
    DIR="LTR | RTL"
    ID="unique alphanumeric identifier"
    LANG="language code"
    STYLE="style information"
    TITLE="advisory text"
    onclick="script"
    ondblclick="script"
    onkeydown="script"
    onkeypress="script"
    onkeyup="script"
    onmousedown="script"
    onmousemove="script"
    onmouseout="script"
```

```
onmouseover="script"
onmouseup="script">
```

`</BIG>`

Attributes and Events Defined by Internet Explorer 4

```
LANGUAGE="JAVASCRIPT | JSCRIPT | VBS | VBSCRIPT"
ondragstart="script"
onhelp="script"
onselectstart="script"
```

Attributes

CLASS   See "Core Attributes Reference," earlier in this chapter.

DIR   See "Language Reference," earlier in this chapter.

ID   See "Core Attributes Reference," earlier in this chapter.

LANG   See "Language Reference," earlier in this chapter.

LANGUAGE   This attribute specifies the language the current script is written in and invokes the proper scripting engine. The default value is **JAVASCRIPT**. **JAVASCRIPT** and **JSCRIPT** represent that the scripting language is written in JavaScript. **VBS** and **VBSCRIPT** represent that the scripting language is written in VBScript.

STYLE   See "Core Attributes Reference," earlier in this chapter.

TITLE   See "Core Attributes Reference," earlier in this chapter.

Attribute and Event Support

NETSCAPE 4   **CLASS**, **ID**, **LANG**, and **STYLE** are implied.

INTERNET EXPLORER 4   All attributes and events except **DIR**.

Event Handlers
See "Events Reference," earlier in this chapter.

Example
This text is regular size. **<BIG>**This text is larger.**</BIG>**

Compatibility
HTML 3.2, 4; Netscape 2, 3, 4; Internet Explorer 2, 3, 4; and WebTV

Notes
HTML 3.2 does not support any attributes for this element.

<BLACKFACE> (Blackface Font)

This WebTV element renders the enclosed text in a double-weight boldface font. It is used for headings and other terms needing special emphasis.

Syntax
<BLACKFACE> *Text* </BLACKFACE>

Attributes
None.

Event Handlers
None.

Example
<BLACKFACE>Buy now!**</BLACKFACE>** This offer expires in five minutes.

Compatibility
WebTV

Notes
This element is supported only by WebTV.

<BLINK> (Blinking Text Display)

This Netscape-specific element causes the enclosed text to flash slowly.

Syntax (Defined by Netscape)

```
<BLINK
    CLASS="class name(s)"
    ID="unique alphanumeric identifier"
    LANG="language code"
    STYLE="style information">

</BLINK>
```

Attributes

CLASS   See "Core Attributes Reference," earlier in this chapter.

ID   See "Core Attributes Reference," earlier in this chapter.

LANG   See "Language Reference," earlier in this chapter.

STYLE   See "Core Attributes Reference," earlier in this chapter.

Attribute and Event Support

NETSCAPE 4   All attributes.

Event Handlers

None.

Example

```
<BLINK>Annoying, isn't it?</BLINK>
```

Compatibility

Netscape 1, 2, 3, 4

Notes

While not defined explicitly in Netscape documentation, the **CLASS**, **ID**, **LANG**, and **STYLE** attributes are mentioned to be universal to all elements under Netscape 4 and may have meaning here.

<BLOCKQUOTE> (Block Quote)

This block element indicates that the enclosed text is an extended quotation. Usually this is rendered visually by indentation.

Syntax

```
<BLOCKQUOTE
     CITE="URL of source information"
     CLASS="class name(s)"
     DIR="LTR | RTL"
     ID="unique alphanumeric identifier"
     LANG="language code"
     STYLE="style information"
     TITLE="advisory text"
     onclick="script"
     ondblclick="script"
     onkeydown="script"
     onkeypress="script"
     onkeyup="script"
     onmousedown="script"
     onmousemove="script"
     onmouseout="script"
     onmouseover="script"
     onmouseup="script">

</BLOCKQUOTE>
```

Attributes and Events Defined by Internet Explorer 4

```
     LANGUAGE="JAVASCRIPT | JSCRIPT | VBS | VBSCRIPT"
     ondragstart="script"
     onhelp="script"
     onselectstart="script"
```

Attributes

CITE   The value of this attribute should be a URL of the document in which the information cited can be found.

CLASS   See "Core Attributes Reference," earlier in this chapter.

DIR   See "Language Reference," earlier in this chapter.

ID   See "Core Attributes Reference," earlier in this chapter.

LANG   See "Language Reference," earlier in this chapter.

LANGUAGE   This attribute specifies the language the current script is written in and invokes the proper scripting engine. The default value is **JAVASCRIPT**. **JAVASCRIPT** and **JSCRIPT** represent that the scripting language is written in JavaScript. **VBS** and **VBSCRIPT** represent that the scripting language is written in VBScript.

STYLE   See "Core Attributes Reference," earlier in this chapter.

TITLE   See "Core Attributes Reference," earlier in this chapter.

Attribute and Event Support

NETSCAPE 4   **CLASS**, **ID**, **LANG**, and **STYLE**.

INTERNET EXPLORER 4   All attributes and events except **CITE** and **DIR**.

Event Handlers

See "Events Reference," earlier in this chapter.

Example

```
The following paragraph is taken from our March report:
<BLOCKQUOTE CITE="marchreport.htm"> ... text ...
</BLOCKQUOTE>
```

Compatibility

HTML 2, 3.2, 4; Netscape 1, 2, 3, 4; Internet Explorer 2, 3, 4; and WebTV

Notes

- HTML 2 and 3.2 do not support any attributes for this element.
- WebTV only indents the left margin of text enclosed in the <BLOCKQUOTE> element.
- Some browsers understand the <BQ> shorthand notation.

<BODY>   (Document Body)

This element encloses a document's displayable content, in contrast to the descriptive and informational content contained in the <HEAD> element.

Syntax

```
<BODY
    ALINK="color name | #RRGGBB" (transitional)
    BACKGROUND="URL of background image" (transitional)
    BGCOLOR="color name | #RRGGBB" (transitional)
    CLASS="class name(s)"
    DIR="LTR | RTL"
    ID="unique alphanumeric identifier"
    LANG="language code"
    LINK="color name | #RRGGBB" (transitional)
    STYLE="style information"
    TEXT="color name | #RRGGBB" (transitional)
    TITLE="advisory text"
    VLINK="color name | #RRGGBB" (transitional)
    onclick="script"
    ondblclick="script"
    onkeydown="script"
    onkeypress="script"
    onkeyup="script"
    onload="script"
    onmousedown="script"
    onmousemove="script"
    onmouseout="script"
    onmouseover="script"
    onmouseup="script"
    onunload="script">

</BODY>
```

Attributes and Events Defined by Internet Explorer 4

```
    BGPROPERTIES="FIXED"
    BOTTOMMARGIN="pixels"
    LANGUAGE="JAVASCRIPT | JSCRIPT | VBS | VBSCRIPT"
    LEFTMARGIN="pixels"
    RIGHTMARGIN="pixels"
    SCROLL="NO | YES"
    TOPMARGIN="pixels"
    onafterupdate="script"
    onbeforeunload="script"
    onbeforeupdate="script"
    ondragstart="script"
    onhelp="script"
    onrowenter="script"
```

```
onrowexit="script"
onscroll="script"
onselect="script"
onselectstart="script"
```

Events Defined by Netscape 4

```
onblur="script"
onfocus="script"
```

Attributes Defined by WebTV

```
CREDITS="URL"
INSTRUCTIONS="URL"
LOGO="URL"
```

Attributes

ALINK   This attribute sets the color for active links within the document. Active links represent the state of a link as it is being pressed. The value of the attribute can either be a browser-dependent named color or a color specified in the hexadecimal #*RRGGBB* format.

BACKGROUND   This attribute contains a URL for an image file, which will be tiled to provide the document background.

BGCOLOR   This attribute sets the background color for the document. Its value can either be a browser-dependent named color or a color specified using the hexadecimal #*RRGGBB* format.

BGPROPERTIES   This attribute, first introduced in Internet Explorer 2, has one value, **FIXED**, which causes the background image to act as a fixed watermark and not to scroll.

BOTTOMMARGIN   This attribute specifies the bottom margin for the entire body of the page and overrides the default margin. When set to **0** or "", the bottom margin is the bottom edge of the window or frame the content is displayed in.

CLASS   See "Core Attributes Reference," earlier in this chapter.

CREDITS   In the WebTV implementation, this attribute contains the URL of the document to retrieve when the viewer presses the credits button on the Info Panel.

DIR   See "Language Reference," earlier in this chapter.

ID   See "Core Attributes Reference," earlier in this chapter.

INSTRUCTIONS   In the WebTV implementation, this attribute contains the URL of the document to retrieve when the viewer presses the instructions button on the Info Panel.

LANG   See "Language Reference," earlier in this chapter.

LANGUAGE   This attribute specifies the language the current script is written in and invokes the proper scripting engine. The default value is **JAVASCRIPT**. **JAVASCRIPT** and **JSCRIPT** represent that the scripting language is written in JavaScript. **VBS** and **VBSCRIPT** represent that the scripting language is written in VBScript.

LEFTMARGIN   This Internet Explorer–specific attribute sets the left margin for the page in pixels, overriding the default margin. When set to **0** or **""**, the left margin is the left edge of the window or the frame.

LINK   This attribute sets the color for hyperlinks within the document that have not yet been visited. Its value can either be a browser-dependent named color or a color specified using the hexadecimal *#RRGGBB* format.

LOGO   In the WebTV implementation, this attribute contains the URL of a 70×52–pixel thumbnail image for the page, which is used in the history and bookmarks for WebTV.

RIGHTMARGIN   This attribute, specific to Internet Explorer, sets the right margin for the page in pixels, overriding the default margin. When set to **0** or **""**, the right margin is the right edge of the window or the frame.

SCROLL   This attribute turns the scroll bars on or off. The default value is **YES**.

STYLE   See "Core Attributes Reference," earlier in this chapter.

TEXT   This attribute sets the text color for the document. Its value can either be a browser-dependent named color or a color specified using the hexadecimal *#RRGGBB* format.

TITLE   See "Core Attributes Reference," earlier in this chapter.

TOPMARGIN   This Internet Explorer–specific attribute sets the top margin for the document in pixels. If set to **0** or "", the top margin will be exactly on the top edge of the window or frame.

VLINK   This attribute sets the color for links within the document that have already been visited. Its value can either be a browser-dependent named color or a color specified using the hexadecimal *#RRGGBB* format.

Attribute and Event Support

NETSCAPE 4   ALINK, BACKGROUND, BGCOLOR, LINK, TEXT, VLINK, onblur, onfocus, onload, and onunload. (CLASS, ID, LANG, and **STYLE** are implied.)

INTERNET EXPLORER 4   All W3C-defined attributes and events except **DIR**, all attributes and events defined by Internet Explorer 4, and **onblur** and **onfocus**.

WEBTV   BACKGROUND, BGCOLOR, CREDITS, INSTRUCTIONS, LINK, LOGO, TEXT, VLINK, onload, and onunload.

Event Handlers
See "Events Reference," earlier in this chapter.

Example
```
<BODY BACKGROUND="checkered.gif"
      BGCOLOR="White"
      ALINK="Red"
      LINK="Blue"
      VLINK="Red"
      TEXT="Black"> ... </BODY>

<!-- myLoadFunction defined in document head in
      <SCRIPT> element -->
<BODY onload="myLoadFunction()"> ... </BODY>
```

Compatibility
HTML 2, 3.2, 4; Netscape 1, 2, 3, 4; Internet Explorer 2, 3, 4; and WebTV

Notes

- When defining text colors, it is important to be careful to specify both foreground and background explicitly so that they are not masked out by browser defaults set by the user.

- Under the HTML 4 strict definition, all color-setting attributes and background attributes are not allowed. This includes the **ALINK**, **BACKGROUND**, **BGCOLOR**, **LINK**, **TEXT**, and **VLINK** attributes.

- This element must be present in all documents except those declaring a frame set.

<BQ>   (Block Quote)

This obsolete element signifies that the enclosed text is an extended quotation. Though it has been defined in early HTML specifications, it is currently supported only by the WebTV browser as an alias for the **<BLOCKQUOTE>** element.

Syntax (Obsolete)

```
<BQ>
</BQ>
```

Attributes

None.

Event Handlers

None.

Example

```
<BQ>The HTML Programmer's Reference says "Don't use this
element."</BQ>
```

Compatibility

WebTV

Notes

This element o riginated in the early days of HTML and is considered obsolete. It should not be used.

  (Line Break)

This empty element forces a line break.

Syntax

```
<BR
    CLASS="class name(s)"
    CLEAR="ALL | LEFT | NONE | RIGHT" (transitional)
    ID="unique alphanumeric identifier"
    STYLE="style information"
    TITLE="advisory text">
```

Attributes Defined by Internet Explorer 4

```
    LANGUAGE="JAVASCRIPT | JSCRIPT | VBS | VBSCRIPT"
```

Attributes

CLASS   See "Core Attributes Reference," earlier in this chapter.

CLEAR   This attribute forces the insertion of vertical space so that the tagged text may be positioned with respect to images. A value of **LEFT** clears text that flows around left-aligned images to the next full left margin, a value of **RIGHT** clears text that flows around right-aligned images to the next full right margin, and a value of **ALL** clears text until it can reach both full margins. The default value according to the HTML 4 transitional specification is **NONE**, but its meaning is generally supported as just introducing a return and nothing more.

ID   See "Core Attributes Reference," earlier in this chapter.

LANGUAGE   This attribute specifies the language the current script is written in and invokes the proper scripting engine. The default value is **JAVASCRIPT**. **JAVASCRIPT** and **JSCRIPT** represent that the scripting language is written in JavaScript. **VBS** and **VBSCRIPT** represent that the scripting language is written in VBScript.

STYLE   See "Core Attributes Reference," earlier in this chapter.

TITLE   See "Core Attributes Reference," earlier in this chapter.

Attribute and Event Support

NETSCAPE 4   **CLEAR.** (**CLASS**, **ID**, and **STYLE** are implied by Netscape documentation.)

INTERNET EXPLORER 4   All attributes.

WEBTV   **CLEAR.**

Event Handlers

None.

Examples

```
This text will be broken here <BR> and continued on a
new line.

<IMG SRC="test.gif" ALIGN="RIGHT">
This is the image caption.<BR CLEAR="RIGHT">
```

Compatibility

HTML 3.2, 4; Netscape 1, 2, 3, 4; Internet Explorer 2, 3, 4; and WebTV

Notes

- This is an empty element. A closing tag is illegal.
- Under the HTML 4 strict specification, the **CLEAR** attribute is not valid. Style sheet rules provide the functionality of the **CLEAR** attribute.

<BUTTON> (Form Button)

This element defines a nameable region known as a button, which may be used together with scripts.

Syntax

```
<BUTTON
    ACCESSKEY="key"
    CLASS="class name(s)"
    DIR="LTR | RTL"
```

```
DISABLED
ID="unique alphanumeric identifier"
LANG="language code"
NAME="button name"
STYLE="style information"
TABINDEX="number"
TITLE="advisory text"
TYPE="BUTTON | RESET | SUBMIT"
VALUE="button value"
onblur="script"
onclick="script"
ondblclick="script"
onfocus="script"
onkeydown="script"
onkeypress="script"
onkeyup="script"
onmousedown="script"
onmousemove="script"
onmouseout="script"
onmouseover="script"
onmouseup="script">
```

```
</BUTTON>
```

Attributes and Events Defined by Internet Explorer 4

```
DATAFLD="name of column supplying bound data"
DATAFORMATAS="HTML | TEXT"
DATASRC="ID of data source object supplying data"
LANGUAGE="JAVASCRIPT | JSCRIPT | VBS | VBSCRIPT"
onafterupdate="script"
onbeforeupdate="script"
ondragstart="script"
onhelp="script"
onresize="script"
onrowenter="script"
onrowexit="script"
onselectstart="script"
```

Attributes

ACCESSKEY   This attribute specifies a keyboard navigation accelerator for the element. Pressing ALT or a similar key in association with the specified key selects the anchor element correlated with that key.

CLASS   See "Core Attributes Reference," earlier in this chapter.

DATAFLD   This attribute specifies the column name from the data source object that supplies the bound data that defines the information for the **<BUTTON>** element's content.

DATAFORMATAS   This attribute indicates if the bound data is plain text or HTML.

DATASRC   This attribute indicates the **ID** of the data source object that supplies the data that is bound to the **<BUTTON>** element.

DIR   See "Language Reference," earlier in this chapter.

DISABLED   This attribute is used to disable the button.

ID   See "Core Attributes Reference," earlier in this chapter.

LANG   See "Language Reference," earlier in this chapter.

LANGUAGE   This attribute specifies the language that the current script associated with the event handlers is written in and invokes the proper scripting engine. The default value is **JAVASCRIPT**. **JAVASCRIPT** and **JSCRIPT** represent that the scripting language is written in JavaScript. **VBS** and **VBSCRIPT** represent that the scripting language is written in VBScript.

NAME   This attribute is used to define a name for the button so that it can be scripted by older browsers or used to provide a name for submit buttons when there is more than one in a page.

STYLE   See "Core Attributes Reference," earlier in this chapter.

TABINDEX   This attribute uses a number to identify the object's position in the tabbing order.

TITLE   See "Core Attributes Reference," earlier in this chapter.

TYPE   Defines the type of button. According to the HTML 4 specification, by default the button is undefined. Possible values include **BUTTON**, **RESET**, and **SUBMIT**, which are used to indicate the button is a plain button, submit button, or reset button, respectively.

VALUE   Defines the value that is sent to the server when the button is pressed. This may be useful when using multiple **SUBMIT** buttons that perform different actions to indicate which button was pressed to the handling CGI program.

2

Attribute and Event Support

INTERNET EXPLORER 4   All attributes and events except **DIR**, **NAME, TABINDEX**, and **VALUE**.

Event Handlers

See "Events Reference," earlier in this chapter.

Examples

```
<BUTTON NAME="Submit"
        VALUE="Submit"
        TYPE="Submit">Submit Request</BUTTON>

<BUTTON TYPE="BUTTON"
        onclick="doSomething()">Click This Button</BUTTON>

<BUTTON TYPE="BUTTON">
<IMG SRC="polkadot.gif" ALT="Polkadot"></BUTTON>
```

Compatibility

HTML 4; Internet Explorer 4

Notes

- It is illegal to associate an image map with an **<IMG>** that appears as the contents of a **BUTTON** element.
- The HTML 4 specification reserves the data-binding attributes **DATAFLD**, **DATAFORMATAS**, and **DATASRC** for future use.

<CAPTION>   (Figure or Table Caption)

This element is used within both the figure and table elements to define a caption.

Syntax

```
<CAPTION
    ALIGN="BOTTOM | LEFT | RIGHT | TOP" (transitional)
    CLASS="class name(s)"
    DIR="LTR | RTL"
    ID="unique alphanumeric identifier"
    LANG="language code"
    STYLE="style information"
    TITLE="advisory text"
    onclick="script"
    ondblclick="script"
    onkeydown="script"
    onkeypress="script"
    onkeyup="script"
    onmousedown="script"
    onmousemove="script"
    onmouseout="script"
    onmouseover="script"
    onmouseup="script">

</CAPTION>
```

Attributes and Events Defined by Internet Explorer 4

```
    LANGUAGE="JAVASCRIPT | JSCRIPT | VBS | VBSCRIPT"
    VALIGN="BOTTOM | TOP"
    onafterupdate="script"
    onbeforeupdate="script"
    onblur="script"
    onchange="script"
    ondragstart="script"
    onfocus="script"
    onhelp="script"
    onresize="script"
    onrowenter="script"
    onrowexit="script"
    onselect="script"
    onselectstart="script"
```

Attributes

ALIGN   This attribute specifies the alignment of the caption. HTML 4 defines **BOTTOM, LEFT, RIGHT**, and **TOP** as legal values. Internet Explorer and WebTV also support **CENTER**. Because this does not provide the possibility to combine vertical and horizontal

alignments, Microsoft has introduced the **VALIGN** attribute for the
<CAPTION> element.

CLASS   See "Core Attributes Reference," earlier in this chapter.

DIR   See "Language Reference," earlier in this chapter.

ID   See "Core Attributes Reference," earlier in this chapter.

LANG   See "Language Reference," earlier in this chapter.

LANGUAGE   This attribute specifies the language the current
script is written in and invokes the proper scripting engine. The
default value is **JAVASCRIPT**. **JAVASCRIPT** and **JSCRIPT**
represent that the scripting language is written in JavaScript. **VBS**
and **VBSCRIPT** represent that the scripting language is written in
VBScript.

STYLE   See "Core Attributes Reference," earlier in this chapter.

TITLE   See "Core Attributes Reference," earlier in this chapter.

VALIGN   This Internet Explorer–specific attribute specifies
whether the table caption appears at the top or bottom.

Attribute and Event Support

NETSCAPE 4   **ALIGN**. (**CLASS**, **ID**, **LANG**, and **STYLE** are
implied.)

INTERNET EXPLORER 4   All attributes and events except **DIR**.

WEBTV   **ALIGN (CENTER | LEFT | RIGHT)**.

Event Handlers

See "Events Reference," earlier in this chapter.

Example

```
<TABLE>
    <CAPTION ALIGN="TOP">Our High-Priced Menu</CAPTION>
        <TR>
            <TD>Escargot</TD>
            <TD>Filet Mignon</TD>
            <TD>Big Mac</TD>
        </TR>
</TABLE>
```

Compatibility

HTML 3.2, 4; Netscape 1.1, 2, 3, 4; Internet Explorer 2, 3, 4; and WebTV

Notes

- There should be only one caption per table.

- HTML 3.2 defines only the **ALIGN** attribute with values of **BOTTOM** and **TOP**. No other attributes are defined prior to HTML 4. WebTV adds a **CENTER** value to the **ALIGN** attribute.

\<CENTER\>   (Center Alignment)

This element causes the enclosed content to be centered within the margins currently in effect. Margins are either the default page margins or those imposed by overriding elements such as tables.

Syntax (Transitional Only)

```
<CENTER
    CLASS="class name(s)"
    DIR="LTR | RTL"
    ID="unique alphanumeric identifier"
    LANG="language code"
    STYLE="style information"
    TITLE="advisory text"
    onclick="script"
    ondblclick="script"
    onkeydown="script"
    onkeypress="script"
    onkeyup="script"
    onmousedown="script"
    onmousemove="script"
    onmouseout="script"
    onmouseover="script"
    onmouseup="script">

</CENTER>
```

Attributes and Events Defined by Internet Explorer 4

```
    LANGUAGE="JAVASCRIPT | JSCRIPT | VBS | VBSCRIPT"
    ondragstart="script"
```

```
onhelp="script"
onselectstart="script"
```

Attributes

CLASS   See "Core Attributes Reference," earlier in this chapter.

DIR   See "Language Reference," earlier in this chapter.

ID   See "Core Attributes Reference," earlier in this chapter.

LANG   See "Language Reference," earlier in this chapter.

LANGUAGE   This attribute specifies the language the current script is written in and invokes the proper scripting engine. The default value is **JAVASCRIPT**. **JAVASCRIPT** and **JSCRIPT** represent that the scripting language is written in JavaScript. **VBS** and **VBSCRIPT** represent that the scripting language is written in VBScript.

STYLE   See "Core Attributes Reference," earlier in this chapter.

TITLE   See "Core Attributes Reference," earlier in this chapter.

Attribute and Event Support

NETSCAPE 4   **CLASS**, **ID**, **LANG**, and **STYLE** are implied.

INTERNET EXPLORER 4   All attributes and events except **DIR**.

Event Handlers
See "Events Reference," earlier in this chapter.

Example
<CENTER>This is in the center of the page.**</CENTER>**

Compatibility
HTML 3.2, 4 (transitional); Netscape 1.1, 2, 3, 4; Internet Explorer 2, 3, 4; and WebTV

Notes

- The **<CENTER>** element defined by the W3C is a shorthand notation for **<DIV ALIGN="CENTER">**. The strict version of HTML 4 does not include the **<CENTER>** element.

- HTML 3.2 does not support any attributes for this element.

<CITE> (Citation)

This element indicates a citation from a book or other published source and is usually rendered in italics by a browser.

Syntax

```
<CITE
     CLASS="class name(s)"
     DIR="LTR | RTL"
     ID="unique alphanumeric identifier"
     LANG="language code"
     STYLE="style information"
     TITLE="advisory text"
     onclick="script"
     ondblclick="script"
     onkeydown="script"
     onkeypress="script"
     onkeyup="script"
     onmousedown="script"
     onmousemove="script"
     onmouseout="script"
     onmouseover="script"
     onmouseup="script">

</CITE>
```

Attributes and Events Defined by Internet Explorer 4

```
     LANGUAGE="JAVASCRIPT | JSCRIPT | VBS | VBSCRIPT"
     ondragstart="script"
     onhelp="script"
     onselectstart="script"
```

Attributes

CLASS   See "Core Attributes Reference," earlier in this chapter.

DIR   See "Language Reference," earlier in this chapter.

ID   See "Core Attributes Reference," earlier in this chapter.

LANG   See "Language Reference," earlier in this chapter.

LANGUAGE This attribute specifies the language the current script is written in and invokes the proper scripting engine. The default value is **JAVASCRIPT**. **JAVASCRIPT** and **JSCRIPT** represent that the scripting language is written in JavaScript. **VBS** and **VBSCRIPT** represent that the scripting language is written in VBScript.

STYLE See "Core Attributes Reference," earlier in this chapter.

TITLE See "Core Attributes Reference," earlier in this chapter.

Attribute and Event Support

NETSCAPE 4 **CLASS**, **ID**, **LANG**, and **STYLE** are implied.

INTERNET EXPLORER 4 All events and attributes except **DIR**.

Event Handlers

See "Events Reference," earlier in this chapter.

Example

```
This example is taken from <CITE> The HTML
Programmer's Reference.</CITE>
```

Compatibility

HTML 2, 3.2, 4; Netscape 1, 2, 3, 4; Internet Explorer 2, 3, 4; and WebTV

Notes

HTML 2 and 3.2 do not indicate any attributes for this element.

<CODE> (Code Listing)

This element indicates that the enclosed text is source code in a programming language. Usually it is rendered in a monospaced font.

Syntax

```
<CODE
    CLASS="class name(s)"
    DIR="LTR | RTL"
    ID="unique alphanumeric identifier"
    LANG="language code"
    STYLE="style information"
```

```
TITLE="advisory text"
onclick="script"
ondblclick="script"
onkeydown="script"
onkeypress="script"
onkeyup="script"
onmousedown="script"
onmousemove="script"
onmouseout="script"
onmouseover="script"
onmouseup="script">
```

```
</CODE>
```

Attributes and Events Defined by Internet Explorer 4

```
LANGUAGE="JAVASCRIPT | JSCRIPT | VBS | VBSCRIPT"
ondragstart="script"
onhelp="script"
onselectstart="script"
```

Attributes

CLASS   See "Core Attributes Reference," earlier in this chapter.

DIR   See "Language Reference," earlier in this chapter.

ID   See "Core Attributes Reference," earlier in this chapter.

LANG   See "Language Reference," earlier in this chapter.

LANGUAGE   This attribute specifies the language the current script is written in and invokes the proper scripting engine. The default value is **JAVASCRIPT**. **JAVASCRIPT** and **JSCRIPT** represent that the scripting language is written in JavaScript. **VBS** and **VBSCRIPT** represent that the scripting language is written in VBScript.

STYLE   See "Core Attributes Reference," earlier in this chapter.

TITLE   See "Core Attributes Reference," earlier in this chapter.

Attribute and Event Support

NETSCAPE 4   **CLASS**, **ID**, **LANG**, and **STYLE** are implied.

INTERNET EXPLORER 4   All attributes and events except **DIR**.

2

Event Handlers

See "Events Reference," earlier in this chapter.

Example

To increment a variable called *count,* use

`<CODE>` count++ `</CODE>`

Compatibility

HTML 2, 3.2, 4; Netscape 1, 2, 3, 4; Internet Explorer 2, 3, 4; and WebTV

Notes

- This element is best for short code fragments because it does not preserve special indentation. For multiline code fragments, page authors tend to use the **<PRE>** element.
- HTML 2 and 3.2 do not support any attributes for this element.

<COL> (Column)

This element defines a column within a table and is used for grouping and alignment purposes. It is generally found within a **<COLGROUP>** element.

Syntax

```
<COL
      ALIGN="CENTER | CHAR | JUSTIFY | LEFT | RIGHT"
      CHAR="character"
      CHAROFF="number"
      CLASS="class name(s)"
      DIR="LTR | RTL"
      ID="unique alphanumeric identifier"
      LANG="language code"
      SPAN="number"
      STYLE="style information"
      TITLE="advisory text"
      VALIGN="BASELINE | BOTTOM | MIDDLE | TOP"
      WIDTH="column width specification"
      onclick="script"
      ondblclick="script"
      onkeydown="script"
```

```
onkeypress="script"
onkeyup="script"
onmousedown="script"
onmousemove="script"
onmouseout="script"
onmouseover="script"
onmouseup="script">
```

Attributes

ALIGN   This attribute specifies horizontal alignment of cell's contents.

CHAR   This attribute is used to set the character to align the cells in a column on. Typical values for this include a period (.) when attempting to align numbers or monetary values.

CHAROFF   This attribute is used to indicate the number of characters to offset the column data from the alignment characters specified by the **CHAR** value.

CLASS   See "Core Attributes Reference," earlier in this chapter.

DIR   See "Language Reference," earlier in this chapter.

ID   See "Core Attributes Reference," earlier in this chapter.

LANG   See "Language Reference," earlier in this chapter.

SPAN   When present, this attribute applies the attributes of the <COL> element to additional consecutive columns.

STYLE   See "Core Attributes Reference," earlier in this chapter.

TITLE   See "Core Attributes Reference," earlier in this chapter.

VALIGN   This attribute specifies the vertical alignment of the text within the cell. Possible values for this attribute are **BASELINE, BOTTOM, MIDDLE,** and **TOP**.

WIDTH   This attribute specifies a default width for each column in the current column group. In addition to the standard pixel and percentage values, this attribute may take the special form **0***, which means that the width of each column in the group should be the minimum width necessary to hold the column's contents. Relative widths like **0.5*** can also be used.

Attribute and Event Support

INTERNET EXPLORER 4 **ALIGN (CENTER | LEFT | RIGHT), CLASS, ID, SPAN, STYLE, TITLE, VALIGN,** and **WIDTH.**

Event Handlers

See "Events Reference," earlier in this chapter.

Example

```
<TABLE BORDER="1" WIDTH="400">
<COLGROUP>
<COL ALIGN="CENTER" WIDTH="150"><COL ALIGN="RIGHT">

<TR>
   <TD>This column is aligned to the center.</TD>
   <TD>This one is aligned to the right.</TD>
</TR>

<TR><TD>!</TD><TD>?</TD></TR>

<TR><TD>!</TD><TD>?</TD></TR>
</TABLE>
```

Compatibility

HTML 4; Internet Explorer 4

Notes

- As an empty element, **<COL>** does not require a closing tag.
- This element generally appears within a **<COLGROUP>** element and like that element is somewhat of a convenience feature used to set attributes with one or more table columns.

<COLGROUP>   (Column Group)

This element creates an explicit column group to access a group of table columns for scripting or formatting.

Syntax

```
<COLGROUP
    ALIGN="CENTER | CHAR | JUSTIFY | LEFT | RIGHT"
    CHAR="character"
    CHAROFF="number"
    CLASS="class name(s)"
    DIR="LTR | RTL"
    ID="unique alphanumeric identifier"
    LANG="language code"
    SPAN="number"
    STYLE="style information"
    TITLE="advisory text"
    VALIGN="BASELINE | BOTTOM | MIDDLE | TOP"
    WIDTH="column width specification"
    onclick="script"
    ondblclick="script"
    onkeydown="script"
    onkeypress="script"
    onkeyup="script"
    onmousedown="script"
    onmousemove="script"
    onmouseout="script"
    onmouseover="script"
    onmouseup="script">

    <COL> elements

</COLGROUP>
```

Attributes

ALIGN   This attribute specifies horizontal alignment of contents of the cells in the column group. The values of **CENTER**, **LEFT**, and **RIGHT** have obvious meanings. A value of **JUSTIFY** for the attribute should attempt to justify all the column's contents. A value of **CHAR** attempts to align the contents based on the value of the **CHAR** attribute in conjunction with **CHAROFF**.

CHAR   This attribute is used to set the character to align the cells in a column on. Typical values for this include a period (.) when attempting to align numbers or monetary values.

CHAROFF   This attribute is used to indicate the number of characters to offset the column data from the alignment characters specified by the **CHAR** value.

2

CLASS   See "Core Attributes Reference," earlier in this chapter.

DIR   See "Language Reference," earlier in this chapter.

ID   See "Core Attributes Reference," earlier in this chapter.

LANG   See "Language Reference," earlier in this chapter.

SPAN   When present, this attribute specifies the default number of columns in this group. Browsers should ignore this attribute if the current column group contains one or more **<COL>** elements. The default value of this attribute is **1**.

STYLE   See "Core Attributes Reference," earlier in this chapter.

TITLE   See "Core Attributes Reference," earlier in this chapter.

VALIGN   This attribute specifies the vertical alignment of the contents of the cells within the column group.

WIDTH   This attribute specifies a default width for each column and its cells in the current column group. In addition to the standard pixel and percentage values, this attribute may take the special form **0***, which means that the width of each column in the group should be the minimum width necessary to hold the column's contents.

Attribute and Event Support

INTERNET EXPLORER 4   **ALIGN (CENTER | LEFT | RIGHT)**, **CLASS, ID, SPAN, STYLE, TITLE, VALIGN,** and **WIDTH.**

Event Handlers

See "Events Reference," earlier in this chapter.

Examples

```
<COLGROUP SPAN="10" ALIGN="CHAR" CHAR=":"
        VALIGN="CENTER">

<COLGROUP STYLE="{background: green}">
<COL ALIGN="LEFT">
<COL ALIGN="CENTER">
</COLGROUP>
```

Compatibility

HTML 4; Internet Explorer 4

Notes

Each column group defined by a **<COLGROUP>** may contain zero or more **<COL>** elements.

<COMMENT>   (Comment Information)

This nonstandard element treats enclosed text as nondisplaying comments while processing enclosed HTML. This element should not be used.

Syntax (Defined by Internet Explorer 4)

```
<COMMENT
     ID="unique alphanumeric identifier"
     LANG="language code"
     TITLE="advisory text">

     Commented information

</COMMENT>
```

Attributes

ID   See "Core Attributes Reference," earlier in this chapter.

LANG   See "Language Reference," earlier in this chapter.

TITLE   See "Core Attributes Reference," earlier in this chapter.

Attribute and Event Support

INTERNET EXPLORER 4   All attributes.

Event Handlers

None.

Example

```
<COMMENT>This is not the proper way to form
comments.</COMMENT>
```

Compatibility

Internet Explorer 4; WebTV

Notes

- It is better to use the <!-- ... --> element, an alternate comment element that does not process enclosed HTML in all specification-conforming browsers.

- Because the **<COMMENT>** element is not supported by all browsers, commented text done in this fashion will appear in Netscape browsers. While Internet Explorer still supports this elements, IE documentation recommends use of the <!-- ... --> element.

- While some notes indicate that the **<COMMENT>** element will render HTML included within it, in practice this does not seem to be the case.

<DD> (Definition in a Definition List)

This element indicates the definition of a term within a list of defined terms (**<DT>**) enclosed by a definition list (**<DL>**).

Syntax

```
<DD
      CLASS="class name(s)"
      DIR="LTR | RTL"
      ID="unique alphanumeric identifier"
      LANG="language code"
      STYLE="style information"
      TITLE="advisory text"
      onclick="script"
      ondblclick="script"
      onkeydown="script"
      onkeypress="script"
      onkeyup="script"
      onmousedown="script"
      onmousemove="script"
      onmouseout="script"
      onmouseover="script"
      onmouseup="script">

</DD>
```

Attributes and Events Defined by Internet Explorer 4

```
LANGUAGE="JAVASCRIPT | JSCRIPT | VBS | VBSCRIPT"
ondragstart="script"
onhelp="script"
onselectstart="script"
```

Attributes

CLASS   See "Core Attributes Reference," earlier in this chapter.

DIR   See "Language Reference," earlier in this chapter.

ID   See "Core Attributes Reference," earlier in this chapter.

LANG   See "Language Reference," earlier in this chapter.

LANGUAGE   This attribute specifies the language the current script is written in and invokes the proper scripting engine. The default value is **JAVASCRIPT**. **JAVASCRIPT** and **JSCRIPT** represent that the scripting language is written in JavaScript. **VBS** and **VBSCRIPT** represent that the scripting language is written in VBScript.

STYLE   See "Core Attributes Reference," earlier in this chapter.

TITLE   See "Core Attributes Reference," earlier in this chapter.

Attribute and Event Support

NETSCAPE 4   CLASS, ID, LANG, and STYLE.

INTERNET EXPLORER 4   All attributes and events except DIR.

Event Handlers

See "Events Reference," earlier in this chapter.

Example

```
<DL>
    <DT>DOG
        <DD>A domesticated animal that craves
            attention all the time
    <DT>CAT
        <DD>An animal that would just as soon
            ignore you until it gets hungry
</DL>
```

Compatibility

HTML 2, 3.2, 4; Netscape 1, 2, 3, 4; Internet Explorer 2, 3, 4; and WebTV

Notes

- The close tag for this element is optional, though encouraged when it will help make the list more understandable.

- This element occurs within a list of defined terms enclosed by the **<DL>** element. Typically associated with it is the term it defines, indicated by the **<DT>** element that just proceeds it.

- HTML 2 and 3.2 define no attributes for this element.

<DEL> (Deleted Text)

This element is used to indicate that text has been deleted from a document. A browser may render deleted text as strikethrough text.

Syntax

```
<DEL
    CITE="URL"
    CLASS="class name(s)"
    DATETIME="date"
    DIR="LTR | RTL"
    ID="unique alphanumeric identifier"
    LANG="language code"
    STYLE="style information"
    TITLE="advisory text"
    onclick="script"
    ondblclick="script"
    onkeydown="script"
    onkeypress="script"
    onkeyup="script"
    onmousedown="script"
    onmousemove="script"
    onmouseout="script"
    onmouseover="script"
    onmouseup="script"
    onselectstart="script">

</DEL>
```

Attributes and Events Defined by Internet Explorer 4

```
LANGUAGE="JAVASCRIPT | JSCRIPT | VBS | VBSCRIPT"
ondragstart="script"
onhelp="script"
```

Attributes

CITE   The value of this attribute is a URL that designates a source document or message that may give a reason why the information was deleted.

CLASS   See "Core Attributes Reference," earlier in this chapter.

DATETIME   This attribute is used to indicate the date and time the deletion was made. The value of the attribute is a date in a special format as defined by ISO 8601. The basic date format is

```
YYYY-MM-DDThh:mm:ssTZD
```

where the following is true:

```
YYYY=four-digit year such as 1997
MM=two-digit month (01=January, 02=February, and so on)
DD=two-digit day of the month (01 to 31)
hh=two-digit hour (00 to 23) (24-hour clock, not AM or PM)
mm=two-digit minute (00 to 59)
ss=two-digit second (00 to 59)
TZD=time zone designator
```

The time zone designator is either **Z**, which indicates UTC (Universal Time Coordinate, or coordinated universal time format), or **+_hh_:_mm_**, which indicates that the time is a local time that is _hh_ hours and _mm_ minutes ahead of UTC. Alternatively, the format for the time zone designator could be **-_hh_:_mm_**, which indicates that the local time is behind UTC. Note that the letter "T" actually appears in the string, all digits must be used, and **00** values for minutes and seconds may be required. An example value for the **DATETIME** attribute might be **1997-10-6T09:15:00-05:00**, which corresponds to October 6, 1997, 9:15 A.M., U.S. Eastern Standard Time.

DIR   See "Language Reference," earlier in this chapter.

ID   See "Core Attributes Reference," earlier in this chapter.

LANG   See "Language Reference," earlier in this chapter.

LANGUAGE   In the Microsoft implementation, this attribute specifies the scripting language to be used with an associated script bound to the element, typically through an event handler attribute. Possible values may include **JAVASCRIPT**, **JSCRIPT**, **VBS**, and **VBSCRIPT**. Other values, which include the version of the language used, such as **JavaScript1.1**, may also be possible.

STYLE   See "Core Attributes Reference," earlier in this chapter.

TITLE   See "Core Attributes Reference," earlier in this chapter.

Attribute and Event Support

INTERNET EXPLORER 4   All attributes and events except **CITE**, **DATETIME**, and **DIR**.

Event Handlers
See "Events Reference," earlier in this chapter.

Example
```
<DEL CITE="http://www.bigcompany.com/changes/oct97.htm"
    DATETIME="1998-10-06T09:15:00-05:00">
The penalty clause applies to client lateness as well.
</DEL>
```

Compatibility
HTML 4; Internet Explorer 4

Notes

- Browsers may render deleted (**<DEL>**) text in a different style to show the changes that have been made to the document. Internet Explorer 4 renders the text as strikethrough text. Eventually, a browser may have a way to show a revision history on a document. User agents that do not understand **<DEL>** or **<INS>** will show the information anyway, so there is no harm in adding information—only in deleting it. Because of the fact that **<DEL>**-enclosed text may show up, it may be wise to comment it out within the element, as shown here:

```
<DEL>
<!-- This is old information. -->
</DEL>
```

- The **<DEL>** element is not supported under the HTML 2 and 3.2 specifications.

<DFN>   (Defining Instance of a Term)

This element encloses the defining instance of a term. It is usually rendered as bold or bold italic text.

Syntax

```
<DFN
    CLASS="class name(s)"
    DIR="LTR | RTL"
    ID="unique alphanumeric identifier"
    LANG="language code"
    STYLE="style information"
    TITLE="advisory text"
    onclick="script"
    ondblclick="script"
    onkeydown="script"
    onkeypress="script"
    onkeyup="script"
    onmousedown="script"
    onmousemove="script"
    onmouseout="script"
    onmouseover="script"
    onmouseup="script">

</DFN>
```

Attributes and Events Defined by Internet Explorer 4

```
    LANGUAGE="JAVASCRIPT | JSCRIPT | VBS | VBSCRIPT"
    ondragstart="script"
    onhelp="script"
    onselectstart="script"
```

Attributes

CLASS   See "Core Attributes Reference," earlier in this chapter.

DIR   See "Language Reference," earlier in this chapter.

ID   See "Core Attributes Reference," earlier in this chapter.

LANG   See "Language Reference," earlier in this chapter.

LANGUAGE   This attribute specifies the language the current script is written in and invokes the proper scripting engine. The default value is **JAVASCRIPT**. **JAVASCRIPT** and **JSCRIPT** represent that the scripting language is written in JavaScript. **VBS** and **VBSCRIPT** represent that the scripting language is written in VBScript.

2

STYLE   See "Core Attributes Reference," earlier in this chapter.

TITLE   See "Core Attributes Reference," earlier in this chapter.

Attribute and Event Support

INTERNET EXPLORER 4   All attributes and events except **DIR**.

Event Handlers

See "Events Reference," earlier in this chapter.

Example

An **<DFN>**elephant**</DFN>** is too large to make a viable pet for anyone poorer than Bill Gates.

Compatibility

HTML 2, 3.2, 4; Internet Explorer 2, 3, 4; and WebTV

Notes

HTML 2 and 3.2 define no attributes for this element.

<DIR>   (Directory List)

This element encloses a list of brief, unordered items, such as might occur in a menu or DIRectory. The individual items are indicated by the **<LI>** element. Use of this element is not encouraged, as it is not part of the HTML 4 strict specification and provides little extra benefit over the **<UL>** element.

Syntax (Transitional Only)

```
<DIR
     CLASS="class name(s)"
     COMPACT
     DIR="LTR | RTL"
     ID="unique alphanumeric identifier"
     LANG="language code"
```

```
STYLE="style information"
TITLE="advisory text"
onclick="script"
ondblclick="script"
onkeydown="script"
onkeypress="script"
onkeyup="script"
onmousedown="script"
onmousemove="script"
onmouseout="script"
onmouseover="script"
onmouseup="script">
```

```
</DIR>
```

Attributes and Events Defined by Internet Explorer 4

```
LANGUAGE="JAVASCRIPT | JSCRIPT | VBS | VBSCRIPT"
ondragstart="script"
onhelp="script"
onselectstart="script"
```

Attributes

CLASS   See "Core Attributes Reference," earlier in this chapter.

COMPACT   This attribute reduces the white space between list items.

DIR   See "Language Reference," earlier in this chapter.

ID   See "Core Attributes Reference," earlier in this chapter.

LANG   See "Language Reference," earlier in this chapter.

LANGUAGE   This attribute specifies the language the current script is written in and invokes the proper scripting engine. The default value is **JAVASCRIPT**. **JAVASCRIPT** and **JSCRIPT** represent that the scripting language is written in JavaScript. **VBS** and **VBSCRIPT** represent that the scripting language is written in VBScript.

STYLE   See "Core Attributes Reference," earlier in this chapter.

TITLE   See "Core Attributes Reference," earlier in this chapter.

Attribute and Event Support

NETSCAPE 4   **CLASS, ID, LANG,** and **STYLE** are explicit.

INTERNET EXPLORER 4   All events and attributes except **COMPACT** and **DIR.**

WEBTV   No attributes. (Note: WebTV bolds text enclosed in the <DIR> element.)

Event Handlers

See "Events Reference," earlier in this chapter.

Example

```
<DIR>
  <LI>Header Files
  <LI>Code Files
  <LI>Comment Files
</DIR>
```

Compatibility

HTML 2, 3.2, 4 (transitional); Netscape 1, 2, 3, 4; Internet Explorer 2, 3, 4; and WebTV

Notes

- Because the **<DIR>** element is supposed to be used with short lists, the items in the list should have a maximum width of 20 characters.

- The HTML 4 strict specification does not support this element.

- Many browsers will not to render the **<DIR>** element any differently than the **<UL>** element.

- Many browsers will not render the **COMPACT** list style.

- HTML 2 and 3.2 support only the **COMPACT** attribute.

<DIV>   (Division)

This element indicates a block of document content, which should be treated as a logical unit.

Syntax

```
<DIV
    ALIGN="CENTER | JUSTIFY | LEFT | RIGHT"
        (transitional)
    CLASS="class name(s)"
    DATAFLD="name of column supplying bound data"
        (reserved)
    DATAFORMATAS="HTML | TEXT" (reserved)
    DATASRC="ID of data source object supplying data"
        (reserved)
    DIR="LTR | RTL"
    ID="unique alphanumeric identifier"
    LANG="language code"
    STYLE="style information"
    TITLE="advisory text"
    onclick="script"
    ondblclick="script"
    onkeydown="script"
    onkeypress="script"
    onkeyup="script"
    onmousedown="script"
    onmousemove="script"
    onmouseout="script"
    onmouseover="script"
    onmouseup="script">

</DIV>
```

Attributes and Events Defined by Internet Explorer 4

```
    LANGUAGE="JAVASCRIPT | JSCRIPT | VBS | VBSCRIPT"
    onafterupdate="script"
    onbeforeupdate="script"
    onblur="script"
    ondragstart="script"
    onfocus="script"
    onhelp="script"
    onresize="script"
    onrowenter="script"
    onrowexit="script"
    onscroll="script"
    onselectstart="script"
```

Attributes

ALIGN This attribute indicates how the tagged text should be horizontally aligned on the page. The default value is **LEFT**. The **JUSTIFY** value is supported only by the Microsoft implementation.

2

CHARSET This attribute defines the character encoding of the linked resource specified by the **HREF** attribute. The value is a space- and/or comma-delimited list of character sets as defined in RFC 2045. The default value is **ISO-8859-1**.

CLASS See "Core Attributes Reference," earlier in this chapter.

DATAFLD This attribute specifies the column name from the data source object that supplies the bound data.

DATAFORMATAS This attribute indicates if the bound data is plain text or HTML.

DATASRC This attribute indicates the **ID** of the data source object that supplies the data that is bound to this element.

DIR See "Language Reference," earlier in this chapter.

ID See "Core Attributes Reference," earlier in this chapter.

LANG See "Language Reference," earlier in this chapter.

LANGUAGE This attribute specifies the language the current script is written in and invokes the proper scripting engine. The default value is **JAVASCRIPT**. **JAVASCRIPT** and **JSCRIPT** represent that the scripting language is written in JavaScript. **VBS** and **VBSCRIPT** represent that the scripting language is written in VBScript.

STYLE See "Core Attributes Reference," earlier in this chapter.

TITLE See "Core Attributes Reference," earlier in this chapter.

Attribute and Event Support

NETSCAPE 4 **ALIGN**, **CLASS**, **ID**, **LANG**, and **STYLE**.

INTERNET EXPLORER 4 All attributes and events except **DIR**.

WEBTV **ALIGN (CENTER | LEFT | RIGHT)**.

Event Handlers

See "Events Reference," earlier in this chapter.

Examples

```
<DIV ALIGN="JUSTIFY">
All text within this division will be justified
(but only under Netscape 4).
</DIV>

<DIV CLASS="special" ID="div1"
    STYLE="{background: yellow}">
Get ready to animate and stylize this.
</DIV>
```

Compatibility

HTML 3.2, 4; Netscape 2, 3, 4; Internet Explorer 2, 3, 4; and WebTV

Notes

- Many users are confused by the proper use of the **<DIV>** element, since all it does is create a block element. It is very useful for binding scripts or styles to an arbitrary section of a document. In this sense, **<DIV>** complements **<SPAN>**, which is used inline.

- The HTML 4 specification specifies that the **DATAFLD**, **DATAFORMATAS**, and **DATASRC** attributes are reserved for **<DIV>** and may be supported in the future. Internet Explorer 4 already supports these reserved attributes.

- Under the strict specification of HTML 4, the **ALIGN** attribute is not supported.

- HTML 3.2 supports only the **ALIGN** attribute.

<DL> (Definition List)

This element encloses a list of terms and definition pairs. A common use for this element is to implement a glossary.

Syntax

```
<DL
    CLASS="class name(s)"
    COMPACT
```

```
DIR="LTR | RTL"
ID="unique alphanumeric identifier"
LANG="language code"
STYLE="style information"
TITLE="advisory text"
onclick="script"
ondblclick="script"
onkeydown="script"
onkeypress="script"
onkeyup="script"
onmousedown="script"
onmousemove="script"
onmouseout="script"
onmouseover="script"
onmouseup="script">
```

```
</DL>
```

Attributes and Events Defined by Internet Explorer 4

```
LANGUAGE="JAVASCRIPT | JSCRIPT | VBS | VBSCRIPT"
ondragstart="script"
onhelp="script"
onselectstart="script"
```

Attributes

CLASS   See "Core Attributes Reference," earlier in this chapter.

COMPACT   This attribute reduces the white space between list items.

DIR   See "Language Reference," earlier in this chapter.

ID   See "Core Attributes Reference," earlier in this chapter.

LANG   See "Language Reference," earlier in this chapter.

LANGUAGE   This attribute specifies the language the current script is written in and invokes the proper scripting engine. The default value is **JAVASCRIPT**. **JAVASCRIPT** and **JSCRIPT** represent that the scripting language is written in JavaScript. **VBS** and **VBSCRIPT** represent that the scripting language is written in VBScript.

STYLE   See "Core Attributes Reference," earlier in this chapter.

TITLE   See "Core Attributes Reference," earlier in this chapter.

Attribute and Event Support

NETSCAPE 4   **CLASS, COMPACT, ID, LANG,** and **STYLE.**

INTERNET EXPLORER 4   All attributes and events except **DIR.**

Event Handlers

See "Events Reference," earlier in this chapter.

Example

```
<DL>
    <DT>Cat
        <DD>A domestic animal that likes fish
    <DT>Skunk
        <DD>A wild animal that needs deodorant
</DL>
```

Compatibility

HTML 2, 3.2, 4; Netscape 1, 2, 3, 4; Internet Explorer 2, 3, 4; and WebTV

Notes

- The items in the list comprise two parts: the term, indicated by the **<DT>** element, and its definition, indicated by the **<DD>** element.

- Some page designers may use the **<DL>** element or **<UL>** element to help create text indent. While this is a common practice on the Web, it is not advisable because it confuses the meaning of the element by making it a physical layout device rather than a list.

- Under the strict HTML 4 definition, the **COMPACT** attribute is not allowed.

- HTML 2 and 3.2 support only the **COMPACT** attribute for this element.

<DT> (Term in a Definition List)

This element identifies a definition list term in a definition list term-definition pair.

Syntax

```
<DT
    CLASS="class name(s)"
    DIR="LTR | RTL"
    ID="unique alphanumeric identifier"
    LANG="language code"
    STYLE="style information"
    TITLE="advisory text"
    onclick="script"
    ondblclick="script"
    onkeydown="script"
    onkeypress="script"
    onkeyup="script"
    onmousedown="script"
    onmousemove="script"
    onmouseout="script"
    onmouseover="script"
    onmouseup="script">
```

Attributes and Events Defined by Internet Explorer 4

```
    LANGUAGE="JAVASCRIPT | JSCRIPT | VBS | VBSCRIPT"
    ondragstart="script"
    onhelp="script"
    onselectstart="script"
```

Attributes

CLASS   See "Core Attributes Reference," earlier in this chapter.

DIR   See "Language Reference," earlier in this chapter.

ID   See "Core Attributes Reference," earlier in this chapter.

LANG   See "Language Reference," earlier in this chapter.

LANGUAGE   This attribute specifies the language the current script is written in and invokes the proper scripting engine. The default value is **JAVASCRIPT**. **JAVASCRIPT** and **JSCRIPT** represent that the scripting language is written in JavaScript. **VBS** and **VBSCRIPT** represent that the scripting language is written in VBScript.

STYLE   See "Core Attributes Reference," earlier in this chapter.

TITLE   See "Core Attributes Reference," earlier in this chapter.

Attribute and Event Support

NETSCAPE 4   **CLASS**, **ID**, **LANG**, and **STYLE**.

INTERNET EXPLORER 4   All attributes and events except **DIR**.

Event Handlers

See "Events Reference," earlier in this chapter.

Example

```
<DL>
  <DT>Rake
    <DD>A garden tool used to gather leaves and rubbish
  <DT>Trowel
    <DD>A small garden tool used to shovel earth
</DL>
```

Compatibility

HTML 2, 3.2, 4; Netscape 1, 2, 3, 4; Internet Explorer 2, 3, 4; and WebTV

Notes

- This element occurs within a list of defined terms enclosed by the **<DL>** element. It is generally used in conjunction with the **<DD>** element, which indicates its definition. However, **<DT>** elements do not require a one-to-one correspondence with **<DD>** elements.

- The close tag for the element is optional but suggested when it will make things more clear, particularly with multiple-line definitions.

- HTML 2 and 3.2 support no attributes for this element.

<EM>   (Emphasis)

This element indicates emphasized text, which many browsers will display as italic text.

Syntax

```
<EM
        CLASS="class name(s)"
        DIR="LTR | RTL"
        ID="unique alphanumeric identifier"
        LANG="language code"
        STYLE="style information"
        TITLE="advisory text"
        onclick="script"
        ondblclick="script"
        onkeydown="script"
        onkeypress="script"
        onkeyup="script"
        onmousedown="script"
        onmousemove="script"
        onmouseout="script"
        onmouseover="script"
        onmouseup="script">

</EM>
```

Attributes and Events Defined by Internet Explorer 4

```
        LANGUAGE="JAVASCRIPT | JSCRIPT | VBS | VBSCRIPT"
        ondragstart="script"
        onhelp="script"
        onselectstart="script"
```

Attributes

CLASS   See "Core Attributes Reference," earlier in this chapter.

DIR   See "Language Reference," earlier in this chapter.

ID   See "Core Attributes Reference," earlier in this chapter.

LANG   See "Language Reference," earlier in this chapter.

LANGUAGE   This attribute specifies the language the current script is written in and invokes the proper scripting engine. The default value is **JAVASCRIPT**. **JAVASCRIPT** and **JSCRIPT** represent that the scripting language is written in JavaScript. **VBS** and **VBSCRIPT** represent that the scripting language is written in VBScript.

STYLE   See "Core Attributes Reference," earlier in this chapter.

TITLE   See "Core Attributes Reference," earlier in this chapter.

Attribute and Event Support

NETSCAPE 4   **CLASS**, **ID**, **LANG**, and **STYLE** are implied.

INTERNET EXPLORER 4   All attributes and events except **DIR**.

Event Handlers

See "Events Reference," earlier in this chapter.

Example

```
This is an <EM>important point</EM> to consider.
```

Compatibility

HTML 2, 3.2, 4; Netscape 1, 2, 3, 4; Internet Explorer 2, 3, 4; and
WebTV

Notes

- As a logical element, `<EM>` is a prime candidate to bind style
  information to. For example, to define emphasis to mean a
  larger font size in the Impact font, you might use a CSS rule
  like the following in a document-wide style sheet.

  ```
  EM  {font-size: larger; font-family: Impact;}
  ```

- HTML 2 and 3.2 support no attributes for this element.

`<EMBED>` (Embedded Object)

This widely supported but nonstandard element specifies an
object, typically a multimedia element, to be embedded in an
HTML document.

Syntax (Defined by Internet Explorer 4)

```
<EMBED
        ALIGN="ABSBOTTOM | ABSMIDDLE | BASELINE | BOTTOM |
               LEFT | MIDDLE | RIGHT | TEXTTOP | TOP"
        ALT="alternative text"
        CLASS="class name(s)"
```

```
CODE="filename"
CODEBASE="URL"
HEIGHT="pixels"
HSPACE="pixels"
ID="unique alphanumeric identifier"
NAME="string"
SRC="URL"
STYLE="style information"
TITLE="advisory text"
VSPACE="pixels"
WIDTH="pixels">

</EMBED>
```

Attributes Defined by Netscape 4

```
BORDER="pixels"
HIDDEN="TRUE | FALSE"
PALETTE="BACKGROUND | FOREGROUND"
PLUGINSPAGE="URL"
TYPE="MIME type"
UNITS="EN | PIXELS"
```

Attributes

ALIGN   This attribute controls the alignment of adjacent text with respect to the embedded object. The default value is **LEFT**.

ALT   This attribute indicates the text to be displayed if the applet cannot be executed.

BORDER   This attribute specifies the size in pixels of the border around the embedded object.

CLASS   See "Core Attributes Reference," earlier in this chapter.

CODE   This attribute specifies the name of the file containing the compiled Java class if the **<EMBED>** element is used to include a Java applet. This is a strange alternate form of Java inclusion documented by Microsoft.

CODEBASE   This specifies the base URL for the plug-in or potential applet in the case of the alternative form under Internet Explorer.

HEIGHT   This attribute sets the height in pixels of the embedded object.

HIDDEN   If this attribute is set to the value **TRUE**, the embedded object is not visible on the page and implicitly has a size of zero.

HSPACE   This attribute specifies in pixels the size of the left and right margin between the embedded object and surrounding text.

ID   See "Core Attributes Reference," earlier in this chapter.

NAME   This attribute specifies a name for the embedded object, which can be referenced by client-side programs in an embedded scripting language.

PALETTE   This attribute is used only on Windows systems to select the color palette used for the plug-in and may be set to **BACKGROUND** or **FOREGROUND**. The default is **BACKGROUND**.

PLUGINSPAGE   This attribute contains the URL of instructions for installing the plug-in required to render the embedded object.

SRC   This attribute specifies the URL of source content for the embedded object.

STYLE   See "Core Attributes Reference," earlier in this chapter.

TITLE   See "Core Attributes Reference," earlier in this chapter.

TYPE   This attribute specifies the MIME type of the embedded object. It is used by the browser to determine an appropriate plug-in for rendering the object. It can be used instead of the **SRC** attribute for plug-ins that have no content or that fetch it dynamically.

UNITS   This Netscape-specific attribute is used to set the units for measurement for the embedded object either in **EN** or in the default, **PIXELS**.

VSPACE   This attribute specifies in pixels the size of the top and bottom margin between the embedded object and surrounding text.

WIDTH   This attribute sets the width in pixels of the embedded object.

Attribute and Event Support

NETSCAPE 4 **ALIGN (BOTTOM | LEFT | RIGHT | TOP)**, **HEIGHT**, **SRC**, **WIDTH**, and all Netscape-defined attributes. (**CLASS**, **ID**, **LANG**, and **STYLE** are implied.)

INTERNET EXPLORER 4 All Microsoft-defined attributes and events.

WEBTV **ALIGN (BOTTOM | LEFT | RIGHT | TOP)**, **BORDER**, **HEIGHT**, **HIDDEN**, **HSPACE**, **NAME**, **SRC**, **VSPACE**, and **WIDTH**.

Event Handlers

See "Events Reference," earlier in this chapter.

Examples

```
<!-- EMBED without a close tag -->
<EMBED SRC="testmovie.mov" HEIGHT="150" WIDTH="150">
<NOEMBED>
 <IMG SRC="testgif.gif" HEIGHT="150" WIDTH="150"
     ALT="Test Image">
</NOEMBED>

<!-- EMBED with a close tag -->
<EMBED SRC="testmovie.mov" HEIGHT="150" WIDTH="150">
<NOEMBED>
 <IMG SRC="testgif.gif" HEIGHT="150" WIDTH="150"
     ALT="Test Image">
</NOEMBED>
</EMBED>
```

Compatibility

Netscape 2, 3, 4; Internet Explorer 3, 4; and WebTV

Notes

- It is unclear whether or not the close tag for **<EMBED>** is required. Many sites tend not to use it, and documentation is not consistent. Some people claim that a close tag is required and should surround any alternative content in a **<NOEMBED>** element; others do not use a close tag. Since this element should eventually be phased out in favor of **<OBJECT>**, this may be a moot issue.

- While WebTV may support the **<EMBED>** element, it can deal only with media types the equipment knows how to handle, such as Macromedia Flash or certain standard audio files. Other plug-ins cannot be added to the system.

- The **<EMBED>** element is not favored by the W3C and is not part of any official HTML specification; however, it is very common. The HTML specification says to use the **<OBJECT>** element, which can be used in conjunction with the **<EMBED>** element to provide backward compatibility.

- Embedded objects are multimedia content files of arbitrary type, which are rendered by browser plug-ins. The **TYPE** attribute uses a file's MIME type to determine an appropriate browser plug-in. Any attributes not defined are treated as object-specific parameters and passed through to the embedded object. Consult the plug-in or object documentation to determine these. The standard parameters supported by the Microsoft implementation are **HEIGHT**, **NAME**, **PALETTE**, **SRC**, **UNITS**, and **WIDTH**.

<FIELDSET> (Form Field Set)

This element allows form designers to group thematically related controls together.

Syntax

```
<FIELDSET
    CLASS="class name(s)"
    DIR="LTR | RTL"
    ID="unique alphanumeric identifier"
    LANG="language code"
    STYLE="style information"
    TITLE="advisory text"
    onclick="script"
    ondblclick="script"
    onkeydown="script"
    onkeypress="script"
    onkeyup="script"
    onmousedown="script"
    onmousemove="script"
    onmouseout="script"
```

2

```
          onmouseover="script"
          onmouseup="script">

</FIELDSET>
```

Attributes and Events Defined by Internet Explorer 4

```
     ALIGN="CENTER | LEFT | RIGHT"
     LANGUAGE="JAVASCRIPT | JSCRIPT | VBS | VBSCRIPT"
     onblur="script"
     onchange="script"
     ondragstart="script"
     onfilterchange="script"
     onfocus="script"
     onhelp="script"
     onresize="script"
     onscroll="script"
     onselect="script"
     onselectstart="script"
```

Attributes

ALIGN   Internet Explorer defines the **ALIGN** attribute, which sets how the element and its contents are positioned in a table or the window.

CLASS   See "Core Attributes Reference," earlier in this chapter.

DIR   See "Language Reference," earlier in this chapter.

ID   See "Core Attributes Reference," earlier in this chapter.

LANG   See "Language Reference," earlier in this chapter.

LANGUAGE   This attribute specifies the language the current script is written in and invokes the proper scripting engine. The default value is **JAVASCRIPT**. **JAVASCRIPT** and **JSCRIPT** represent that the scripting language is written in JavaScript. **VBS** and **VBSCRIPT** represent that the scripting language is written in VBScript.

STYLE   See "Core Attributes Reference," earlier in this chapter.

TITLE   See "Core Attributes Reference," earlier in this chapter.

Attribute and Event Support

INTERNET EXPLORER 4   All attributes and events except **DIR**.

Event Handlers

See "Events Reference," earlier in this chapter.

Example

```
<FIELDSET>
<LEGEND>Customer Identification</LEGEND>
<BR>
<LABEL>Customer Name:
<INPUT TYPE="TEXT" ID="CustName" SIZE="25">
</FIELDSET>
```

Compatibility

HTML 4; Internet Explorer 4

Notes

- Grouping controls makes it easier for users to understand the purposes of the controls while simultaneously facilitating tabbing navigation for visual user agents and speech navigation for speech-oriented user agents. The proper use of this element makes documents more accessible to people with disabilities.

- The caption for this element is defined by the **<LEGEND>** element within the **<FIELDSET>** element.

<FN>　(Footnote)

This WebTV-specific element indicates either a reference to a footnote or the footnote itself.

Syntax (Defined by WebTV)

```
<FN
    HREF="URL"
    ID="unique alphanumeric identifier">

</FN>
```

Attributes

HREF　This attribute contains a URL that references the footnote. Typically the URL is a fragment in the form of the pound sign (#) followed by the name of the footnote anchor. It indicates that the tagged text is a reference to a footnote.

ID This attribute contains the name of the footnote anchor. It indicates that the tagged text is a footnote.

Attribute and Event Support

WEBTV **HREF** and **ID**.

Event Handlers
None.

Example
This wonderful idea came from **<FN HREF="#smith">** Smith.**</FN>**

<FN ID="smith">Smith, Fred, Journal of Really Good Ideas**</FN>**

Compatibility
WebTV

Notes

- Footnotes are implemented as internal links within a document. Use the **HREF** attribute to indicate a reference to a footnote. Use the **ID** attribute to indicate the footnote itself.

- Footnotes are not to be used outside the WebTV environment. They are a leftover of the failed HTML 3 proposal.

<FONT> (Font Definition)

This element allows specification of the size, color, and font of the text it encloses. Use of this element is not encouraged as it is not part of the HTML 4 strict specification. Style sheets provide a cleaner way of providing the same functionality when they are supported.

Syntax (Transitional Only)

```
<FONT
    CLASS="class name(s)"
    COLOR="color name | #RRGGBB"
    DIR="LTR | RTL"
    FACE="font name"
    ID="unique alphanumeric identifier"
```

```
LANG="language code"
SIZE="1 to 7 | +1 to +6 | -1 to -6"
STYLE="style information"
TITLE="advisory text">
```

```
</FONT>
```

Attributes and Events Defined by Internet Explorer 4

```
LANGUAGE="JAVASCRIPT | JSCRIPT | VBS | VBSCRIPT"
onclick="script"
ondblclick="script"
ondragstart="script"
onhelp="script"
onkeydown="script"
onkeypress="script"
onkeyup="script"
onmousedown="script"
onmousemove="script"
onmouseout="script"
onmouseover="script"
onmouseup="script"
onselectstart="script"
```

Attributes Defined by Netscape 4

```
POINT-SIZE="point size for font"
WEIGHT="100 | 200 | 300 | 400 | 500 | 600 | 700 |
        800 | 900"
```

Attributes Defined by WebTV

```
EFFECT="EMBOSS | RELIEF | SHADOW"
TRANSPARENCY="number (0-100)"
```

Attributes

CLASS   See "Core Attributes Reference," earlier in this chapter.

COLOR   This attribute sets the text color using either a browser-dependent named color or a color specified in the hexadecimal *#RRGGBB* format.

DIR   See "Language Reference," earlier in this chapter.

EFFECT   In the WebTV implementation, this attribute renders the tagged text in a special way. The **RELIEF** value causes the text to appear raised off the page. The **EMBOSS** value causes the text to appear embossed into the page.

FACE This attribute contains a list of one or more font names separated by commas. The user agent looks through the specified font names and renders the text in the first font that is supported.

ID See "Core Attributes Reference," earlier in this chapter.

LANG See "Language Reference," earlier in this chapter.

LANGUAGE This attribute specifies the language the current script is written in and invokes the proper scripting engine. The default value is **JAVASCRIPT**. **JAVASCRIPT** and **JSCRIPT** represent that the scripting language is written in JavaScript. **VBS** and **VBSCRIPT** represent that the scripting language is written in VBScript.

POINT-SIZE This Netscape 4–specific attribute specifies the point size of text and is used with downloadable fonts.

SIZE This attribute specifies the font size as either a numeric or relative value. Numeric values range from **1** to **7** with **1** being the smallest and **3** the default. The relative values, + and –, increment or decrement the font size relative to the current size. The value for increment or decrement should range only from **+1** to **+ 6** or **–1** to **–6**.

STYLE See "Core Attributes Reference," earlier in this chapter.

TITLE See "Core Attributes Reference," earlier in this chapter.

TRANSPARENCY WebTV's proprietary **TRANSPARENCY** attribute is used to set the transparency level of the text. A value of **0** indicates the text is opaque; a value of **100** indicates text is fully transparent, allowing the background to show through. The default value for this attribute is **0**.

WEIGHT Under Netscape 4, this attribute specifies the weight of the font, with a value of **100** being lightest and **900** being heaviest.

Attribute and Event Support

NETSCAPE 4 COLOR, POINT-SIZE, SIZE, and **WEIGHT**. (**CLASS**, **ID**, **LANG**, and **STYLE** are implied.)

INTERNET EXPLORER 4 All W3C-defined attributes and events except **DIR**, and all attributes and events defined by Internet Explorer 4.

WEBTV   **COLOR**, **EFFECT**, **SIZE**, and **TRANSPARENCY**.

Event Handlers

See "Events Reference," earlier in this chapter.

Example

```
<FONT COLOR="#FF0000" FACE="Helvetica, Times Roman"
    SIZE="+1">
Relatively large red text in Helvetica or Times
</FONT>
```

Compatibility

HTML 3.2, 4; Netscape 1.1, 2, 3, 4; Internet Explorer 2, 3, 4; and WebTV

Notes

- The default text size for a document can be set using the **SIZE** attribute of the **<BASEFONT>** element.

- The HTML 3.2 specification supports only the **COLOR** and **SIZE** attributes for this element.

- The HTML 4 transitional specification supports the **CLASS**, **COLOR**, **DIR**, **FACE**, **ID**, **LANG**, **SIZE**, **STYLE**, and **TITLE** attributes.

- The HTML 4 strict specification does not support the **<FONT>** element at all.

<FORM>   (Form for User Input)

The element defines a fill-in form to contain labels and form controls, such as menus and text entry boxes that may be filled in by a user.

Syntax

```
<FORM
    ACCEPT-CHARSET="list of supported character sets"
    ACTION="URL"
    CLASS="class name(s)"
    DIR="LTR | RTL"
    ENCTYPE="application/x-www-form-urlencoded |
             multipart/form-data | text/plain |
```

2

```
                  Media Type as per RFC 2045"
     ID="unique alphanumeric identifier"
     LANG="language code"
     METHOD="GET | POST"
     STYLE="style information"
     TARGET="_blank | frame name | _parent | _self |
           _top" (transitional)
     TITLE="advisory text"
     onclick="script"
     ondblclick="script"
     onkeydown="script"
     onkeypress="script"
     onkeyup="script"
     onmousedown="script"
     onmousemove="script"
     onmouseout="script"
     onmouseover="script"
     onmouseup="script"
     onreset="script"
     onsubmit="script">

</FORM>
```

Attributes and Events Defined by Internet Explorer 4

```
     LANGUAGE="JAVASCRIPT | JSCRIPT | VBS | VBSCRIPT"
     NAME="string"
     ondragstart="script"
     onhelp="script"
     onselectstart="script"
```

Attributes

ACCEPT-CHARSET   This attribute specifies the list of character encodings for input data that must be accepted by the server processing form. The value is a space- or comma-delimited list of character sets as defined in RFC 2045. The default value for this attribute is the reserved value **UNKNOWN**.

ACTION   This attribute contains the URL of the server program, which will process the contents of the form. Some browsers may also support a mailto URL, which may mail the results to the specified address.

CLASS   See "Core Attributes Reference," earlier in this chapter.

DIR   See "Language Reference," earlier in this chapter.

ENCTYPE   This attribute indicates how form data should be encoded before being sent to the server. The default is **application/x-www-form-urlencoded**. This encoding replaces blank characters in the data with a + and all other nonprinting characters with a % followed by the character's ASCII HEX representation. The multipart/form-data option does not perform character conversion and transfers the information as a compound MIME document. This must be used when using **<INPUT TYPE="FILE">**. It may also be possible to use another encoding like text/plain to avoid any form of hex encoding that may be useful with mailed forms.

ID   See "Core Attributes Reference," earlier in this chapter.

LANG   See "Language Reference," earlier in this chapter.

LANGUAGE   This attribute specifies the language the current script is written in and invokes the proper scripting engine. The default value is **JAVASCRIPT**. **JAVASCRIPT** and **JSCRIPT** represent that the scripting language is written in JavaScript. **VBS** and **VBSCRIPT** represent that the scripting language is written in VBScript.

METHOD   This attribute indicates how form information should be transferred to the server. The **GET** option appends data to the URL specified by the **ACTION** attribute. This approach gives best performance, but imposes a size limitation determined by the command-line length supported by the server. The **POST** option transfers data using an HTTP post transaction. This approach is more secure and imposes no data size limitation.

NAME   This attribute specifies a name for the form and can be used by client-side programs to reference form data.

STYLE   See "Core Attributes Reference," earlier in this chapter.

TARGET   In documents containing frames, this attribute specifies the target frame to display the results of a form submission. In addition to named frames, several special values exist. The **_blank** value indicates a new window. The **_parent** value indicates the parent frame set containing the source link. The **_self** value indicates the frame containing the source link. The **_top** value indicates the full browser window.

TITLE   See "Core Attributes Reference," earlier in this chapter.

Attribute and Event Support

NETSCAPE 4   **ACTION, ENCTYPE, METHOD, NAME, TARGET, onreset,** and **onsubmit.** (**CLASS, ID, LANG,** and **STYLE** are implied.)

INTERNET EXPLORER 4   All attributes and events except **ACCEPT-CHARSET** and **DIR.**

WEBTV   **ACTION, METHOD, TARGET, onreset,** and **onsubmit.**

Event Handlers

See "Events Reference," earlier in this chapter.

Example

```
<FORM ACTION="http://www.bigcompany.com/cgi-bin/
              processit.exe"
METHOD="POST" NAME="testform" onsubmit="validate()">
Enter your comments here:<BR>
<TEXTAREA NAME="comments" COLS="30" ROWS="8"></TEXTAREA>
<BR>
<INPUT TYPE="SUBMIT">
<INPUT TYPE="RESET">
</FORM>
```

Compatibility

HTML 2, 3.2, 4; Netscape 1, 2, 3, 4; Internet Explorer 2, 3, 4; and WebTV

Notes

- Form content is defined using the **<BUTTON>, <INPUT>, <SELECT>,** and **<TEXTAREA>** elements as well as other HTML formatting and structuring elements. Special grouping elements like **<FIELDSET>, <LABEL>,** and **<LEGEND>** have been introduced to provide better structuring for forms, but other HTML elements such as **<DIV>** and **<TABLE>** may also be used to improve form layout.

- HTML 2 and 3.2 support only the **ACTION, ENCTYPE,** and **METHOD** attributes for the **<FORM>** element.

<FRAME> (Window Region)

This element defines a nameable window region, known as a *frame*, that can independently display its own content.

Syntax (Transitional Only)

```
<FRAME
    CLASS="class name(s)"
    FRAMEBORDER="0 | 1"
    ID="unique alphanumeric identifier"
    LONGDESC="URL of description"
    MARGINHEIGHT="pixels"
    MARGINWIDTH="pixels"
    NAME="string"
    NORESIZE
    SCROLLING="AUTO | NO | YES"
    SRC="URL" of frame contents"
    STYLE="style information"
    TITLE="advisory text">
```

Attributes and Events Defined by Internet Explorer 4

```
    BORDERCOLOR="color name | #RRGGBB"
    DATAFLD="name of column supplying bound data"
    DATASRC="ID of data source object supplying data"
    FRAMEBORDER="NO | YES | 0 | 1"
    HEIGHT="pixels"
    LANG="language code"
    LANGUAGE="JAVASCRIPT | JSCRIPT | VBS | VBSCRIPT"
    WIDTH="pixels"
    onreadystatechange="script"
```

Attributes Defined by WebTV

```
    ALIGN="BOTTOM | CENTER | LEFT | RIGHT | TOP"
```

Attributes

BORDERCOLOR   This attribute sets the color of the frame's border using either a named color or a color specified in the hexadecimal *#RRGGBB* format.

CLASS   See "Core Attributes Reference," earlier in this chapter.

DATAFLD   This Internet Explorer attribute specifies the column name from the data source object that supplies the bound data.

DATASRC   This Internet Explorer attribute indicates the **ID** of the data source object that supplies the data that is bound to this element.

2

FRAMEBORDER   This attribute determines whether the frame is surrounded by an outlined three-dimensional border. The HTML specification prefers the use of **1** for the frame border on and **0** for off; most browsers also acknowledge the use of **NO** and **YES**.

ID   See "Core Attributes Reference," earlier in this chapter.

LANG   See "Language Reference," earlier in this chapter.

LANGUAGE   This attribute specifies the language the current script is written in and invokes the proper scripting engine. The default value is **JAVASCRIPT**. **JAVASCRIPT** and **JSCRIPT** represent that the scripting language is written in JavaScript. **VBS** and **VBSCRIPT** represent that the scripting language is written in VBScript.

LONGDESC   This attribute specifies a URL of a document that contains a long description of the frame's content. This attribute shoud be used in conjunction with the **<TITLE>** element.

MARGINHEIGHT   This attribute sets the height in pixels between the frame's contents and its top and bottom borders.

MARGINWIDTH   This attribute sets the width in pixels between the frame's contents and its left and right borders.

NAME   This attribute assigns the frame a name so that it can be the target destination of hyperlinks as well as be a possible candidate for manipulation via a script.

NORESIZE   This attribute overrides the default ability to resize frames and gives the frame a fixed size.

SCROLLING   This attribute determines if the frame has scroll bars. A **YES** value forces scroll bars, a **NO** value prohibits them, and an **AUTO** value lets the browser decide. When not specified, the default value of **AUTO** is used. Authors are recommended to leave the value as **AUTO**. If you turn off scrolling and the contents end up being too large for the frame (due to rendering differences, window size, etc.), the user will not be able to scroll to see the rest of the contents. If you turn scrolling on and the contents all fit in the frame, the scroll bars will needlessly consume screen space. With the **AUTO** value, scroll bars appear only when needed.

SRC   This attribute contains the URL of the contents to be displayed in the frame. If absent, nothing will be loaded in the frame.

STYLE   See "Core Attributes Reference," earlier in this chapter.

TITLE   See "Core Attributes Reference," earlier in this chapter.

Attribute and Event Support

NETSCAPE 4   BORDERCOLOR, FRAMEBORDER, MARGINHEIGHT, MARGINWIDTH, NAME, NORESIZE, SCROLLING, and SRC. (CLASS, ID, LANG, and STYLE are implied.)

INTERNET EXPLORER 4   All W3C-defined attributes except LONGDESC and STYLE, and all attributes and events defined by Internet Explorer 4. (Note: Internet Explorer 4 supports the values NORESIZE and RESIZE.)

WEBTV   ALIGN, FRAMEBORDER (0 | 1), MARGINHEIGHT, MARGINWIDTH, NAME, and SRC.

Event Handlers

See "Events Reference," earlier in this chapter.

Example

```
<FRAMESET ROWS="20%,80%">
  <FRAME SRC="controls.htm" NAME="controls"
         NORESIZE SCROLLING="NO">
  <FRAME SRC="content.htm">
</FRAMESET>
```

Compatibility

HTML 4; Netscape 2, 3, 4; Internet Explorer 2, 3, 4; and WebTV

Notes

- A frame must be declared as part of a frame set as set by the **<FRAMESET>** element, which specifies the frame's relationship to other frames on a page. A frame set occurs in a special

HTML document in which the **<FRAMESET>** element replaces the **<BODY>** element. Another form of frames called *independent frames*, or *floating frames*, is also supported by Microsoft as well as the HTML 4 transitional specification. Floating frames can be directly embedded in a document without belonging to a frameset. These are defined with the **<IFRAME>** element.

2

- Numerous browsers do not support frames and require the use of the **<NOFRAMES>** element.

- Frames introduce potential navigation difficulties; their use should be limited to instances where they can be shown to help navigation rather than hinder it.

<FRAMESET> (Frameset Definition)

This element is used to define the organization of a set of independent window regions known as *frames*, as defined by the **<FRAME>** element. This element replaces the **<BODY>** element in framing documents.

Syntax (Transitional Only)

```
<FRAMESET
    CLASS="class name(s)"
    COLS="list of columns"
    ID="unique alphanumeric identifier"
    ROWS="list of rows"
    STYLE="style information"
    TITLE="advisory text"
    onload="script"
    onunload="script">

    <FRAME> elements and <NOFRAMES>

</FRAMESET>
```

Attributes and Events Defined by Internet Explorer 4

```
    BORDER="pixels"
    BORDERCOLOR="color name | #RRGGBB"
    FRAMEBORDER="NO | YES | 0 | 1"
    FRAMESPACING="pixels"
    LANG="language code"
    LANGUAGE="JAVASCRIPT | JSCRIPT | VBS | VBSCRIPT"
```

Attributes and Events Defined by Netscape 4

```
BORDER="pixels"
BORDERCOLOR="color name | #RRGGBB"
FRAMEBORDER="NO | YES | 0 | 1"
LANG="language code"
onblur="script"
onfocus="script"
```

Attributes Defined by WebTV

```
BORDER="pixels"
FRAMEBORDER="0 | 1"
```

Attributes

BORDER   This attribute sets the width in pixels of frame borders within the frame set. Setting **BORDER="0"** eliminates all frame borders. This attribute is not defined in the HTML specification but is widely supported.

BORDERCOLOR   This attribute sets the color for frame borders within the frame set using either a named color or a color specified in the hexadecimal *#RRGGBB* format.

CLASS   See "Core Attributes Reference," earlier in this chapter.

COLS   This attribute contains a comma-delimited list, which specifies the number and size of columns contained within a set of frames. List items indicate columns, left to right. Column size is specified in three formats, which may be mixed. A column can be assigned a fixed width in pixels. It can also be assigned a percentage of the available width, such as 50 percent. Last, a column can be set to expand to fill the available space by setting the value to *, which acts as a wildcard.

FRAMEBORDER   This attribute controls whether or not frame borders should be displayed. Netscape supports **NO** and **YES** values. Microsoft uses **1** and **0** as well as **NO** and **YES**.

FRAMESPACING   This attribute indicates the space between frames in pixels.

ID   See "Core Attributes Reference," earlier in this chapter.

LANG   See "Language Reference," earlier in this chapter.

LANGUAGE This attribute specifies the language the current script is written in and invokes the proper scripting engine. The default value is **JAVASCRIPT**. **JAVASCRIPT** and **JSCRIPT** represent that the scripting language is written in JavaScript. **VBS** and **VBSCRIPT** represent that the scripting language is written in VBScript.

2

ROWS This attribute contains a comma-delimited list, which specifies the number and size of rows contained within a set of frames. The number of entries in the list indicates the number of rows. Row size is specified with the same formats used for columns.

STYLE See "Core Attributes Reference," earlier in this chapter.

TITLE See "Core Attributes Reference," earlier in this chapter.

Attribute and Event Support

NETSCAPE 4 BORDER, BORDERCOLOR, COLS, FRAMEBORDER, ROWS, onblur, onfocus, onload, and onunload. (CLASS, ID, LANG, and STYLE are implied.)

INTERNET EXPLORER 4 BORDER, BORDERCOLOR, CLASS, COLS, FRAMEBORDER, ID, LANG, LANGUAGE, ROWS, and TITLE.

WEBTV BORDER, COLS, FRAMEBORDER (0 | 1), FRAMESPACING, ROWS, onload, and onunload.

Event Handlers

See "Events Reference," earlier in this chapter.

Examples

```
<!-- This example defines a frame set of three columns.
     The middle column is 50 pixels wide.
     The first and last columns fill the remaining space.
     The last column takes twice as much space as the first.
-->

<FRAMESET COLS="*,50,*">
<FRAME SRC="column1.htm">
<FRAME SRC="column2.htm">
<FRAME SRC="column3.htm">
</FRAMESET>
```

```
<!-- This example defines a frame set of two columns,
     one of which is 20% of the screen and the
     other 80%.
-->

<FRAMESET COLS="20%, 80%">
<FRAME SRC="controls.htm">
<FRAME SRC="display.htm">
</FRAMESET>

<!-- This example defines two rows, one of which is
     10% of the screen and the other, whatever space
     is left.


-->

<FRAMESET ROWS="10%, *">
 <FRAME SRC="adbanner.htm" NAME="ad_frame">
 <FRAME SRC="contents.htm" NAME="content_frame">
</FRAMESET>
```

Compatibility

HTML 4 (transitional); Netscape 2, 3, 4; Internet Explorer 2, 3, 4; and WebTV

Notes

- The **<FRAMESET>** element contains one or more **<FRAME>** elements, which are used to indicate the framed contents. The **<FRAMESET>** element may also contain a **<NOFRAMES>** element whose contents will be displayed on browsers that do not support frames.

- The **<FRAMESET>** element replaces the **<BODY>** element in a framing document as shown here:

    ```
    <HTML>
    <HEAD>
    <TITLE>Collection of Frames</TITLE>
    </HEAD>
    <FRAMESET COLS="*,50,*">
        <FRAME SRC="column1.htm" NAME="col1">
    ```

```
<FRAME SRC="column2.htm" NAME="col2">
<FRAME SRC="column3.htm" NAME="col3">
<NOFRAMES>
Please visit our <A HREF="noframes.htm">no frames</A>
site.
</FRAMESET>
</HTML>
```

<H1> Through <H6>   (Headings)

These tags implement six levels of document headings; **<H1>** is
the most prominent, and **<H6>** is the least prominent.

Syntax

```
<H1
     ALIGN="CENTER | JUSTIFY | LEFT | RIGHT"
          (transitional)
     CLASS="class name(s)"
     DIR="LTR | RTL"
     ID="unique alphanumeric identifier"
     LANG="language code"
     STYLE="style information"
     TITLE="advisory text"
     onclick="script"
     ondblclick="script"
     onkeydown="script"
     onkeypress="script"
     onkeyup="script"
     onmousedown="script"
     onmousemove="script"
     onmouseout="script"
     onmouseover="script"
     onmouseup="script">

</H1>
```

Attributes and Events Defined by Internet Explorer 4

```
     LANGUAGE="JAVASCRIPT | JSCRIPT | VBS | VBSCRIPT"
     ondragstart="script"
     onhelp="script"
     onselectstart="script"
```

Attributes

ALIGN   This attribute controls the horizontal alignment of the heading with respect to the page. The default value is **LEFT**.

CLASS   See "Core Attributes Reference," earlier in this chapter.

DIR   See "Language Reference," earlier in this chapter.

ID   See "Core Attributes Reference," earlier in this chapter.

LANG   See "Language Reference," earlier in this chapter.

LANGUAGE   This attribute specifies the language the current script is written in and invokes the proper scripting engine. The default value is **JAVASCRIPT**. **JAVASCRIPT** and **JSCRIPT** represent that the scripting language is written in JavaScript. **VBS** and **VBSCRIPT** represent that the scripting language is written in VBScript.

STYLE   See "Core Attributes Reference," earlier in this chapter.

TITLE   See "Core Attributes Reference," earlier in this chapter.

Attribute and Event Support

NETSCAPE 4   **ALIGN**. (**CLASS**, **ID**, **LANG**, and **STYLE** are implied.)

INTERNET EXPLORER 4   All attributes and events except **DIR**. (Note: The **JUSTIFY** value for **ALIGN** is not supported.)

WEBTV   **ALIGN (CENTER | LEFT | RIGHT)**.

Event Handlers

See "Events Reference," earlier in this chapter.

Examples

```
<H1>This is a Major Document Heading</H1>
<H2 ALIGN="CENTER">Second heading, aligned to the
center</H2>
<H3 ALIGN="RIGHT">Third heading, aligned to the
right</H3>
<H4>Fourth heading</H4>
<H5 STYLE="{font-size: 20pt}">Fifth heading with
style information</H5>
<H6>The smallest heading</H6>
```

Compatibility

HTML 2, 3.2, 4; Netscape 1, 2, 3, 4; Internet Explorer 2, 3, 4; and WebTV

Notes

- In most implementations, heading numbers correspond inversely with the six font sizes supported by the **<FONT>** element. For example, **<H1>** corresponds to **<FONT SIZE="6">**. The default font size is **3**. However, this approach to layout is not encouraged and page designers should consider using styles to set even relative sizes.

- HTML 3.2 supports only the **ALIGN** attribute. HTML 2 does not support any attributes for headings.

- The strict definition of HTML 4 does not include support for the **ALIGN** attribute. Style sheets should be used instead.

<HEAD> (Document Head)

This element indicates the document head that contains descriptive information about the HTML document as well as other supplementary information such as style rules or scripts.

Syntax

```
<HEAD
     DIR="LTR | RTL"
     LANG="language code"
     PROFILE="URL">

</HEAD>
```

Attributes and Events Defined by Internet Explorer 4

```
     CLASS="class name(s)"
     ID="unique alphanumeric identifier"
     TITLE="advisory text"
```

Attributes

CLASS   See "Core Attributes Reference," earlier in this chapter.

DIR   See "Language Reference," earlier in this chapter.

ID   See "Core Attributes Reference," earlier in this chapter.

LANG   See "Language Reference," earlier in this chapter.

PROFILE   This attribute specifies a URL for a meta-information dictionary. The specified profile should indicate the format of allowed meta-data and the potential meaning of the data.

TITLE   See "Core Attributes Reference," earlier in this chapter.

Attribute and Event Support

INTERNET EXPLORER 4   CLASS, ID, and TITLE.

Event Handlers

None.

Example

```
<HEAD>
<TITLE>Big Company Home Page</TITLE>
<BASE HREF="http://www.bigcompany.com">
<META NAME="Keywords" CONTENT="BigCompany, SuperWidget">
</HEAD>
```

Compatibility

HTML 2, 3.2, 4; Netscape 1, 2, 3, 4; Internet Explorer 2, 3, 4; and WebTV

Notes

- The **<HEAD>** element must contain a **<TITLE>** element. It may also contain the **<BASE>**, **<ISINDEX>**, **<LINK>**, **<META>**, **<SCRIPT>**, and **<STYLE>** elements. Internet Explorer 4 supports the inclusion of the **<BASEFONT>** element in the **<HEAD>** element, but **<BASEFONT>** has been depreciated under HTML 4.

- While the HTML 4 specification shows support for the **PROFILE** attribute, no browsers appear to support it.

- Internet Explorer 4 defines the **<BGSOUND>** element as another legal element within **<HEAD>**.

- HTML 2 and 3.2 support no attributes for this element.

<HR> (Horizontal Rule)

This element is used to insert a horizontal rule to visually separate document sections. Rules are usually rendered as a raised or etched line.

Syntax
```
<HR
    ALIGN="CENTER | LEFT | RIGHT" (transitional)
    CLASS="class name(s)"
    ID="unique alphanumeric identifier"
    NOSHADE (transitional)
    SIZE="pixels" (transitional)
    STYLE="style information"
    TITLE="advisory information"
    WIDTH="percentage | pixels" (transitional)
    onclick="script"
    ondblclick="script"
    onkeydown="script"
    onkeypress="script"
    onkeyup="script"
    onmousedown="script"
    onmousemove="script"
    onmouseout="script"
    onmouseover="script"
    onmouseup="script">
```

Attributes and Events Defined by Internet Explorer 4
```
    COLOR="color name | #RRGGBB"
    LANG="language code"
    LANGUAGE="JAVASCRIPT | JSCRIPT | VBS | VBSCRIPT"
    SRC="URL"
    onbeforeupdate="script"
    onblur="script"
    ondragstart="script"
    onfocus="script"
    onhelp="script"
    onresize="script"
    onrowenter="script"
```

```
onrowexit="script"
onselectstart="script"
```

Attributes Defined by WebTV

INVERTBORDER

Attributes

ALIGN   This attribute controls the horizontal alignment of the rule with respect to the page. The default value is **LEFT**.

CLASS   See "Core Attributes Reference," earlier in this chapter.

COLOR   This attribute sets the rule color using either a named color or a color specified in the hexadecimal *#RRGGBB* format. This attribute is currently supported only by Internet Explorer.

ID   See "Core Attributes Reference," earlier in this chapter.

INVERTBORDER   This WebTV-specific attribute creates a horizontal rule that appears raised, as opposed to embossed, on the surface of the page.

LANG   See "Language Reference," earlier in this chapter.

LANGUAGE   This attribute specifies the language the current script is written in and invokes the proper scripting engine. The default value is **JAVASCRIPT**. **JAVASCRIPT** and **JSCRIPT** represent that the scripting language is written in JavaScript. **VBS** and **VBSCRIPT** represent that the scripting language is written in VBScript.

NOSHADE   This attribute causes the rule to be rendered as a solid bar without shading.

SIZE   This attribute indicates the height in pixels of the rule.

SRC   This attribute specifies a URL for an associated file.

STYLE   See "Core Attributes Reference," earlier in this chapter.

TITLE   See "Core Attributes Reference," earlier in this chapter.

WIDTH   This attribute indicates how wide the rule should be specified either in pixels or as a percent of screen width, such as 80 percent.

Attribute and Event Support

NETSCAPE 4 **ALIGN, NOSHADE, SIZE,** and **WIDTH**. (**CLASS, ID,** and **STYLE** are implied.)

INTERNET EXPLORER 4 All attributes and events defined by W3C and Internet Explorer 4.

WEBTV **ALIGN, INVERTBORDER, NOSHADE, SIZE,** and **WIDTH**.

Event Handlers

See "Events Reference," earlier in this chapter.

Examples

```
<HR ALIGN="LEFT" NOSHADE SIZE="1" WIDTH="420">

<HR ALIGN="center" WIDTH="100%" SIZE="3" COLOR="#000000">
```

Compatibility

HTML 2, 3.2, 4; Netscape 1, 2, 3, 4; Internet Explorer 2, 3, 4; and WebTV

Notes

- The strict definition of HTML 4 removes support for the **ALIGN, NOSHADE, SIZE,** and **WIDTH** attributes for horizontal rules. These effects are possible using style sheets.

- An empty element, **<HTML>** requires no closing tag.

<HTML> (HTML Document)

This element identifies a document as containing HTML-tagged content.

Syntax

```
<HTML
     DIR="LTR | RTL"
     LANG="language code"
     VERSION="URL" (transitional)>

</HTML>
```

Attributes Defined by Internet Explorer 4

`TITLE="advisory text"`

Attributes

DIR   See "Language Reference," earlier in this chapter.

LANG   See "Language Reference," earlier in this chapter.

TITLE   See "Core Attributes Reference," earlier in this chapter.

VERSION   The **VERSION** attribute is used to set the URL of the location of the document type definition (DTD) that the current document conforms to. The DTD is also specified by the <!DOCTYPE> comment. Since few if any browsers support the **VERSION** attribute, it should be used only in conjunction with a <!DOCTYPE> comment and not instead of one.

Attribute and Event Support

INTERNET EXPLORER 4   **LANG** and **TITLE**.

Event Handlers

None.

Example

```
<!-- Minimal HTML document -->
<HTML>
<HEAD><TITLE>Minimal Document</TITLE></HEAD>
<BODY></BODY>
</HTML>
```

Compatibility

HTML 4; Netscape 4; Internet Explorer 4; and WebTV

Notes

The **<HTML>** element is the first element in an **<HTML>** document. Except for comments, the only tags it directly contains are the **<HEAD>** element followed by either a **<BODY>** element or a **<FRAMESET>** element.

<I> (Italic)

This element indicates that the enclosed text should be displayed in an italic typeface.

2

Syntax

```
<I
    CLASS="class name(s)"
    DIR="LTR | RTL"
    ID="unique alphanumeric identifier"
    LANG="language code"
    STYLE="style information"
    TITLE="advisory text"
    onclick="script"
    ondblclick="script"
    onkeydown="script"
    onkeypress="script"
    onkeyup="script"
    onmousedown="script"
    onmousemove="script"
    onmouseout="script"
    onmouseover="script"
    onmouseup="script">

</I>
```

Attributes and Events Defined by Internet Explorer 4

```
    LANGUAGE="JAVASCRIPT | JSCRIPT | VBS | VBSCRIPT"
    ondragstart="script"
    onhelp="script"
    onselectstart="script"
```

Attributes

CLASS   See "Core Attributes Reference," earlier in this chapter.

DIR   See "Language Reference," earlier in this chapter.

ID   See "Core Attributes Reference," earlier in this chapter.

LANG   See "Language Reference," earlier in this chapter.

LANGUAGE   This attribute specifies the language the current script is written in and invokes the proper scripting engine. The default value is **JAVASCRIPT**. **JAVASCRIPT** and **JSCRIPT** represent that the scripting language is written in JavaScript. **VBS** and **VBSCRIPT** represent that the scripting language is written in VBScript.

STYLE   See "Core Attributes Reference," earlier in this chapter.

TITLE   See "Core Attributes Reference," earlier in this chapter.

Attribute and Event Support

NETSCAPE 4   **CLASS**, **ID**, **LANG**, and **STYLE** are implied.

INTERNET EXPLORER 4   All attributes and events except **DIR**.

Event Handlers

See "Events Reference," earlier in this chapter.

Example

```
Here is some <I>italicized</I> text.
```

Compatibility

HTML 4; Netscape 4; Internet Explorer 4; and WebTV

<IFRAME>   (Floating Frame)

This element indicates a floating frame, an independently controllable content region that can be embedded in a page.

Syntax (Transitional Only)

```
<IFRAME
     ALIGN="BOTTOM | LEFT | MIDDLE | RIGHT | TOP"
     CLASS="class name(s)"
     FRAMEBORDER="0 | 1"
     HEIGHT="percentage | pixels"
     ID="unique alphanumeric identifier"
     LONGDESC="URL of description"
     MARGINHEIGHT="pixels"
     MARGINWIDTH="pixels"
     NAME="string"
     SCROLLING="AUTO | NO | YES"
     SRC="URL of frame contents"
```

```
STYLE="style information"
TITLE="advisory text"
WIDTH="percentage | pixels">
```

`</IFRAME>`

Attributes Defined by Internet Explorer 4

```
ALIGN="ABSBOTTOM | ABSMIDDLE | BASELINE | TEXTTOP"
BORDER="pixels"
BORDERCOLOR="color name | #RRGGBB"
DATAFLD="name of column supplying bound data"
DATASRC="ID of data source object supplying data"
FRAMEBORDER="No | YES | 0 | 1"
FRAMESPACING="pixels"
HSPACE="pixels"
LANG="language code"
LANGUAGE="JAVASCRIPT | JSCRIPT | VBS | VBSCRIPT"
NORESIZE="noresize | resize"
VSPACE="pixels"
```

Attributes

ALIGN   This attribute controls the horizontal alignment of the floating frame with respect to the page. The default is **LEFT**.

BORDER   This attribute specifies the thickness of the border in pixels.

BORDERCOLOR   This attribute specifies the color of the border.

CLASS   See "Core Attributes Reference," earlier in this chapter.

DATAFLD   This attribute specifies the column name from the data source object that supplies the bound data.

DATASRC   This attribute indicates the **ID** of the data source object that supplies the data that is bound to this element.

FRAMEBORDER   This attribute determines whether the frame is surrounded by a border. The HTML 4 specification defines **0** to be off and **1** to be on. The default value is **1**. Internet Explorer also defines the values **NO** and **YES**.

FRAMESPACING   This attribute creates additional space between the frames.

HEIGHT   The attribute sets the floating frame's height in pixels.

HSPACE   This attribute specifies margins for the frame.

ID   See "Core Attributes Reference," earlier in this chapter.

LANG   See "Language Reference," earlier in this chapter.

LANGUAGE   This attribute specifies the language the current script is written in and invokes the proper scripting engine. The default value is **JAVASCRIPT**. **JAVASCRIPT** and **JSCRIPT** represent that the scripting language is written in JavaScript. **VBS** and **VBSCRIPT** represent that the scripting language is written in VBScript.

LONGDESC   This attribute specifies a URL of a document that contains a long description of the frame's contents. This may be particularly useful as a complement to the **<TITLE>** element.

MARGINHEIGHT   This attribute sets the height in pixels between the floating frame's content and its top and bottom borders.

MARGINWIDTH   This attribute sets the width in pixels between the floating frame's content and its left and right borders.

NAME   This attribute assigns the floating frame a name so that it can be the target destination of hyperlinks.

NORESIZE   When **NORESIZE** is included, the frame cannot be resized by the user.

SCROLLING   This attribute determines if the frame has scroll bars. A **YES** value forces scroll bars; a **NO** value prohibits them.

SRC   This attribute contains the URL of the content to be displayed in the floating frame. If absent, the frame is blank.

STYLE   See "Core Attributes Reference," earlier in this chapter.

TITLE   See "Core Attributes Reference," earlier in this chapter.

VSPACE   This attribute specifies margins for the frame.

WIDTH   This attribute sets the floating frame's width in pixels.

Attribute and Event Support

INTERNET EXPLORER 4   All attributes and events except **LONGDESC**.

Event Handlers
See "Events Reference," earlier in this chapter.

Example
```
<IFRAME SRC="http://www.bigcompany.com" HEIGHT="150"
        WIDTH="200" NAME="FloatingFrame1">
Sorry, your browser doesn't support inlined frames.
</IFRAME>
```

Compatibility
HTML 4 (transitional); Internet Explorer 3, 4

Notes

- A floating frame does not need to be declared by the **<FRAMESET>** element as part of a frame set.
- WebTV and Netscape 4 do not support floating frames.
- Under HTML 4's strict definition, the **<IFRAME>** element is not defined. Floating frames may be imitated using the **<DIV>** element and CSS positioning facilities.

<ILAYER>   (Inflow Layer)

This Netscape-specific element allows the definition of overlapping content layers that can be positioned, hidden or shown, rendered transparent or opaque, reordered front to back, and nested. An *inflow layer* is a layer with a relative position that appears where it would naturally occur in the document, in contrast to a *general layer*, which may be positioned absolutely regardless of its location in a document. The functionality of layers is available using CSS positioning, and page developers are advised not to use this element.

Syntax (Defined by Netscape 4)
```
<ILAYER
     ABOVE="layer"
     BACKGROUND="URL of image"
     BELOW="layer"
     BGCOLOR="color name | #RRGGBB"
     CLASS="class name(s)"
     CLIP="x1, y1, x2, y2"
     HEIGHT="percentage | pixels"
```

```
ID="unique alphanumeric identifier"
LEFT="pixels"
NAME="string"
PAGEX="pixels"
PAGEY="pixels"
SRC="URL of layer contents"
STYLE="style information"
TOP="pixels"
VISIBILITY="HIDE | INHERIT | SHOW"
WIDTH="percentage | pixels"
Z-INDEX="number"
onblur="script"
onfocus="script"
onload="script"
onmouseout="script"
onmouseover="script">
```

`</ILAYER>`

Attributes

ABOVE   This attribute contains the name of the layer to be rendered above the current layer.

BACKGROUND   This attribute contains the URL of a background image for the layer.

BELOW   This attribute contains the name of the layer to be rendered below the current layer.

BGCOLOR   This attribute specifies a layer's background color. Its value can be either a named color or a color specified in the hexadecimal *#RRGGBB* format.

CLASS   This attribute specifies the class name(s) for access via a style sheet.

CLIP   This attribute specifies the clipping region or viewable area of the layer. All layer content outside that rectangle will be rendered as transparent. The **CLIP** rectangle is defined by two *x,y* pairs: top *x*, left *y*, bottom *x*, and right *y*. Coordinates are relative to the layer's origin point, **0,0** in its top-left corner.

HEIGHT   This attribute specifies the height of a layer in pixels or percentage values.

ID   See "Core Attributes Reference," earlier in this chapter.

LEFT   This attribute specifies in pixels the horizontal offset of the layer. The offset is relative to its parent layer if it has one, or to the left page margin if it does not.

NAME   This attribute assigns the layer a name that can be referenced by programs in a client-side scripting language. The **ID** attribute can also be used.

PAGEX   This attribute specifies the horizontal position of the layer relative to the browser window.

PAGEY   This attribute specifies the vertical position of the layer relative to the browser window.

SRC   This attribute is used to set the URL of a file that contains the content to load into the layer.

STYLE   This attribute specifies an inline style for the layer.

TOP   This attribute specifies in pixels the top offset of the layer. The offset is relative to its parent layer if it has one, or the top page margin if it does not.

VISIBILITY   This attribute specifies whether a layer is hidden, shown, or inherits its visibility from the layer that includes it.

WIDTH   This attribute specifies a layer's width in pixels.

Z-INDEX   This attribute specifies a layer's stacking order relative to other layers. Position is specified with positive integers, with **1** indicating the bottommost layer.

Attribute and Event Support

NETSCAPE 4   All attributes.

Event Handlers
None.

Example
```
<P>Content comes before</P>
<ILAYER NAME="background" BGCOLOR="green">
<P>Layered information goes here.</P>
</ILAYER>
<P>Content comes after.</P>
```

Compatibility

Netscape 4

Notes

- This element will likely fall out of fashion because of its lack of cross-browser compatibility. The functionality of **<ILAYER>** is possible using the positioning features in CSS, and page developers are encouraged not to use this element.

- Applets, plug-ins, and other embedded media forms, generically called *objects*, may be included in a layer; however, they will float to the top of all other layers, even if their containing layer is obscured.

<IMG>   (Image)

This element indicates a media object to include in an HTML document. Usually, the object is a graphic image, but some implementations support movies and animations.

Syntax

```
<IMG
     ALIGN="BOTTOM | LEFT | MIDDLE | RIGHT | TOP"
          (transitional)
     ALT="alternative text"
     BORDER="pixels" (transitional)
     CLASS="class name(s)"
     DIR="LTR | RTL"
     HEIGHT="pixels"
     HSPACE="pixels" (transitional)
     ID="unique alphanumeric identifier"
     ISMAP
     LANG="language code"
     LONGDESC="URL of description file"
     SRC="URL of image"
     STYLE="style information"
     TITLE="advisory text"
     USEMAP="URL of map file"
     VSPACE="pixels" (transitional)
     WIDTH="pixels"
     onclick="script"
     ondblclick="script"
```

```
onkeydown="script"
onkeypress="script"
onkeyup="script"
onmousedown="script"
onmousemove="script"
onmouseout="script"
onmouseover="script"
onmouseup="script">
```

Attributes and Events Defined by Internet Explorer 4

```
ALIGN="ABSBOTTOM | ABSMIDDLE | BASELINE | TEXTTOP"
DATAFLD="name of column supplying bound data"
DATASRC="ID of data source object supplying data"
DYNSRC="URL of movie"
LANGUAGE="JAVASCRIPT | JSCRIPT | VBS | VBSCRIPT"
LOOP="INFINITE | number"
LOWSRC="URL of low-resolution image"
NAME="unique alphanumeric identifier"
onabort="script"
onafterupdate="script"
onbeforeupdate="script"
onblur="script"
ondragstart="script"
onerror="script"
onfocus="script"
onhelp="script"
onload="script"
onresize="script"
onrowenter="script"
onrowexit="script"
onselectstart="script"
```

Attributes Defined by Netscape 4

```
ALIGN="ABSBOTTOM | ABSMIDDLE | BASELINE | TEXTTOP"
LOWSRC="URL of low-resolution image"
NAME="unique alphanumeric identifier"
SUPPRESS="TRUE | FALSE"
```

Attributes Defined by WebTV

```
CONTROLS
NAME="unique alphanumeric identifier"
RELOAD="seconds"
SELECTED="x,y pair"
TRANSPARENCY="number (1-100)"
```

Attributes

ALIGN   This attribute controls the horizontal alignment of the image with respect to the page. The default value is **LEFT**. Only the Netscape, Internet Explorer 4, and WebTV implementations support the **ABSBOTTOM, ABSMIDDLE, BASELINE,** and **TEXTTOP** values.

ALT   This attribute contains a string to display instead of the image for browsers that cannot display images.

BORDER   This attribute indicates the width in pixels of the border surrounding the image.

CLASS   See "Core Attributes Reference," earlier in this chapter.

CONTROLS   Under Internet Explorer 3 and WebTV, it is possible to set the controls to show by placing this attribute in the <IMG> element. This attribute does not appear to be supported under Internet Explorer 4, and users are encouraged to use the <OBJECT> element to embed video for Internet Explorer.

DATAFLD   This attribute specifies the column name from the data source object that supplies the bound data to set the **SRC** of the <IMG> element.

DATASRC   This attribute indicates the **ID** of the data source object that supplies the data that is bound to this <IMG> element.

DIR   See "Language Reference," earlier in this chapter.

DYNSRC   In the Microsoft and WebTV implementations, this attribute indicates the URL of a movie file and is used instead of the **SRC** attribute.

HEIGHT   This attribute indicates the height in pixels of the image.

HSPACE   This attribute indicates the horizontal space in pixels between the image and surrounding text.

ID   See "Core Attributes Reference," earlier in this chapter.

ISMAP   This attribute indicates that the image is a server-side image map. User mouse actions over the image are sent to the server for processing.

LANG   See "Language Reference," earlier in this chapter.

LANGUAGE This attribute specifies the language the current script is written in and invokes the proper scripting engine. The default value is **JAVASCRIPT**. **JAVASCRIPT** and **JSCRIPT** represent that the scripting language is written in JavaScript. **VBS** and **VBSCRIPT** represent that the scripting language is written in VBScript.

LONGDESC This attribute specifies a URL of a document that contains a long description of the image. This attribute is used as a complement to the **ALT** attribute.

LOOP In the Microsoft implementation, this attribute is used with the **DYNSRC** attribute to cause a movie to loop. Its value is either a numeric loop count or the keyword **INFINITE**.

LOWSRC In the Netscape implementation, this attribute contains the URL of an image to be initially loaded. Typically, the **LOWSRC** image is a low-resolution or black-and-white image that provides a quick preview of the image to follow. Once the primary image is loaded, it replaces the **LOWSRC** image.

NAME This common attribute is used to bind a name to the image. Older browsers understand the **NAME** field, and in conjunction with scripting languages it is possible to manipulate images by their defined names to create effects like "rollover" buttons. The **ID** attribute under HTML 4 specifies element identifiers; for backward compatibility, **NAME** may still be used.

RELOAD In the WebTV implementation, this attribute indicates in seconds how frequently an image should be reloaded.

SELECTED In the WebTV implementation, this attribute indicates the initial x, y coordinate location on the image. The cursor is placed at that location when the image is loaded. It requires either the **ISMAP** or the **USEMAP** attribute.

SRC This attribute indicates the URL of an image file to be displayed.

STYLE See "Core Attributes Reference," earlier in this chapter.

SUPPRESS This Netscape-specific attribute determines if a placeholder icon will appear during image loading. Values are **TRUE** and **FALSE**. **SUPPRESS="TRUE"** will suppress display of the placeholder icon as well as display of any **ALT** information until the image is loaded. **SUPPRESS="FALSE"** will allow the placeholder icon and any tool tips defined by the **ALT** information to display while the image is loading. The default value is **FALSE**. If the browser is set to not load images automatically, the **SUPPRESS** attribute is ignored.

TITLE   See "Core Attributes Reference," earlier in this chapter.

TRANSPARENCY   In the WebTV implementation, this attribute allows the background to show through the image. It takes a numeric argument indicating the degree of transparency, from fully opaque (**0**) to fully transparent (**100**).

USEMAP   This attribute makes the image support client-side image mapping. Its argument is a URL specifying the map file, which associates image regions with hyperlinks.

VSPACE   This attribute indicates the vertical space in pixels between the image and surrounding text.

WIDTH   This attribute indicates the width in pixels of the image.

Attribute and Event Support

NETSCAPE 4   ALIGN, ALT, BORDER, HEIGHT, HSPACE, ISMAP, LOWSRC, NAME, SRC, SUPPRESS, USEMAP, VSPACE, and WIDTH.

INTERNET EXPLORER 4   All W3C-defined attributes and events except **DIR** and **LONGDESC**, and all attributes and events defined by Internet Explorer 4.

WEBTV   ALIGN, BORDER, HEIGHT, HSPACE, ID, ISMAP, NAME, SELECTED, SRC, START, TRANSPARENCY, USEMAP, VSPACE, WIDTH, onabort, onerror, and onload.

Event Handlers
See "Events Reference," earlier in this chapter.

Examples
```
<IMG SRC="lakers.jpg" LOWSRC="lakersbw.jpg"
     ALT="Los Angeles Lakers" HEIGHT="100" WIDTH="300">

<IMG SRC="hugeimagemap.gif" USEMAP="mainmap" BORDER="0"
     HEIGHT="200" WIDTH="200" ALT="Image Map Here">

<A HREF="home.htm"><IMG SRC="homebutton.gif" WIDTH="50"
   HEIGHT="20" ALT="Link to Home Page"></A>
```

Compatibility

HTML 2, 3.2, 4; Netscape 1, 2, 3, 4; Internet Explorer 2, 3, 4; and WebTV

Notes

- No browser currently appears to support **LONGDESC**.

- Typically, when you use the **USEMAP** attribute, the URL is a fragment, such as #map1, rather than a full URL. Some browsers do not support external client-side map files.

- Under the HTML 4 strict definition, the **<IMG>** element does not support **ALIGN, BORDER, HEIGHT, HSPACE, VSPACE,** and **WIDTH**. The functionality of these attributes should be possible using style sheet rules.

- While the HTML 4 specification reserves data-binding attributes like **DATAFLD** or **DATASRC**, it is not specified for **<IMG>**, although Internet Explorer provides support for these attributes.

<INPUT>   (Input Form Control)

This element specifies an input control for a form. The type of input is set by the **TYPE** attribute and may be a variety of different types, including single-line text field, multiline text field, password style, check box, radio button, or push button.

Syntax

```
<INPUT
     ACCEPT="MIME TYPES"
     ACCESSKEY="character"
     ALIGN="BOTTOM I LEFT I MIDDLE I RIGHT I TOP"
          (transitional)
     ALT="text"
     CHECKED
     CLASS="class name(s)"
     DIR="LTR I RTL"
     DISABLED
     ID="unique alphanumeric identifier"
     LANG="language code"
     MAXLENGTH="maximum field size"
     NAME="field name"
     READONLY
```

```
SIZE="field size"
SRC="URL of image file"
STYLE="style information"
TABINDEX="number"
TITLE="advisory text"
TYPE="BUTTON | CHECKBOX | FILE | HIDDEN | IMAGE |
      PASSWORD | RADIO | RESET | SUBMIT | TEXT"
USEMAP="URL of map file"
VALUE="field value"
onblur="script"
onchange="script"
onclick="script"
ondblclick="script"
onfocus="script"
onkeydown="script"
onkeypress="script"
onkeyup="script"
onmousedown="script"
onmousemove="script"
onmouseout="script"
onmouseover="script"
onmouseup="script"
onselect="script">
```

Attributes and Events Defined by Internet Explorer 4

```
ALIGN="CENTER"
LANGUAGE="JAVASCRIPT | JSCRIPT | VBS | VBSCRIPT"
onafterupdate="script"
onbeforeupdate="script"
ondragstart="script"
onhelp="script"
onselectstart="script"
```

Attributes Defined by Netscape 4

```
ALIGN="ABSBOTTOM | ABSMIDDLE | BASELINE | TEXTTOP"
```

Attributes Defined by WebTV

```
BGCOLOR="color name | #RRGGBB"
BORDERIMAGE="URL"
CURSOR="color name | #RRGGBB"
USESTYLE
WIDTH="pixels"
```

Attributes

ACCEPT   This attribute is used to list the MIME types accepted for file uploads when **<INPUT TYPE="FILE">**.

ACCESSKEY   This attribute specifies a keyboard navigation accelerator for the element. Pressing ALT or a similar key in association with the specified character selects the form control correlated with that key sequence. Page designers are forewarned to avoid key sequences already bound to browsers.

ALIGN   With image form controls (**TYPE="IMAGE"**), this attribute aligns the image with respect to surrounding text. The HTML 4 transitional specification defines **BOTTOM, LEFT, MIDDLE, RIGHT**, and **TOP** as allowable values. Netscape and Microsoft browsers may also allow the use of attribute values like **ABSBOTTOM** or **ABSMIDDLE**. Like other presentation-specific aspects of HTML, the **ALIGN** attribute is dropped under the strict HTML 4 specification.

ALT   This attribute is used to display an alternative description of image buttons for text-only browsers. The meaning of **ALT** for forms of **<INPUT>** beyond **TYPE="INPUT"** is unclear.

BGCOLOR   In the WebTV implementation, this attribute specifies the background color of a text form control (**TYPE= "TEXT"**). The value of the attribute can be either a named color or a color specified in the hexadecimal *#RRGGBB* format.

BORDERIMAGE   In the WebTV implementation, this attribute allows specification of a graphical border for **RESET, SUBMIT**, and **TEXT** controls. Its value is the URL of a .bif (Border Image File) graphics file that specifies the border. Border image files tend to reside in WebTV ROM; the common values are **file://ROM/Border/ ButtonBorder2.bif** and **file://ROM/Border/ButtonBorder3.bif**, though other values may be present under later versions of WebTV.

CHECKED   The **CHECKED** attribute should be used only for check box (**TYPE="CHECKBOX"**) and radio (**TYPE="RADIO"**) form controls. The presence of this attribute indicates that the control should be displayed in its checked state.

CLASS   See "Core Attributes Reference," earlier in this chapter.

CURSOR   In the WebTV implementation, this attribute sets the cursor color for a text form control (**TYPE="TEXT"**). The attribute's value is either a named color or a color specified in the hexadecimal *#RRGGBB* format.

DIR   See "Language Reference," earlier in this chapter.

DISABLED   This attribute is used to turn off a form control. Elements will not be submitted, nor may they receive any focus from the keyboard or mouse. Disabled form controls will not be part of the tabbing order. The browser may also gray out the form that is disabled, in order to indicate to the user that the form control is inactive. This attribute requires no value.

ID   See "Core Attributes Reference," earlier in this chapter.

LANG   See "Language Reference," earlier in this chapter.

LANGUAGE   In the Microsoft implementation, this attribute specifies the scripting language to be used with an associated script bound to the element typically through an event handler attribute. Possible values may include **JAVASCRIPT**, **JSCRIPT**, **VBS**, and **VBSCRIPT**. Other values that include the version of the language used, such as **JavaScript1.1**, may also be possible.

MAXLENGTH   This attribute indicates the maximum content length that can be entered in a text form control (**TYPE="TEXT"**). The maximum number of characters allowed differs from the visible dimension of the form control, which is set with the **SIZE** attribute.

NAME   This attribute allows a form control to be assigned a name so that it can be referenced by a scripting language. **NAME** is supported by older browsers such as Netscape 2–generation browsers, but the W3C encourages the use of the **ID** attribute. For compatibility purposes, both may have to be used.

READONLY   This attribute prevents the form control's value from being changed. Form controls with this attribute set may receive focus from the user but may not be modified. Since it receives focus, a **READONLY** form control will be part of the form's tabbing order. Last, the control's value will be sent on form submission. This attribute can only be used with <INPUT> when **TYPE** is set to **TEXT** or **PASSWORD**. The attribute is also used with the <TEXTAREA> element.

SIZE This attribute indicates the visible dimension, in characters, of a text form control (**TYPE="TEXT"**). This differs from the maximum length of content, which can be entered in a form control set by the **MAXLENGTH** attribute.

SRC This attribute is used with image form controls (**TYPE="IMAGE"**) to specify the URL of the image file to load.

STYLE See "Core Attributes Reference," earlier in this chapter.

TABINDEX This attribute takes a numeric value that indicates the position of the form control in the tabbing index for the form. Tabbing proceeds from the lowest positive **TABINDEX** value to the highest. Negative values for **TABINDEX** will leave the form control out of the tabbing order. When tabbing is not explicitly set, the browser may tab through items in the order they are encountered. Form controls that are disabled due to the presence of the **DISABLED** attribute will not be part of the tabbing index, though read-only controls will be.

TITLE See "Core Attributes Reference," earlier in this chapter.

TYPE This attribute specifies the type of the form control. A value of **BUTTON** indicates a general-purpose button with no well-defined meaning. However, an action can be associated with the button using an event handler attribute, such as **onclick**. A value of **CHECKBOX** indicates a check box control. Check box form controls have a checked and nonchecked set, but even if these controls are grouped together, they allow a user to select multiple check boxes at once. In contrast, a value of RADIO indicates a radio button control. When grouped, radio buttons allow only one of the many choices to be selected at a given time.

A form control type of **HIDDEN** indicates a field that is not visible to the viewer but is used to store information. A hidden form control is often used to preserve state information between pages. A value of **FILE** for the **TYPE** attribute indicates a control that allows the viewer to upload a file to a server. The filename can be entered in a displayed field, or a user agent may provide a special browse button allowing the user to locate the file. A value of **IMAGE** indicates a graphic image form control that a user can click to invoke an associated action. A value of **PASSWORD** for the **TYPE** attribute indicates a password entry field. A password field will not display text entered as it is typed; it may instead show a series of *dots.* Note that password-entered data is not transferred to the server in any secure fashion. A value of **RESET** for the **TYPE** attribute is used to insert a button that resets all controls within a form to their default values. A value of **SUBMIT** inserts a special submission button that, when pressed, sends the contents of the form to the location indicated by the **ACTION** attribute of the enclosing **<FORM>** element. Last, a value of **TEXT** (the default) for the **TYPE** attribute indicates a single-line text input field.

USEMAP   This HTML 4 attribute is used to indicate the map file to be associated with an image when the form control is set with **TYPE="IMAGE"**. The value of the attribute should be a URL of a map file, but will generally be in the form of a URL fragment referencing a map file within the current file.

USESTYLE   In the WebTV implementation, the presence of this attribute causes control text to be rendered in the default text style for the page. This attribute requires no value.

VALUE   This attribute has two different uses, depending on the value for the **TYPE** attribute. With data entry controls (**TYPE= "TEXT"** and **TYPE="PASSWORD"**), this attribute is used to set the default value for the control. When used with check box or radio form controls, this attribute specifies the return value for the control when it is turned on, rather than the default Boolean value submitted.

WIDTH   This WebTV attribute is used to set the size of the form control in pixels.

Attribute and Event Support

NETSCAPE 4   **NAME**, **VALUE**, and **onclick**. (**CLASS**, **ID**, **LANG**, and **STYLE** are implied.)

INTERNET EXPLORER 4   All W3C-defined attributes and events except **ACCEPT**, **CHECKED**, **DIR**, and **USEMAP**, and all attributes and events defined by Internet Explorer 4. (Note: Internet Explorer 4 supports only the **CENTER**, **LEFT**, and **RIGHT** values for the **ALIGN** attribute.)

WEBTV   **ALIGN**, **BGCOLOR**, **CHECKED**, **CURSOR**, **ID**, **MAXLENGTH**, **NAME**, **SIZE**, **TYPE**, **USESTYLE**, **VALUE**, **WIDTH**, **onblur**, **onchange**, **onclick**, **onfocus**, and **onselect**.

Event Handlers

See "Events Reference," earlier in this chapter.

2

Examples

```
<FORM>
    Which is your favorite food?
    <INPUT TYPE="RADIO" NAME="favorite"
           VALUE="Mexican">Mexican
    <INPUT TYPE="RADIO" NAME="favorite"
           VALUE="Russian">Russian
    <INPUT TYPE="RADIO" NAME="favorite"
           VALUE="Japanese">Japanese
    <INPUT TYPE="RADIO" CHECKED NAME="favorite"
           VALUE="Other">Other
</FORM>

<FORM>
    Enter your name: <INPUT TYPE="TEXT" MAXLENGTH="35"
                            SIZE="20"><BR>
    Enter your password: <INPUT TYPE="PASSWORD"
                                MAXLENGTH="35"
                                SIZE="20"><BR>
    <BR>
    <INPUT TYPE="SUBMIT" VALUE="Submit">
    <INPUT TYPE="RESET" VALUE="Reset">
</FORM>
```

Compatibility

HTML 2, 3.2, 4; Netscape 1, 2, 3, 4; Internet Explorer 2, 3, 4; and WebTV

Notes

- The **<INPUT>** element is an empty element and requires no closing tag.

- Some documents suggest the use of **TYPE="TEXTAREA"**. Even if this style is supported, it should be avoided in favor of the **<TEXTAREA>** element, which is common to all browsers.

- The HTML 2 and 3.2 specifications support only the **ALIGN**, **CHECKED**, **MAXLENGTH**, **NAME**, **SIZE**, **SRC**, **TYPE**, and **VALUE** attributes for the **<INPUT>** element.

- The HTML 4 specification also reserves the use of the **DATAFLD**, **DATAFORMATAS**, and **DATASRC** data-binding attributes.

- Under the strict HTML 4 specification, the **ALIGN** attribute is not allowed.

<INS> (Inserted Text)

This element is used to indicate that text has been added to the document.

Syntax

```
<INS
    CITE="URL"
    CLASS="class name(s)"
    DATETIME="date"
    ID="unique alphanumeric identifier"
    LANG="language code"
    STYLE="style information"
    TITLE="advisory text"
    onclick="script"
    ondblclick="script"
    onkeydown="script"
    onkeypress="script"
    onkeyup="script"
    onmousedown="script"
    onmousemove="script"
    onmouseout="script"
    onmouseover="script"
    onmouseup="script">

</INS>
```

Attributes and Events Defined by Internet Explorer 4

```
    LANGUAGE="JAVASCRIPT | JSCRIPT | VBS | VBSCRIPT"
    ondragstart="script"
    onhelp="script"
```

Attributes

CITE   The value of this attribute is a URL that designates a source document or message for the information inserted. This attribute is intended to point to information explaining why the text was changed.

CLASS   See "Core Attributes Reference," earlier in this chapter.

DATETIME   This attribute is used to indicate the date and time the insertion was made. The value of the attribute is a date in a special format as defined by ISO 8601. The basic date format is

```
YYYY-MM-DDThh:mm:ssTZD
```

where the following is true:

```
YYYY=four-digit year such as 1997
MM=two-digit month (01=January, 02=February, and so on)
DD=two-digit day of the month (01 to 31)
hh=two-digit hour (00 to 23) (24-hour clock not AM or PM)
mm=two-digit minute (00 to 59)
ss=two-digit second (00 to 59)
TZD=time zone designator
```

The time zone designator is either **Z**, which indicates UTC (Universal Time Coordinate, or coordinated universal time format), or **+hh:mm**, which indicates that the time is a local time that is *hh* hours and *mm* minutes ahead of UTC. Alternatively, the format for the time zone designator could be **-hh:mm**, which indicates that the local time is behind UTC. Note that the letter "T" actually appears in the string, all digits must be used, and **00** values for minutes and seconds may be required. An example value for the **DATETIME** attribute might be **1997-10-6T09:15:00-05:00**, which corresponds to October 6, 1997, 9:15 A.M., U.S. Eastern Standard Time.

ID   See "Core Attributes Reference," earlier in this chapter.

LANG   See "Language Reference," earlier in this chapter.

LANGUAGE   In the Microsoft implementation, this attribute specifies the scripting language to be used with an associated script bound to the element, typically through an event handler attribute. Possible values may include **JAVASCRIPT**, **JSCRIPT**, **VBS**, and **VBSCRIPT**. Other values that include the version of the language used, such as **JavaScript1.1**, may also be possible.

STYLE   See "Core Attributes Reference," earlier in this chapter.

TITLE   See "Core Attributes Reference," earlier in this chapter.

Attribute and Event Support

INTERNET EXPLORER 4   All attributes and events except **CITE** and **DATETIME**.

Event Handlers

See "Events Reference," earlier in this chapter.

Example

```
<INS CITE="http://www.bigcompany.com/changes/oct97.htm"
     DATE="1997-10-06T09:15:00-05:00">The penalty clause
```

```
applies to client lateness as well.
</INS>
```

Compatibility
HTML 4; Internet Explorer 4

Notes

- Browsers may render inserted (**<INS>**) or deleted (**<DEL>**) text in a different style to show the changes that have been made to the document. Eventually, a browser may have a way to show a revision history on a document. User agents that do not understand **<DEL>** or **<INS>** will show the information anyway, so there is no harm in adding information, only in deleting it.

- The **<INS>** element is not supported under the HTML 2 and 3.2 specifications.

<ISINDEX> (Index Prompt)

This element indicates that a document has an associated searchable keyword index. When a browser encounters this element, it inserts a query entry field at that point in the document. The viewer can enter query terms to perform a search. This element is depreciated under the strict HTML 4 specification and should not be used.

Syntax (Transitional Only)

```
<ISINDEX
        CLASS="class name(s)"
        DIR="LTR | RTL"
        HREF="URL" (nonstandard but common)
        ID="unique alphanumeric identifier"
        LANG="language code"
        PROMPT="string"
        STYLE="style information"
        TITLE="advisory text">
```

Attributes Defined by Internet Explorer 4

```
        LANGUAGE="JAVASCRIPT | JSCRIPT | VBS | VBSCRIPT"
```

Attributes

ACTION   This attribute specifies the URL of the query action to be executed when the viewer presses the ENTER key. While this attribute is not defined under any HTML specification, it is common to many browsers, particularly Internet Explorer 3, which defined it.

CLASS   See "Core Attributes Reference," earlier in this chapter.

DIR   See "Language Reference," earlier in this chapter.

HREF   The **HREF** attribute is used with the <**ISINDEX**> element as a way to indicate what the search document is. Another approach is to use the <**BASE**> element for the document. The HTML 2 documentation suggests that this is a legal approach and browsers appear to support it; however, it is poorly documented at best.

ID   See "Core Attributes Reference," earlier in this chapter.

LANG   See "Language Reference," earlier in this chapter.

LANGUAGE   In the Microsoft implementation, this attribute specifies the scripting language to be used with an associated script bound to the element, typically through an event handler attribute. Possible values may include **JAVASCRIPT**, **JSCRIPT**, **VBS**, and **VBSCRIPT**. Other values that include the version of the language used, such as **JavaScript1.1**, may also be possible.

PROMPT   This attribute allows a custom query prompt to be defined. The default prompt is "This is a searchable index. Enter search keywords." WebTV does not implement this attribute.

STYLE   See "Core Attributes Reference," earlier in this chapter.

TITLE   See "Core Attributes Reference," earlier in this chapter.

Attribute and Event Support

NETSCAPE 4   **PROMPT**. (**CLASS**, **ID**, **LANG**, and **STYLE** are implied.)

INTERNET EXPLORER 4   **CLASS**, **ID**, **LANG**, **LANGUAGE**, **PROMPT**, and **STYLE**.

Event Handlers
None.

Examples
```
<ISINDEX ACTION="cgi-bin/search" PROMPT="Enter search
                terms">

<ISINDEX HREF="cgi-bin/search" PROMPT="Keywords:">

<BASE HREF="cgi-bin/search">
<ISINDEX PROMPT="Enter search terms">
```

Compatibility
HTML 2, 3.2, 4 (transitional); Netscape 1, 2, 3, 4; Internet Explorer 2, 3, 4; and WebTV

Notes

- An empty element, **<ISINDEX>** requires no closing tag.

- The HTML 3.2 specification only allows the **PROMPT** attribute, while HTML 2 expected a text description to accompany the search field.

- Netscape 1.1 originated the use of the **PROMPT** attribute. WebTV does not support this attribute.

- Originally, the W3C intended this element to be used in a document's header. Browser vendors have relaxed this usage to allow the element in a document's body. Early implementations did not support the **ACTION** attribute and used the **<BASE>** element or an **HREF** attribute to specify a search function's URL.

- Older versions of Internet Explorer also support the **ACTION** attribute, which specifies the URL to use for the query rather than relying on the URL set in the **<BASE>** element. Internet Explorer 4 does not support the **ACTION**, **DIR**, **HREF**, or **TITLE** attributes. Microsoft documentation suggests using **<INPUT>** instead of this depreciated element.

<KBD> (Keyboard Input)

This element logically indicates text as keyboard input. A browser generally renders text enclosed by this element in a monospaced font.

Syntax

```
<KBD
    CLASS="class name(s)"
    DIR="LTR | RTL"
    ID="unique alphanumeric identifier"
    LANG="language code"
    STYLE="style information"
    TITLE="advisory text"
    onclick="script"
    ondblclick="script"
    onkeydown="script"
    onkeypress="script"
    onkeyup="script"
    onmousedown="script"
    onmousemove="script"
    onmouseout="script"
    onmouseover="script"
    onmouseup="script">

</KBD>
```

Attributes and Events Defined by Internet Explorer 4

```
    LANGUAGE="JAVASCRIPT | JSCRIPT | VBS | VBSCRIPT"
    ondragstart="script"
    onhelp="script"
    onselectstart="script"
```

Attributes

CLASS   See "Core Attributes Reference," earlier in this chapter.

DIR   See "Language Reference," earlier in this chapter.

ID   See "Core Attributes Reference," earlier in this chapter.

LANG   See "Language Reference," earlier in this chapter.

LANGUAGE   In the Microsoft implementation, this attribute specifies the scripting language to be used with an associated script bound to the element, typically through an event handler attribute. Possible values may include **JAVASCRIPT**, **JSCRIPT**, **VBS**, and **VBSCRIPT**. Other values that include the version of the language used, such as **JavaScript1.1**, may also be possible.

STYLE   See "Core Attributes Reference," earlier in this chapter.

TITLE   See "Core Attributes Reference," earlier in this chapter.

Attribute and Event Support

NETSCAPE 4   **CLASS, ID, LANG,** and **STYLE** are implied.

INTERNET EXPLORER 4   All attributes and events except **DIR**.

Event Handlers
See "Events Reference," earlier in this chapter.

Example
```
Enter the change directory command at the prompt as
shown below.<BR>
<BR>
<KBD>CD .. </KBD>
```

Compatibility
HTML 2, 3.2, 4; Netscape 1, 2, 3, 4; Internet Explorer 2, 3, 4; and
WebTV

Notes
The HTML 2 and 3.2 specifications support no attributes for this
element.

<LABEL>   (Form Control Label)

This HTML 4 element is used to relate descriptions to form
controls.

Syntax
```
<LABEL
    ACCESSKEY="key"
    CLASS="class name(s)"
    DIR="LTR | RTL"
    FOR="ID of control"
    ID="unique alphanumeric identifier"
    LANG="language code"
    STYLE="style information"
    TITLE="advisory text"
    onblur="script"
    onclick="script"
    ondblclick="script"
```

```
onfocus="script"
onkeydown="script"
onkeypress="script"
onkeyup="script"
onmousedown="script"
onmousemove="script"
onmouseout="script"
onmouseover="script"
onmouseup="script">
```

```
</LABEL>
```

Attributes and Events Defined by Internet Explorer 4

```
DATAFLD="column name"
DATAFORMATAS="HTML | TEXT"
DATASRC="data source ID"
LANGUAGE="JAVASCRIPT | JSCRIPT | VBS | VBSCRIPT"
ondragstart="script"
onhelp="script"
onselectstart="script"
```

Attributes

ACCESSKEY   This attribute specifies a keyboard navigation accelerator for the element. Pressing ALT or a similar key in association with the specified key selects the anchor element correlated with that key.

CLASS   See "Core Attributes Reference," earlier in this chapter.

DATAFLD   This attribute is used to indicate the column name in the data source that is bound to the content of the **<LABEL>** element.

DATAFORMATAS   This attribute indicates if the bound data is plain text (**TEXT**) or HTML (**HTML**). The data bound with **<LABEL>** is used to set the content of the label.

DATASRC   The value of this attribute is an identifier indicating the data source to pull data from.

DIR   See "Language Reference," earlier in this chapter.

FOR   This attribute specifies the **ID** for the form control element the label references. This is optional when the label encloses the form control it is bound to. In many cases, particularly when a table is used to structure the form, the **<LABEL>** element will not be able to enclose the associated form control, so the **FOR** attribute should be used. This attribute allows more than one label to be associated with the same control by creating multiple references.

ID   See "Core Attributes Reference," earlier in this chapter.

LANG   See "Language Reference," earlier in this chapter.

LANGUAGE   In the Microsoft implementation, this attribute specifies the scripting language to be used with an associated script bound to the element, typically through an event handler attribute. Possible values may include **JAVASCRIPT**, **JSCRIPT**, **VBS**, and **VBSCRIPT**. Other values that include the version of the language used, such as **JavaScript1.1**, may also be possible.

STYLE   See "Core Attributes Reference," earlier in this chapter.

TITLE   See "Core Attributes Reference," earlier in this chapter.

Attribute and Event Support

INTERNET EXPLORER 4   All W3C-defined attributes and events except **DIR**, **onblur**, and **onfocus**, and all attributes and events defined by Internet Explorer 4.

Event Handlers

See "Events Reference," earlier in this chapter.

Examples

```
<FORM>
    <LABEL ID="usernamelabel">Name
<INPUT TYPE="TEXT" ID="username">
    </LABEL>
</FORM>


<FORM>
  <TABLE>
    <TR>
      <TD><LABEL FOR="username">Name</LABEL></TD>
      <TD><INPUT TYPE="TEXT" ID="username"></TD>
    </TR>
  </TABLE>
</FORM>
```

Compatibility
HTML 4; Internet Explorer 4

Notes

2

- To associate a label with another control implicitly, make the control the contents of the **LABEL**. In this case, a **<LABEL>** element may only contain one other control element. The label itself may be positioned before or after the associated control. If it is impossible to enclose the associated form control, the **FOR** attribute may be used.

- The HTML 4 specification defines the **onblur** and **onfocus** events for **<LABEL>**. However, Internet Explorer 4 does not document their use.

<LAYER> (Content Layers)

This Netscape-specific element allows the definition of overlapping content layers that can be exactly positioned, hidden or shown, rendered transparent or opaque, reordered front to back, and nested. The functionality of layers is available using CSS positioning facilities; page developers are advised not to use the **<LAYER>** element.

Syntax (Defined by Netscape 4)

```
<LAYER
    ABOVE="layer name"
    BACKGROUND="URL of background image"
    BELOW="layer name"
    BGCOLOR="color value"
    CLASS="class name(s)"
    CLIP="clip region coordinates in x1, y1, x2, y2 form"
    HEIGHT="percentage | pixels"
    ID="unique alphanumeric identifier"
    LEFT="pixels"
    NAME="string"
    PAGEX="horizontal pixel position of layer"
    PAGEY="vertical pixel position of layer"
    SRC="URL of layer's contents"
    STYLE="style information"
    TITLE="advisory text"
    TOP="pixels"
```

```
VISIBILITY="HIDE | INHERIT | SHOW"
WIDTH="percentage | pixels"
Z-INDEX="number"
onblur="script"
onfocus="script"
onload="script"
onmouseout="script"
onmouseover="script">
```

```
</LAYER>
```

Attributes

ABOVE   This attribute contains the name of the layer (as set with the **NAME** attribute) to be rendered directly above the current layer.

BACKGROUND   This attribute contains the URL of a background pattern for the layer. Like backgrounds for the document as a whole, the image may tile.

BELOW   This value of this attribute is the name of the layer to be rendered below the current layer.

BGCOLOR   This attribute specifies a layer's background color. The attribute's value can be either a named color, such as **red**, or a color specified in the hexadecimal *#RRGGBB* format, such as **#FF0000**.

CLASS   See "Core Attributes Reference," earlier in this chapter.

CLIP   This attribute clips a layer's content to a specified rectangle. All layer content outside that rectangle will be rendered transparent. The **CLIP** rectangle is defined by two *x,y* pairs that correspond to the top *x*, left *y*, bottom *x*, and right *y* coordinate of the rectangle. The coordinates are relative to the layer's origin point, **0,0** in its top-left corner, and may have nothing to do with the pixel coordinates of the screen.

HEIGHT   This attribute is used to set the height of the layer either in pixels or as a percentage of the screen or region the layer is contained within.

ID   See "Core Attributes Reference," earlier in this chapter.

LEFT   This attribute specifies in pixels the left offset of the layer. The offset is relative to its parent layer, if it has one, or to the left browser margin if it does not.

NAME   This attribute assigns the layer a name that can be referenced by programs in a client-side scripting language. The **ID** attribute can also be used.

PAGEX   This attribute is used to set the horizontal pixel position of the layer relative to the document window rather than any enclosing layer.

PAGEY   This attribute is used to set the vertical pixel position of the layer relative to the document window rather than any enclosing layer.

SRC   This attribute specifies the URL that contains the content to include in the layer. Using this attribute with an empty element is a good way to preserve layouts under older browsers.

STYLE   See "Core Attributes Reference," earlier in this chapter.

TITLE   See "Core Attributes Reference," earlier in this chapter.

TOP   This attribute specifies in pixels the top offset of the layer. The offset is relative to its parent layer if it has one, or the top browser margin if it is not enclosed in another layer.

VISIBILITY   This attribute specifies whether a layer is hidden (**HIDDEN**), shown (**SHOW**), or inherits (**INHERITS**) its visibility from the layer enclosing it.

WIDTH   This attribute specifies a layer's width in pixels or as a percentage value of the enclosing layer or browser width.

Z-INDEX   This attribute specifies a layer's stacking order relative to other layers. Position is specified with positive integers, with "1" indicating the bottommost layer.

Attribute and Event Support

NETSCAPE 4   All attributes.

Event Handlers

See "Events Reference," earlier in this chapter.

Examples

```
<LAYER NAME="scene" BGCOLOR="#00FFFF">
  <LAYER NAME="Shaq" LEFT="100" TOP="100">
    <IMG SRC="shaq.gif">
  </LAYER>
  <LAYER NAME="Rodman" LEFT="200" TOP="100"
         VISIBLITY="HIDDEN">
    <IMG SRC="pinkhair.gif">
  </LAYER>
</LAYER>

<!-- The better way to do layers -->
<LAYER SRC="contents.htm" LEFT="20" TOP="20"
       HEIGHT="80%" WIDTH="80%">
</LAYER>
```

Compatibility

Netscape 4

Notes

- This element will likely fall out of fashion because it lacks
  cross-browser compatibility. The functionality of **\<LAYER\>** is
  possible using the positioning features in CSS; page developers are encouraged not to use the **\<LAYER\>** element.

- Applets, plug-ins, and other embedded media forms, generically called *objects*, may be included in a layer; however, they
  will float to the top of all other layers even if their containing
  layer is obscured.

\<LEGEND\>   (Field Legend)

This HTML 4 element is used to assign a caption to a set of form
fields as defined by the **\<FIELDSET\>** element.

Syntax

```
<LEGEND
    ACCESSKEY="character"
    ALIGN="BOTTOM | LEFT | RIGHT | TOP" (transitional)
    CLASS="class name(s)"
    DIR="LTR | RTL"
```

```
ID="unique alphanumeric identifier"
LANG="language code"
STYLE="style information"
TITLE="advisory text"
onclick="script"
ondblclick="script"
onkeydown="script"
onkeypress="script"
onkeyup="script"
onmousedown="script"
onmousemove="script"
onmouseout="script"
onmouseover="script"
onmouseup="script">
```

`</LEGEND>`

Attributes and Events Defined by Internet Explorer 4

```
ALIGN="CENTER"
LANGUAGE="JAVASCRIPT | JSCRIPT | VBS | VBSCRIPT"
VALIGN="BOTTOM | TOP"
ondragstart="script"
onhelp="script"
```

Attributes

ACCESSKEY   This attribute specifies a keyboard navigation accelerator for the element. Pressing ALT or a similar key in association with the specified key selects the form section or the legend itself.

ALIGN   This attribute indicates where the legend value should be positioned within the border created by a **<FIELDSET>** element. The default position for the legend is the upper-left corner. It is also possible to position the legend to the right by setting the attribute to **RIGHT**. The specification defines **BOTTOM** and **TOP** as well. Microsoft defines the use of the **CENTER** and also defines another attribute, **VALIGN**, to set the vertical alignment separately. Future support for **VALIGN** is unclear; page designers are encouraged to use only the **ALIGN** attribute and to eventually rely on style sheets for legend positioning.

CLASS   See "Core Attributes Reference," earlier in this chapter.

DIR   See "Language Reference," earlier in this chapter.

ID   See "Core Attributes Reference," earlier in this chapter.

LANG   See "Language Reference," earlier in this chapter.

LANGUAGE   In the Microsoft implementation, this attribute specifies the scripting language to be used with an associated script bound to the element, typically through an event handler attribute. Possible values may include **JAVASCRIPT**, **JSCRIPT**, **VBS**, and **VBSCRIPT**. Other values that include the version of the language used, such as **JavaScript1.1**, may also be possible.

STYLE   See "Core Attributes Reference," earlier in this chapter.

TITLE   See "Core Attributes Reference," earlier in this chapter.

VALIGN   This Microsoft-specific attribute is used to set whether the legend appears on the **BOTTOM** or the **TOP** of the border defined by the enclosing **<FIELDSET>** element. The attribute will probably be dropped, as it is nonstandard.

Attribute and Event Support

INTERNET EXPLORER 4   All attributes and events except **ACCESSKEY** and **DIR**.

Event Handlers

See "Events Reference," earlier in this chapter.

Example

```
<FORM>
<FIELDSET>
   <LEGEND ALIGN="TOP">User Information</LEGEND>
   First Name: <INPUT TYPE="TEXT" ID="firstname"
                      SIZE="20"><BR>
   Last Name: <INPUT TYPE="TEXT" ID="lastname"
                      SIZE="20"><BR>
 </FIELDSET>
</FORM>
```

Compatibility

HTML 4; Internet Explorer 4

Notes

- The **<LEGEND>** element should occur only within the **<FIELDSET>** element. There should be only one **<LEGEND>** per **<FIELDSET>** element.

- The legend improves accessibility when the **FIELDSET** is rendered nonvisually.

- The Microsoft implementation can use the **CENTER** option in the **ALIGN** attribute. Microsoft also defines the **VALIGN** attribute for legend positioning. However, the **VALIGN** attribute does not appear to work consistently.

- WebTV and Netscape do not yet support this element.

<LI> (List Item)

This element is used to indicate a list item as contained in an ordered list (**<OL>**), unordered list (**<UL>**), or older list styles like **<DIR>** and **<MENU>**.

Syntax

```
<LI
    CLASS="class name(s)"
    DIR="LTR I RTL"
    ID="unique alphanumeric identifier"
    LANG="language code"
    STYLE="style information"
    TITLE="advisory text"
    TYPE="CIRCLE I DISC I SQUARE I a I A I i I I I 1"
        (transitional)
    VALUE="number" (transitional)
    onclick="script"
    ondblclick="script"
    onkeydown="script"
    onkeypress="script"
    onkeyup="script"
    onmousedown="script"
    onmousemove="script"
    onmouseout="script"
    onmouseover="script"
    onmouseup="script">
```

Attributes and Events Defined by Internet Explorer 4

```
LANGUAGE="JAVASCRIPT | JSCRIPT | VBS | VBSCRIPT"
ondragstart="script"
onhelp="script"
onselectstart="script"
```

Attributes

CLASS   See "Core Attributes Reference," earlier in this chapter.

DIR   See "Language Reference," earlier in this chapter.

ID   See "Core Attributes Reference," earlier in this chapter.

LANG   See "Language Reference," earlier in this chapter.

LANGUAGE   In the Microsoft implementation, this attribute specifies the scripting language to be used with an associated script bound to the element, typically through an event handler attribute. Possible values may include **JAVASCRIPT**, **JSCRIPT**, **VBS**, and **VBSCRIPT**. Other values that include the version of the language used, such as **JavaScript1.1**, may also be possible.

STYLE   See "Core Attributes Reference," earlier in this chapter.

TITLE   See "Core Attributes Reference," earlier in this chapter.

TYPE   This attribute indicates the bullet type used in unordered lists or the numbering type used in ordered lists. For ordered lists, a value of **a** indicates lowercase letters, **A** indicates uppercase letters, **i** indicates lowercase Roman numerals, **I** indicates uppercase Roman numerals, and **1** indicates numbers. For unordered lists, values are used to specify bullet types. While the browser is free to set bullet styles, a value of **DISC** generally specifies a filled circle, a value of **CIRCLE** specifies an empty circle, and a value of **b** specifies a filled square. Browsers like WebTV may include other bullet shapes like triangles.

VALUE   This attribute indicates the current number of items in an ordered list as defined by the <OL> element. Regardless of the value of **TYPE** being used to set Roman numerals or letters, the only allowed value for this attribute is a number. List items that follow will continue numbering from the value set. The **VALUE** attribute has no meaning for unordered lists.

Attribute and Event Support

NETSCAPE 4 **CLASS, ID, LANG, STYLE, TYPE,** and **VALUE.**

INTERNET EXPLORER 4 All attributes and events except **DIR.**

WEBTV **TYPE** and **VALUE.**

Event Handlers
See "Events Reference," earlier in this chapter.

Examples
```
<UL>
    <LI TYPE="CIRCLE">First list item is a circle
    <LI TYPE="SQUARE">Second list item is a square
    <LI TYPE="DISC">Third list item is a square
</UL>

<OL>
    <LI TYPE="I">Roman Numerals
    <LI TYPE="A" VALUE="3">Second list item is letter C
    <LI TYPE="a">Continue list in lowercase letters
</OL>
```

Compatibility
HTML 2, 3.2, 4; Netscape 1, 2, 3, 4; Internet Explorer 2, 3, 4; and WebTV

Notes

- Under the strict HTML 4 definition, the **<LI>** element loses the **TYPE** and **VALUE** attributes, as these functions can be performed with style sheets.

- While bullet style can be set explicitly, browsers tend to change styles for bullets when **<UL>** lists are nested. However, ordered lists generally do not change style automatically, nor do they support outline style number (1.1, 1.1.1, and so on).

- The closing tag **</LI>** is optional and is not commonly used.

<LINK>
(Link to External Files or Set Relationship)

This empty element specifies relationships between the current
document and other documents. Possible uses for this element
include defining a relational framework for navigation and linking
the document to a style sheet.

Syntax
```
<LINK
     CHARSET="charset list from RFC 2045"
     CLASS="class name(s)"
     DIR="LTR | RTL"
     HREF="URL"
     HREFLANG="language code"
     ID="unique alphanumeric identifier"
     LANG="language code"
     MEDIA="ALL | AURAL | BRAILLE | PRINT | PROJECTION |
            SCREEN | other"
     REL="relationship value"
     REV="relationship value"
     STYLE="style information"
     TARGET="frame name" (transitional)
     TITLE="advisory information"
     TYPE="content type"
     onclick="script"
     ondblclick="script"
     onkeydown="script"
     onkeypress="script"
     onkeyup="script"
     onmousedown="script"
     onmousemove="script"
     onmouseout="script"
     onmouseover="script"
     onmouseup="script">
```

Attributes Defined by Internet Explorer 4
```
     DISABLED
```

Attributes Defined by Netscape 4
```
     SRC="URL"
```

Attributes

CHARSET   This attribute specifies the character set used by the linked document. Allowed values for this attribute are character set names, such as EUC-JP, as defined in RFC 2045.

CLASS   See "Core Attributes Reference," earlier in this chapter.

DIR   See "Language Reference," earlier in this chapter.

DISABLED   This Microsoft-defined attribute is used to disable a link relationship. The presence of the attribute is all that is required to remove a linking relationship. In conjunction with scripting, this attribute could be used to turn on and off various style sheet relationships.

HREF   This attribute specifies the URL of the linked resource. A URL may be absolute or relative.

HREFLANG   This attribute is used to indicate the language of the linked resource. See "Language Reference," earlier in this chapter, for information on allowed values.

ID   See "Core Attributes Reference," earlier in this chapter.

LANG   See "Language Reference," earlier in this chapter.

MEDIA   This attribute specifies the destination medium for any linked style information, as indicated when the **REL** attribute is set to **STYLESHEET**. The value of the attribute may be a single media descriptor like **SCREEN** or a comma-separated list. Possible values for this attribute include **ALL, AURAL, BRAILLE, PRINT, PROJECTION,** and **SCREEN**. Other values may also be defined, depending on the browser. Internet Explorer supports **ALL, PRINT,** and **SCREEN** as values for this attribute.

REL   This attribute names a relationship between the linked document and the current document. Possible values for this attribute include **ALTERNATE, BOOKMARK, CHAPTER, CHAPTER, CONTENTS, COPYRIGHT, GLOSSARY, HELP, INDEX, NEXT, PREV, SECTION, START, STYLESHEET,** and **SUBSECTION**.

The most common use of this attribute is to specify a link to an external style sheet. The **REL** attribute is set to **STYLESHEET**, and the **HREF** attribute is set to the URL of an external style sheet to format the page. WebTV also supports the use of the value **NEXT** for **REL** to preload the next page in a document series.

REV   The value of the **REV** attribute shows the relationship of the current document to the linked document, as defined by the **HREF** attribute. The attribute thus defines the reverse relationship compared to the value of the **REL** attribute. Values for the **REV** attribute are similar to the possible values for **REL**. They may include **ALTERNATE, BOOKMARK, CHAPTER, CONTENTS, COPYRIGHT, GLOSSARY, HELP, INDEX, NEXT, PREV, SECTION, START, STYLESHEET**, and **SUBSECTION**.

STYLE   See "Core Attributes Reference," earlier in this chapter.

TARGET   The value of the **TARGET** attribute is used to define the frame or window name that has the defined linking relationship or that will show the rendering of any linked resource.

TITLE   See "Core Attributes Reference," earlier in this chapter.

TYPE   This attribute is used to define the type of the content linked to. The value of the attribute should be a MIME type such as **text/html**, **text/css**, and so on. The common use of this attribute is to define the type of style sheet linked and the most common current value is **text/css**, which indicates a Cascading Style Sheet format.

Attribute and Event Support

NETSCAPE 4   REL, SRC, and TYPE. (CLASS, ID, LANG, and STYLE are implied.)

INTERNET EXPLORER 4   DISABLED, HREF, ID, MEDIA (ALL | PRINT | SCREEN), REL, TITLE, and TYPE.

WEBTV   HREF and REL (value="NEXT").

Event Handlers

See "Events Reference," earlier in this chapter.

Examples

```
<LINK HREF="products.htm" REL="parent">

<LINK HREF="corpstyle.css" REL="stylesheet"
      TYPE="text/css" MEDIA="ALL">

<LINK HREF="nextpagetoload.htm" REL="next">
```

Compatibility
HTML 2, 3.2, 4; Netscape 4; Internet Explorer 3, 4; and WebTV

Notes

- As an empty element **<LINK>** has no closing tag.
- The **<LINK>** element can occur only in the **<HEAD>** element; there may be multiple occurrences of the element.
- HTML 3.2 defines only the **HREF, REL, REV**, and **TITLE** attributes for the **<LINK>** element.
- HTML 2 defines the **HREF, METHODS, REL, REV, TITLE**, and **URN** attributes for the **<LINK>** element. The **METHODS** and **URN** attributes were later removed from specifications.
- The HTML 4 specification defines event handlers for the **<LINK>** element, but it is unclear how they would be used.

<LISTING> (Code Listing)

This depreciated element from HTML 2 is used to indicate a code listing; it is no longer part of the HTML standard. Text tends to be rendered in a smaller size within this element. Otherwise, the **<PRE>** element should be used instead of **<LISTING>** to indicate preformatted text.

Syntax (HTML 2; Depreciated)
```
<LISTING
</LISTING>
```

Attributes and Events Defined by Internet Explorer 4
```
CLASS="class name(s)"
ID="unique alphanumeric string"
LANG="language code"
LANGUAGE="JAVASCRIPT | JSCRIPT | VBS | VBSCRIPT"
STYLE="style information"
TITLE="advisory text"
onclick="script"
ondblclick="script"
ondragstart="script"
onhelp="script"
onkeydown="script"
onkeypress="script"
```

```
onkeyup="script"
onmousedown="script"
onmousemove="script"
onmouseout="script"
onmouseover="script"
onmouseup="script"
onselectstart="script"
```

Attributes

CLASS   See "Core Attributes Reference," earlier in this chapter.

ID   See "Core Attributes Reference," earlier in this chapter.

LANG   See "Language Reference," earlier in this chapter.

LANGUAGE   In the Microsoft implementation, this attribute specifies the scripting language to be used with an associated script bound to the element, typically through an event handler attribute. Possible values may include **JAVASCRIPT**, **JSCRIPT**, **VBS**, and **VBSCRIPT**. Other values that include the version of the language used, such as **JavaScript1.1**, may also be possible.

STYLE   See "Core Attributes Reference," earlier in this chapter.

TITLE   See "Core Attributes Reference," earlier in this chapter.

Attribute and Event Support

INTERNET EXPLORER 4   All attributes.

Event Handlers
See "Events Reference," earlier in this chapter.

Example
```
<LISTING>
This is a code listing. The preformatted text element
&lt;PRE&gt; should be used instead of this depreciated
element.
</LISTING>
```

Compatibility
HTML 2; Netscape 1, 2, 3, 4; Internet Explorer 2, 3, 4; and WebTV

Notes

- As a depreciated element, this element should not be used. This element is not supported by HTML 4. It is still documented by many browser vendors, however, and does creep into some pages. The **<PRE>** element should be used instead of **<LISTING>**.

- It appears that Netscape and Internet Explorer browsers also make text within **<LISTING>** one size smaller than normal text, probably because the HTML 2 specification suggested that 132 characters fit to a typical line rather than 80.

- Netscape does not document support for this element, though it is still supported.

<MAP> (Client-Side Image Map)

This element is used to implement client-side image maps. The element is used to define a map to associate locations on an image with a destination URL. Each hot region or hyperlink mapping is defined by an enclosed **<AREA>** element. A map is bound to a particular image through the use of the **USEMAP** attribute in the **<IMG>** element, which is set to the name of the map.

Syntax

```
<MAP
        CLASS="class name(s)"
        DIR="LTR | RTL"
        ID="unique alphanumeric identifier"
        LANG="language code"
        NAME="unique alphanumeric identifier"
        STYLE="style information"
        TITLE="advisory text"
        onclick="script"
        ondblclick="script"
        onkeydown="script"
        onkeypress="script"
        onkeyup="script"
        onmousedown="script"
        onmousemove="script"
        onmouseout="script"
```

```
onmouseover="script"
onmouseup="script">

<AREA> elements
```

`</MAP>`

Events Defined by Internet Explorer 4
```
ondragstart="script"
onhelp="script"
onselectstart="script"
```

Attributes

CLASS   See "Core Attributes Reference," earlier in this chapter.

DIR   See "Language Reference," earlier in this chapter.

ID   See "Core Attributes Reference," earlier in this chapter.

LANG   See "Language Reference," earlier in this chapter.

NAME   Like **ID**, this attribute is used to define a name associated with the element. In the case of the **<MAP>** element, the **NAME** attribute is the common way to define the name of the image map to be referenced by the **USEMAP** attribute within the **<IMG>** element.

STYLE   See "Core Attributes Reference," earlier in this chapter.

TITLE   See "Core Attributes Reference," earlier in this chapter.

Attribute and Event Support

NETSCAPE 4   **NAME**. (**CLASS**, **ID**, **LANG**, and **STYLE** are implied.)

INTERNET EXPLORER 4   All attributes and events except **DIR**.

WEBTV   **NAME**.

Event Handlers
See "Events Reference," earlier in this chapter.

Example

```
<MAP NAME="mainmap">
    <AREA SHAPE="CIRCLE" COORDS="200,250,25"
        HREF="file1.htm">
    <AREA SHAPE="RECTANGLE" COORDS="50,50,100,100"
        HREF="file2.htm#important">
    <AREA SHAPE="DEFAULT" NOHREF>
</MAP>
```

Compatibility

HTML 3.2, 4; Netscape 1, 2, 3, 4; Internet Explorer 2, 3, 4; and WebTV

Notes

- HTML 3.2 supports only the **NAME** attribute for the <**MAP**> element.

- Client-side image maps are not supported under HTML 2. They were first suggested by Spyglass and later incorporated in Netscape and other browsers.

<MARQUEE> (Marquee Display)

This proprietary element specifies a scrolling, sliding, or bouncing text marquee. This is primarily a Microsoft-specific element, though a few other browsers, notably WebTV, support it as well.

Syntax (Defined by Internet Explorer 4)

```
<MARQUEE
    BEHAVIOR="ALTERNATE I SCROLL I SLIDE"
    BGCOLOR="color name I #RRGGBB"
    CLASS="class name(s)"
    DATAFLD="column name"
    DATAFORMATAS="HTML I TEXT"
    DATASRC="data source ID"
    DIRECTION="DOWN I LEFT I RIGHT I UP"
    HEIGHT="pixels or percentage"
    HSPACE="pixels"
    ID="unique alphanumeric identifier"
```

```
LANG="language code"
LANGUAGE="JAVASCRIPT | JSCRIPT | VBS | VBSCRIPT"
LOOP="INFINITE | number"
SCROLLAMOUNT="pixels"
SCROLLDELAY="milliseconds"
STYLE="style information"
TITLE="advisory text"
TRUESPEED
VSPACE="pixels"
WIDTH="pixels or percentage"
onafterupdate="script"
onblur="script"
onbounce="script"
onclick="script"
ondblclick="script"
ondragstart="script"
onfinish="script"
onfocus="script"
onhelp="script"
onkeydown="script"
onkeypress="script"
onkeyup="script"
onmousedown="script"
onmousemove="script"
onmouseout="script"
onmouseover="script"
onmouseup="script"
onresize="script"
onrowenter="script"
onrowexit="script"
onselectstart="script"
onstart="script">

     Marquee text

</MARQUEE>
```

Attributes Defined by WebTV

```
ALIGN="BOTTOM | CENTER | LEFT | RIGHT | TOP"
TRANSPARENCY="number (0-100)"
```

Attributes

ALIGN   This WebTV-specific attribute is used to indicate how the marquee should be aligned with surrounding text. The alignment values and rendering are similar to other embedded objects, like images. The default value for this attribute under WebTV is **LEFT**. Microsoft Internet Explorer no longer supports this attribute.

BEHAVIOR   This attribute controls the movement of marquee text across the marquee. The **ALTERNATE** option causes text to completely cross the marquee field in one direction and then cross in the opposite direction. A value of **SCROLL** for the attribute causes text to wrap around and start over again. This is the default value for a marquee. A value of **SLIDE** for this attribute causes text to cross the marquee field and stop when its leading character reaches the opposite side.

BGCOLOR   This attribute specifies the marquee's background color. The value for the attribute can either be a color name or a color value defined in the hexadecimal *#RRGGBB* format.

CLASS   See "Core Attributes Reference," earlier in this chapter.

DATAFLD   This attribute is used to indicate the column name in the data source that is bound to the <**MARQUEE**> element.

DATAFORMATAS   This attribute indicates if the bound data is plain text (**TEXT**) or HTML (**HTML**). The data bound with <**MARQUEE**> is used to set the message that is scrolled.

DATASRC   The value of this attribute is set to an identifier indicating the data source to pull data from. Bound data is used to set the message that is scrolled in the <**MARQUEE**>.

DIRECTION   This attribute specifies the direction in which the marquee should scroll. The default is **LEFT**. Other possible values for **DIRECTION** include **DOWN**, **RIGHT**, and **UP**. WebTV does not support the **DOWN** and **UP** values.

HEIGHT   This attribute specifies the height of the marquee in pixels or as a percentage of the window.

HSPACE   This attribute indicates the horizontal space in pixels between the marquee and surrounding content.

ID   See "Core Attributes Reference," earlier in this chapter.

LANG   See "Language Reference," earlier in this chapter.

LANGUAGE   In the Microsoft implementation, this attribute specifies the scripting language to be used with an associated script bound to the element, typically through an event handler attribute. Possible values may include **JAVASCRIPT**, **JSCRIPT**, **VBS**, and **VBSCRIPT**. Other values that include the version of the language used, such as **JavaScript1.1**, may also be possible.

LOOP   This attribute indicates the number of times the marquee content should loop. By default, a marquee loops infinitely unless the **BEHAVIOR** attribute is set to **SLIDE**. It is also possible to use a value of **INFINITE** or **–1** to set the text to loop indefinitely.

SCROLLAMOUNT   This attribute specifies the width in pixels between successive displays of the scrolling text in the marquee.

SCROLLDELAY   This attribute specifies the delay in milliseconds between successive displays of the text in the marquee.

STYLE   See "Core Attributes Reference," earlier in this chapter.

TITLE   See "Core Attributes Reference," earlier in this chapter.

TRANSPARENCY   In the WebTV implementation, this attribute specifies the marquee's degree of transparency. Values range from **0** (totally opaque) to **100** (totally transparent). A value of **50** is optimized for fast rendering.

TRUESPEED   When this attribute is present, it indicates that the **SCROLLDELAY** value should be honored for its exact value. If the attribute is not present, any values less than 60 are rounded up to 60 milliseconds.

VSPACE   This attribute indicates the vertical space in pixels between the marquee and surrounding content.

WIDTH   This attribute specifies the width of the marquee in pixels or as a percentage of the enclosing window.

Attribute and Event Support

INTERNET EXPLORER 4   All Microsoft-defined attributes and events.

WEBTV   ALIGN, BEHAVIOR, BGCOLOR, DIRECTION, HEIGHT, HSPACE, LOOP, SCROLLAMOUNT, SCROLLDELAY, TRANSPARENCY, VSPACE, and WIDTH. (Note: WebTV supports only the **LEFT** and **RIGHT** values for the **DIRECTION** attribute.)

Event Handlers

The **<MARQUEE>** element has a few unique events. For example, an event is triggered when the text bounces off one side on the marquee or another. This can be caught with the **onbounce** event handler attribute. When the text first starts scrolling, the start event fires, which can be caught with **onstart**; when the marquee is done, a finish event fires, which can be caught with **onfinish**. The other events are common to HTML 4 elements with Microsoft extensions.

Examples

```
<MARQUEE BEHAVIOR="ALTERNATE">
SPECIAL VALUE !!! This week only !!!
</MARQUEE>

<MARQUEE ID="marquee1" BGCOLOR="RED" DIRECTION="RIGHT"
        HEIGHT="30" WIDTH="80%" HSPACE="10" VSPACE="10">
The super scroller scrolls again!!
More fun than a barrel of &lt;BLINK&gt; elements.
</MARQUEE>
```

Compatibility

Internet Explorer 3, 4; WebTV

Notes

The **<MARQUEE>** element is supported only by Microsoft and WebTV.

<MENU> (Menu List)

This element is used to indicate a short list of items that might occur in a menu of choices. Like the ordered and unordered lists, the individual items in the list are indicated by the **<LI>** element. Most browsers render the **<MENU>** element exactly the same as the unordered list, so there is little reason to use it. Under the HTML 4 strict specification, **<MENU>** is no longer supported.

Syntax (Transitional Only)

```
<MENU
    CLASS="class name(s)"
    COMPACT
```

```
DIR="LTR | RTL"
ID="unique alphanumeric string"
LANG="language code"
STYLE="style information"
TITLE="advisory text"
onclick="script"
ondblclick="script"
onkeydown="script"
onkeypress="script"
onkeyup="script"
onmousedown="script"
onmousemove="script"
onmouseout="script"
onmouseover="script"
onmouseup="script">
```

```
</MENU>
```

Events Defined by Internet Explorer 4

```
ondragstart="script"
onhelp="script"
onselectstart="script"
```

Attributes

CLASS   See "Core Attributes Reference," earlier in this chapter.

COMPACT   This attribute indicates that the list should be rendered in a compact style. Few browsers actually change the rendering of the list regardless of the presence of this attribute. The **COMPACT** attribute requires no value.

DIR   See "Language Reference," earlier in this chapter.

ID   See "Core Attributes Reference," earlier in this chapter.

LANG   See "Language Reference," earlier in this chapter.

STYLE   See "Core Attributes Reference," earlier in this chapter.

TITLE   See "Core Attributes Reference," earlier in this chapter.

Attribute and Event Support

NETSCAPE 4   CLASS, ID, LANG, and STYLE.

2

INTERNET EXPLORER 4   All attributes and events except
COMPACT and **DIR**.

Event Handlers
See "Events Reference," earlier in this chapter.

Example
```
<H2>Taco List</H2>
  <MENU>
    <LI>Fish
    <LI>Pork
    <LI>Beef
    <LI>Chicken
  </MENU>
```

Compatibility
HTML 2, 3.2, 4 (transitional); Netscape 1, 2, 3, 4; Internet Explorer
2, 3, 4; and WebTV

Notes

- Under the HTML 4 strict specification, this element is not
  defined. Since most browsers simply render this style of list
  as an unordered list, using the **<UL>** element instead is
  preferable.

- Most browsers tend not to support the **COMPACT** attribute.

- The HTML 2 and 3.2 specifications support only the **COMPACT**
  attribute.

<META>   (Meta-Information)

This element specifies general information about a document,
which can be used in document indexing. It also allows a
document to define fields in the HTTP response header when it
is sent from the server. A common use of this element is for
client-pull page loading, which allows a document automatically
to load another document after a specified delay.

Syntax
```
<META
    CONTENT="string"
    DIR="LTR | RTL"
```

```
HTTP-EQUIV="http header string"
LANG="language code"
NAME="name of meta-information"
SCHEME="scheme type">
```

Attributes Defined by WebTV

```
URL="url"
```

Attributes

CONTENT   This attribute contains the actual meta-information. The form of the actual meta-information varies greatly, depending on the value set for **NAME**.

DIR   This attribute defines the text direction (left to right or right to left) of the content of the **<META>** element, as defined by the **CONTENT** attribute.

HTTP-EQUIV   This attribute binds the meta-information in the **CONTENT** attribute to an HTTP response header. If this attribute is present, the **NAME** attribute should not be used. The **HTTP-EQUIV** attribute is often used to create a document that automatically loads another document after a set time. This is called *client-pull*. An example of a client-pull **<META>** element is

```
<META HTTP-EQUIV="REFRESH" CONTENT="10;URL='nextpage.htm'">
```

Note that the **CONTENT** attribute contains two values. The first is the number of seconds to wait, and the second is the identifier URL and the URL to load after the specified time.

LANG   This attribute is the language code associated with the language used in the **CONTENT** attribute.

NAME   This attribute associates a name with the meta-information contained in the **CONTENT** attribute. If present, the **HTTP-EQUIV** attribute should not be used.

SCHEME   The scheme attribute is used to indicate the expected format of the value of the **CONTENT** attribute. The particular scheme may also be used in conjunction with the meta-data profile as indicated by the **PROFILE** attribute for the **<HEAD>** element.

Attribute and Event Support

NETSCAPE 4   CONTENT, HTTP-EQUIV, and **NAME**.

INTERNET EXPLORER 4   All attributes except **DIR**.

WEBTV   **CONTENT, HTTP-EQUIV**, and **URL**.

Event Handlers

None.

Examples

```
<!-- Use of the META element to assist document indexing -->
<META NAME="KEYWORDS" CONTENT="HTML, SCRIPTING"
    SCHEME="Lycos">

<!-- Use of the META element to implement client-pull to
    automatically load a page -->
<META HTTP-EQUIV="REFRESH"
    CONTENT="3;URL='http://www.pint.com/'">

<!-- Use of the META element to add rating information -->
<META HTTP-EQUIV="PICS-Label" CONTENT="(PICS-1.1
            'http://www.rsac.org/ratingsv01.html'
            1 gen true comment 'RSACi North America
            Server' by 'webmaster@bigcompany.com'
            for 'http://www.bigcompany.com' on
            '1997.05.26T13:05-0500'
            r (n 0 s 0 v 0 l 1))">
```

Compatibility

HTML 2, 3.2, 4; Netscape 1.1, 2, 3, 4; Internet Explorer 2, 3, 4; and WebTV

Notes

- The **<META>** element can occur only in the **<HEAD>** element. It may be defined multiple times.

- The **<META>** element is an empty element and does not have a closing tag nor contain any content.

- A common use of the **<META>** element is to set information for indexing tools such as search engines. The common values for the **NAME** attribute when performing this function include **AUTHOR, DESCRIPTION**, and **KEYWORDS**; other attributes may also be possible.

- Along the same line as indexing, meta-information is also used for rating pages.

- The HTML 2 and 3.2 specifications define only the **CONTENT**, **HTTP-EQUIV**, and **NAME** attributes.

<MULTICOL>   (Multiple Column Text)

This Netscape-specific element renders the enclosed content in multiple columns. This element should not be used in favor of a table, which is a more standard way to render multiple columns of text across browsers. It is likely that style sheets will provide for multicolumn rendering in the future.

Syntax (Defined by Netscape)

```
<MULTICOL
     CLASS="class name(s)"
     COLS="number of columns"
     GUTTER="pixels"
     ID="unique alphanumeric identifier"
     STYLE="style information"
     WIDTH="pixels">

</MULTICOL>
```

Attributes

CLASS   See "Core Attributes Reference," earlier in this chapter.

COLS   This attribute indicates the number of columns in which to display the text. The browser attempts to fill the columns evenly.

GUTTER   This attribute indicates the width in pixels between the columns. The default value for this attribute is **10** pixels.

ID   See "Core Attributes Reference," earlier in this chapter.

STYLE   See "Core Attributes Reference," earlier in this chapter.

WIDTH   This attribute indicates the column width for all columns. The width of each column is set in pixels and is equivalent for all columns in the group. If the attribute is not specified, the width of columns will be determined by taking the available window size, subtracting the number of pixels for the gutter between the columns as specified by the **GUTTER** attribute, and evenly dividing the result by the number of columns in the group as set by the **COLS** attribute.

Attribute and Event Support

NETSCAPE 4   All attributes.

Event Handlers
None.

Example
```
<MULTICOL COLS="3" GUTTER="20">
Put a long piece of text here ...
</MULTICOL>
```

Compatibility
Netscape 3, 4

Notes

- Do not attempt to use images or other embedded media within a multicolumn layout as defined by **<MULTICOL>**.

- Do not set the number of columns to high or resize the browser window very small, as text will overwrite other lines.

<NOBR>   (No Breaks)

This proprietary element renders enclosed text without line breaks. Break points for where text may wrap can be inserted using the **<WBR>** element.

Syntax
```
<NOBR
    CLASS="class name(s)"
    ID="unique alphanumeric identifier"
    STYLE="style information"
    TITLE="advisory text">

</NOBR>
```

Attributes

CLASS   See "Core Attributes Reference," earlier in this chapter.

ID   See "Core Attributes Reference," earlier in this chapter.

STYLE   See "Core Attributes Reference," earlier in this chapter.

TITLE   See "Core Attributes Reference," earlier in this chapter.

Attribute and Event Support

NETSCAPE 4   All attributes.

INTERNET EXPLORER 4   ID, **STYLE**, and **TITLE**.

Event Handlers

None.

Examples

```
<NOBR>This really long text ... will not be
broken.</NOBR>

<NOBR>With this element it is often important to hint
where a line may be broken using <WBR>.<WBR> This
element acts as a soft return.</NOBR>
```

Compatibility

Netscape 1.1, 2, 3, 4; Internet Explorer 2, 3, 4; and WebTV

Notes

While many browsers support this attribute, it is not part of any
W3C standard.

<NOEMBED>
(No Embedded Media Support)

This Netscape-specific element is used to indicate alternative
content to display on browsers that cannot support an embedded
media object. It should occur in conjunction with the **<EMBED>**
element.

Syntax

```
<NOEMBED>

    Alternative content here

</NOEMBED>
```

Attributes

Netscape does not specifically define attributes for this element; however, Netscape documentation suggests that **CLASS**, **ID**, **STYLE**, and **TITLE** may be supported for this element.

Event Handlers

None.

Example

```
<EMBED SRC="trailer.mov" HEIGHT="150" WIDTH="150">
   <NOEMBED>
      <IMG SRC="trailer.gif">
      <BR>
      Sorry, this browser is not configured to display video.
   </NOEMBED>
</EMBED>
```

Compatibility

Netscape 2, 3, 4; WebTV

Notes

This element will disappear as the **<OBJECT>** style of inserting media into a page becomes more common.

<NOFRAMES>
(No Frame Support Content)

This element is used to indicate alternative content to display on browsers that do not support frames.

Syntax (Transitional Only)

```
<NOFRAMES
    CLASS="class name(s)"
    DIR="LTR | RTL"
    ID="unique alphanumeric identifier"
    LANG="language code"
    STYLE="style information"
    TITLE="advisory text"
    onclick="script"
    ondblclick="script"
    onkeydown="script"
    onkeypress="script"
```

```
onkeyup="script"
onmousedown="script"
onmousemove="script"
onmouseout="script"
onmouseover="script"
onmouseup="script">

Alternative content for non-frame-supporting
browsers

</NOFRAMES>
```

Attributes

CLASS   See "Core Attributes Reference," earlier in this chapter.

DIR   See "Language Reference," earlier in this chapter.

ID   See "Core Attributes Reference," earlier in this chapter.

LANG   See "Language Reference," earlier in this chapter.

STYLE   See "Core Attributes Reference," earlier in this chapter.

TITLE   See "Core Attributes Reference," earlier in this chapter.

Attribute and Event Support

NETSCAPE 4   **CLASS**, **ID**, **LANG**, and **STYLE** are implied.

INTERNET EXPLORER 4   **ID**, **STYLE**, and **TITLE**.

Event Handlers

It is interesting to note that while the **<NOFRAMES>** element does
support the common events for nearly all HTML 4 elements, their
value seems unclear. The only time that content within a
<NOFRAMES> could be rendered is on a browser that does not
support frames; however, browsers that do not support frames are
unlikely to support an event model or similar features. There might
be some possibility with clever scripting to access framed and
nonframed content, but for now the benefit of the events seems
unclear. For more information, see "Events Reference," earlier in
this chapter.

Example

```
<FRAMESET ROWS="100,*">
  <FRAME SRC="controls.htm">
```

```
<FRAME SRC="content.htm
  <NOFRAMES>
  Sorry, this browser does not support frames.
  </NOFRAMES>
</FRAMESET>
```

2

Compatibility

HTML 4 (transitional); Netscape 2, 3, 4; Internet Explorer 2, 3, 4;
and WebTV

Notes

- This element should be used within the scope of the
  <FRAMESET> element.

- The benefit of events and sophisticated attributes like **STYLE**
  is unclear for browsers that would use content within
  <NOFRAMES>, given that older browsers that don't support
  frames would probably not support these features.

<NOSCRIPT>   (No Script Support Content)

This element is used to enclose content that should be rendered on
browsers that do not support scripting or that have scripting
turned off.

Syntax

```
<NOSCRIPT
    CLASS="class name(s)"
    DIR="LTR | RTL"
    ID="unique alphanumeric identifier"
    LANG="language code"
    STYLE="style information"
    TITLE="advisory text"
    onclick="script"
    ondblclick="script"
    onkeydown="script"
    onkeypress="script"
    onkeyup="script"
    onmousedown="script"
    onmousemove="script"
    onmouseout="script"
    onmouseover="script"
```

```
onmouseup="script">
```

Alternative content for non-script-supporting browsers

```
</NOSCRIPT>
```

Attributes

CLASS   See "Core Attributes Reference," earlier in this chapter.

DIR   See "Language Reference," earlier in this chapter.

ID   See "Core Attributes Reference," earlier in this chapter.

LANG   See "Language Reference," earlier in this chapter.

STYLE   See "Core Attributes Reference," earlier in this chapter.

TITLE   See "Core Attributes Reference," earlier in this chapter.

Attribute and Event Support

NETSCAPE 4   **CLASS**, **ID**, **LANG**, and **STYLE** are implied.

Event Handlers

As defined in the preliminary specification of HTML 4, the benefits of event handlers are not very obvious, considering that content within the **<NOSCRIPT>** element assumes the browser does not support scripting, while the script handlers themselves are for browsers that support scripting. These are standard events for nearly all HTML 4 elements. For definitions, see "Events Reference," earlier in this chapter.

Example

```
Last Updated:
<SCRIPT LANGUAGE="JAVASCRIPT">
<!-- document.writeln(document.lastModified); // -->
</SCRIPT>
<NOSCRIPT>
1997
</NOSCRIPT>
```

Compatibility

HTML 4; Netscape 2, 3, 4; Internet Explorer 3, 4; and WebTV

Notes

Improved functionality for the **<NOSCRIPT>** element may come if it is extended to deal with the lack of support for one scripting language or another. Currently, the element is used only to indicate if any scripting is supported or not. It is also useful to "comment out" scripting information so non-scripting-aware browsers will not read it.

<OBJECT> (Embedded Object)

This element specifies an arbitrary object to be included into an HTML document. Initially, this element was used to insert ActiveX controls, but according to the HTML 4 specification, an object may be any media object, document, applet, ActiveX control, or even image.

Syntax

```
<OBJECT
    ALIGN="BOTTOM | LEFT | MIDDLE | RIGHT | TOP"
        (transitional)
    ARCHIVE="URL"
    BORDER="percentage | pixels" (transitional)
    CLASS="class name(s)"
    CLASSID="ID"
    CODEBASE="URL"
    CODETYPE="MIME Type"
    DATA="URL of data"
    DECLARE
    DIR="LTR | RTL"
    HEIGHT="percentage | pixels"
    HSPACE="percentage | pixels" (transitional)
    ID="unique alphanumeric identifier"
    LANG="language code"
    NAME="unique alphanumeric name"
    STANDBY="standby text string"
    STYLE="style information"
    TABINDEX="number"
    TITLE="advisory text"
    TYPE="MIME Type"
    USEMAP="URL"
    VSPACE="percentage | pixels" (transitional)
    WIDTH="percentage | pixels"
```

```
onclick="script"
ondblclick="script"
onkeydown="script"
onkeypress="script"
onkeyup="script"
onmousedown="script"
onmousemove="script"
onmouseout="script"
onmouseover="script"
onmouseup="script">
```

</OBJECT>

Attributes and Events Defined by Internet Explorer 4

```
ACCESSKEY="character"
ALIGN="ABSBOTTOM | ABSMIDDLE | BASELINE | TEXTOP"
CODE="URL"
DATAFLD="column name"
DATASRC="ID for bound data"
LANGUAGE="JAVASCRIPT | JSCRIPT | VBS | VBSCRIPT"
onafterupdate="script"
onbeforeupdate="script"
onblur="script"
ondragstart="script"
onfocus="script"
onhelp="script"
onreadystatechange="script"
onresize="script"
onrowenter="script"
onrowexit="script"
onselectstart="script"
```

Attributes

ACCESSKEY   This Microsoft attribute specifies a keyboard navigation accelerator for the element. Pressing ALT or a similar key in association with the specified character selects the form control correlated with that key sequence. Page designers are forewarned to avoid key sequences already bound to browsers.

ALIGN   This attribute aligns the object with respect to the surrounding text. The default is **LEFT**. The HTML 4 specification defines **BOTTOM**, **MIDDLE**, **RIGHT**, and **TOP** as well. Browsers may provide an even richer set of alignment values. The behavior of alignment for objects is similar to images. Under the strict

HTML 4 specification, the **<OBJECT>** element does not support this attribute.

ARCHIVE   This attribute contains a URL for the location of an archive file. An archive file is typically used to contain multiple object files to improve the efficiency of access.

BORDER   This attribute specifies the width of the object's borders in pixels or as a percentage.

CLASS   See "Core Attributes Reference," earlier in this chapter.

CLASSID   This attribute contains a URL for an object's implementation. The URL syntax depends upon the object's type. With ActiveX controls, the value of this attribute does not appear to be a URL but something of the form *CLSID: object-id*; for example, **CLSID: 99B42120-6EC7-11CF-A6C7-00AA00A47DD2.**

CODE   Under the old Microsoft implementation, this attribute contains the URL referencing a Java applet class file. The way to access a Java applet under the HTML 4 specification is to use **<OBJECT CLASSID="java: classname.class">**. The pseudo URL *java:* is used to indicate a Java applet. Microsoft Internet Explorer 4 and beyond support this style, so **CODE** should not be used.

CODEBASE   This attribute contains a URL to use as a relative base to access the object specified by the **CLASSID** attribute.

CODETYPE   This attribute specifies an object's MIME type. Do not confuse this attribute with **TYPE**, which specifies the MIME type of the data the object may use as defined by the **DATA** attribute.

DATA   This attribute contains a URL for data required by an object.

DATAFLD   This attribute is used to indicate the column name in the data source that is bound to the **<OBJECT>** element.

DATASRC   The value of this attribute is set to an identifier indicating the data source to pull data from.

DECLARE   This attribute declares an object without instantiating it. This is useful when the object will be a parameter to another object.

DIR   See "Language Reference," earlier in this chapter.

HEIGHT   This attribute specifies the height of the object in pixels or as a percentage of the enclosing window.

HSPACE   This attribute indicates the horizontal space in pixels or percentages between the object and surrounding content.

ID   See "Core Attributes Reference," earlier in this chapter.

LANG   See "Language Reference," earlier in this chapter.

LANGUAGE   In the Microsoft implementation, this attribute specifies the scripting language to be used with an associated script bound to the element, typically through an event handler attribute. Possible values may include **JAVASCRIPT**, **JSCRIPT**, **VBS**, and **VBSCRIPT**. Other values that include the version of the language used, such as **JavaScript1.1**, may also be possible.

NAME   This attribute under the Microsoft definition defines the name of the control so scripting can access it. The HTML 4 specification suggests that it is a name for form submission, but this meaning is unclear and not supported by browsers.

STANDBY   This attribute contains a text message to be displayed while the object is loading.

STYLE   See "Core Attributes Reference," earlier in this chapter.

TABINDEX   This attribute takes a numeric value indicating the position of the object in the tabbing index for the document. Tabbing proceeds from the lowest positive **TABINDEX** value to the highest. Negative values for **TABINDEX** will leave the object out of the tabbing order. When tabbing is not explicitly set, the browser may tab through items in the order they are encountered.

TITLE   See "Core Attributes Reference," earlier in this chapter.

TYPE   This attribute specifies the MIME type for the object's data. This is different from the **CODETYPE**, which is the MIME type of the object and not the data it uses.

USEMAP   This attribute contains the URL of the image map to be used with the object. Typically, the URL will be a fragment identifier referencing a **<MAP>** element somewhere else within the file. The presence of this attribute indicates that the type of object being included is an image.

VSPACE   This attribute indicates the vertical space in pixels or percentages between the object and surrounding text.

2

WIDTH This attribute specifies the width of the object in pixels or as a percentage of the enclosing window.

Attribute and Event Support

NETSCAPE 4 ALIGN, CLASSID, CODEBASE, DATA, HEIGHT, TYPE, and WIDTH. (CLASS, ID, LANG, and STYLE are implied.)

INTERNET EXPLORER 4 ALIGN, CLASS, CLASSID, CODE, CODEBASE, CODETYPE, DATA, HEIGHT, ID, LANG, NAME, STYLE, TABINDEX, TITLE, TYPE, WIDTH, all W3C-defined events, and all attributes and events defined by Internet Explorer 4.

Event Handlers

See "Events Reference," earlier in this chapter.

Examples

```
<OBJECT ID="IeLabel1" WIDTH="325" HEIGHT="65"
        CLASSID="CLSID:99B42120-6EC7-11CF-A6C7-00AA00A47DD2">
    <PARAM NAME="_ExtentX" VALUE="6879">
    <PARAM NAME="_ExtentY" VALUE="1376">
    <PARAM NAME="Caption" VALUE="Hello World">
    <PARAM NAME="Alignment" VALUE="4">
    <PARAM NAME="Mode" VALUE="1">
    <PARAM NAME="ForeColor" VALUE="#FF0000">
    <PARAM NAME="FontName" VALUE="Arial">
    <PARAM NAME="FontSize" VALUE="36">
<B>Hello World for non-ActiveX users!</B>
</OBJECT>

<OBJECT CLASSID="java:Blink.class"
        STANDBY="Here it comes"
        HEIGHT="100" WIDTH="300">
    <PARAM NAME="LBL"
           VALUE="Java is fun, exciting, and new.">
    <PARAM NAME="SPEED" VALUE="2">
This will display in non-Java-aware or -enabled
browsers.
</OBJECT>

<OBJECT DATA="pullinthisfile.html">
Data not included!
</OBJECT>

<OBJECT DATA="bigimage.gif" SHAPES>
    <A HREF="page1.htm" SHAPE="RECT" COORDS="10,10,40,40">
```

```
    Page 1</A>
    <A HREF="page2.htm" SHAPE="CIRCLE" COORDS="100,90,20 ">
    Page 2</A>
</OBJECT>
```

Compatibility

HTML 4; Netscape 4; and Internet Explorer 3, 4

Notes

- Under the strict HTML 4 specification the <OBJECT> element loses most of its presentation attributes, including **ALIGN**, **BORDER**, **HEIGHT**, **HSPACE**, **VSPACE**, and **WIDTH**. These attributes are replaced by style sheet rules.

- The HTML 4 specification reserves the **DATAFLD**, **DATAFORMATAS**, and **DATASRC** attributes for future use.

- Alternative content should be defined within the <OBJECT> element after the <PARAM> elements.

- The <OBJECT> element is still mainly used to include binaries in pages. While the specification defines that it can load in HTML files and create image maps, few, if any, browsers support this.

<OL> (Ordered List)

This element is used to define an ordered or numbered list of items. The numbering style comes in many forms, including letters, Roman numerals, and regular numerals. The individual items within the list are specified by <LI> elements included with the <OL> element.

Syntax

```
<OL
    CLASS="class name(s)"
    COMPACT (transitional)
    DIR="LTR | RTL"
    ID="unique alphanumeric identifier"
    LANG="language code"
    START="number" (transitional)
    STYLE="style information"
    TITLE="advisory text"
    TYPE="a | A | i | I | 1" (transitional)
    onclick="script"
    ondblclick="script"
```

```
onkeydown="script"
onkeypress="script"
onkeyup="script"
onmousedown="script"
onmousemove="script"
onmouseout="script"
onmouseover="script"
onmouseup="script">
```

```
</OL>
```

Attributes and Events Defined by Internet Explorer 4

```
LANGUAGE="JAVASCRIPT | JSCRIPT | VBS | VBSCRIPT"
ondragstart="script"
onhelp="script"
onselectstart="script"
```

Attributes

CLASS   See "Core Attributes Reference," earlier in this chapter.

COMPACT   This attribute indicates that the list should be rendered in a compact style. Few browsers actually change the rendering of the list regardless of the presence of this attribute. The **COMPACT** attribute requires no value.

DIR   See "Language Reference," earlier in this chapter.

ID   See "Core Attributes Reference," earlier in this chapter.

LANG   See "Language Reference," earlier in this chapter.

LANGUAGE   In the Microsoft implementation, this attribute specifies the scripting language to be used with an associated script bound to the element, typically through an event handler attribute. Possible values may include **JAVASCRIPT**, **JSCRIPT**, **VBS**, and **VBSCRIPT**. Other values that include the version of the language used, such as **JavaScript1.1**, may also be possible.

START   This attribute is used to indicate the value to start numbering the individual list items from. While the ordering type of list elements may be Roman numerals like **XXXI** or letters, the value of **START** is always represented as a number. To start numbering elements from the letter "C," use **<OL TYPE="A" START="3">**.

STYLE   See "Core Attributes Reference," earlier in this chapter.

TITLE   See "Core Attributes Reference," earlier in this chapter.

TYPE   This attribute indicates the numbering type: "a" indicates lowercase letters, "A" indicates uppercase letters, "i" indicates lowercase Roman numerals, "I" indicates uppercase Roman numerals, and "1" indicates numbers. Type set in the <OL> element is used for the entire list unless a **TYPE** attribute is used within an enclosed <LI> element.

Attribute and Event Support

NETSCAPE 4   **CLASS, ID, LANG, START, STYLE,** and **TYPE.**

INTERNET EXPLORER 4   All attributes and events except **COMPACT** and **DIR.**

WEBTV   **START** and **TYPE.**

Event Handlers
See "Events Reference," earlier in this chapter.

Examples
```
<OL TYPE="1">
   <LI>First step
   <LI>Second step
   <LI>Third step
</OL>

<OL COMPACT TYPE="I" START="30">
   <LI>Clause 30
   <LI>Clause 31
   <LI>Clause 32
</OL>
```

Compatibility
HTML 2, 3.2, 4; Netscape 1, 2, 3, 4; Internet Explorer 2, 3, 4; and WebTV

Notes

- Under the strict HTML 4 specification, the <OL> element no longer supports the **COMPACT, START,** and **TYPE** attributes. These aspects of lists can be controlled with style sheet rules.

- The HTML 3.2 specification supports only the **COMPACT**, **START**, and **TYPE** attributes. The HTML 2 specification supports only the **COMPACT** attribute.

<OPTGROUP> (Option Grouping)

This element specifies a grouping of items in a selection list defined by **<OPTION>** elements so that the menu choices may be presented in a hierarchical menu or similar alternative fashion to improve access via nonvisual browsers.

Syntax

```
<OPTGROUP
      CLASS="class name(s)"
      DIR="LTR | RTL"
      DISABLED
      ID="unique alphanumeric identifier"
      LABEL="text description"
      LANG="language code"
      STYLE="style information"
      TITLE="advisory text"
      onclick="script"
      ondblclick="script"
      onkeydown="script"
      onkeypress="script"
      onkeyup="script"
      onmousedown="script"
      onmousemove="script"
      onmouseout="script"
      onmouseover="script"
      onmouseup="script">

      <OPTION> elements

</OPTGROUP>
```

Attributes

CLASS   See "Core Attributes Reference," earlier in this chapter.

DIR   See "Language Reference," earlier in this chapter.

DISABLED   Occurrence of this attribute indicates that the enclosed set of options is disabled.

ID See "Core Attributes Reference," earlier in this chapter.

LABEL This attribute contains a short label that may be more appealing to use when the selection list is rendered as items in a hierarchy.

LANG See "Language Reference," earlier in this chapter.

STYLE See "Core Attributes Reference," earlier in this chapter.

TITLE See "Core Attributes Reference," earlier in this chapter.

Attribute and Event Support
None.

Event Handlers
See "Events Reference," earlier in this chapter.

Example
```
Where would you like to go for your vacation?<BR>
<SELECT>
    <OPTION ID="ch1" VALUE="China">The Great Wall
  <OPTGROUP LABEL="Mexico">
    <OPTION ID="ch2" LABEL="Los Cabos VALUE="Los Cabos">
    Los Cabos, Mexico
    <OPTION ID="ch3" LABEL="Leon" VALUE="Leon">Leon, Mexico
    <OPTION ID="ch4" VALUE="MXC">Mexico City
  </OPTGROUP>
    <OPTION ID="ch5" VALUE="home" SELECTED>Your backyard
</SELECT>
```

Compatibility
HTML 4

Notes
This element should only occur within the context of a <**SELECT**> element.

<OPTION>   (Option in Selection List)

This element specifies an item in a selection list defined by the <**SELECT**> element.

Syntax

```
<OPTION
      CLASS="class name(s)"
      DIR="LTR | RTL"
      DISABLED
      ID="unique alphanumeric identifier"
      LABEL="text description"
      LANG="language code"
      SELECTED
      STYLE="style information"
      TITLE="advisory text"
      VALUE="option value"
      onclick="script"
      ondblclick="script"
      onkeydown="script"
      onkeypress="script"
      onkeyup="script"
      onmousedown="script"
      onmousemove="script"
      onmouseout="script"
      onmouseover="script"
      onmouseup="script">

</OPTION>
```

Attributes and Events Defined by Internet Explorer 4

```
      LANGUAGE="JAVASCRIPT | JSCRIPT | VBS | VBSCRIPT"
      ondragstart="script"
      onselectstart="script"
```

Attributes

CLASS   See "Core Attributes Reference," earlier in this chapter.

DIR   See "Language Reference," earlier in this chapter.

DISABLED   Presence of this attribute indicates that the particular
item is not selectable.

ID   See "Core Attributes Reference," earlier in this chapter.

LABEL   This attribute contains a short label that may be more
appealing to use when the selection list is rendered as a hierarchy
due to the presence of an **<OPTGROUP>** element.

LANG   See "Language Reference," earlier in this chapter.

LANGUAGE   In the Microsoft implementation, this attribute specifies the scripting language to be used with an associated script bound to the element, typically through an event handler attribute. Possible values may include **JAVASCRIPT**, **JSCRIPT**, **VBS**, and **VBSCRIPT**. Other values that include the version of the language used, such as **JavaScript1.1**, may also be possible.

SELECTED   This attribute indicates that the associated item is the default selection. If not included, the first item in the selection list is the default. If the <SELECT> element enclosing the <OPTION> elements has the **MULTIPLE** attribute, the **SELECTED** attribute may occur in multiple entries. Otherwise, it should occur only in one entry.

STYLE   See "Core Attributes Reference," earlier in this chapter.

TITLE   See "Core Attributes Reference," earlier in this chapter.

VALUE   This attribute indicates the value to include with the form result when the item is selected.

Attribute and Event Support

NETSCAPE 4   **SELECTED** and **VALUE**. (**CLASS**, **ID**, **LANG**, and **STYLE** are implied.)

INTERNET EXPLORER 4   **CLASS**, **ID**, **LANGUAGE**, **SELECTED**, **VALUE**, **ondragstart**, and **onselectstart**.

WEBTV   **SELECTED** and **VALUE**.

Event Handlers

See "Events Reference," earlier in this chapter.

Examples

```
Where would you like to go for your vacation?<BR>
<SELECT>
    <OPTION ID="choice1" VALUE="China">The Great Wall
    <OPTION ID="choice2" VALUE="Mexico">Los Cabos
    <OPTION ID="choice3" VALUE="Home" SELECTED>Your backyard
</SELECT>
```

Compatibility

HTML 2, 3.2. 4; Netscape 1, 2, 3, 4; Internet Explorer 2, 3, 4; and WebTV

Notes

- The closing tag for **<OPTION>** is optional.

- This element should only occur within the context of a **<SELECT>** element.

- The HTML 2 and 3.2 specifications define only the **SELECTED** and **VALUE** attributes for this element.

<P> (Paragraph)

This element is used to define a paragraph of text. Browsers typically insert a blank line before and after a paragraph of text.

Syntax

```
<P
    ALIGN="CENTER | JUSTIFY | LEFT | RIGHT"
        (transitional)
    CLASS="class name(s)"
    DIR="LTR | RTL"
    ID="unique alphanumeric identifier"
    LANG="language code"
    STYLE="style information"
    TITLE="advisory text"
    onclick="script"
    ondblclick="script"
    onkeydown="script"
    onkeypress="script"
    onkeyup="script"
    onmousedown="script"
    onmousemove="script"
    onmouseout="script"
    onmouseover="script"
    onmouseup="script">

</P>
```

Attributes and Events Defined by Internet Explorer 4

```
LANGUAGE="JAVASCRIPT | JSCRIPT | VBS | VBSCRIPT"
ondragstart="script"
onhelp="script"
onselectstart="script"
```

Attributes

ALIGN   This attribute specifies the alignment of text within a paragraph. The default value is **LEFT**. The transitional specification of HTML 4 also defines **CENTER**, **JUSTIFY**, and **RIGHT**. However, under the strict specification of HTML 4 text alignment can be handled through a style sheet rule.

CLASS   See "Core Attributes Reference," earlier in this chapter.

DIR   See "Language Reference," earlier in this chapter.

ID   See "Core Attributes Reference," earlier in this chapter.

LANG   See "Language Reference," earlier in this chapter.

LANGUAGE   In the Microsoft implementation, this attribute specifies the scripting language to be used with an associated script bound to the element, typically through an event handler attribute. Possible values may include **JAVASCRIPT**, **JSCRIPT**, **VBS**, and **VBSCRIPT**. Other values that include the version of the language used, such as **JavaScript1.1**, may also be possible.

STYLE   See "Core Attributes Reference," earlier in this chapter.

TITLE   See "Core Attributes Reference," earlier in this chapter.

Attribute and Event Support

NETSCAPE 4   **ALIGN**. (**CLASS**, **ID**, **LANG**, and **STYLE** are implied.)

INTERNET EXPLORER 4   All attributes and events except **DIR**. (Note: The **JUSTIFY** value for **ALIGN** is not supported by Internet Explorer 4.)

WEBTV   **ALIGN (CENTER | LEFT | RIGHT)**.

Event Handlers

See "Events Reference," earlier in this chapter.

Examples

```
<P ALIGN="RIGHT">A right-aligned paragraph</P>

<P ID="Para1" CLASS="defaultParagraph"
   TITLE="Introduction Paragraph">
This is the introductory paragraph for a very long
paper about nothing.
</P>
```

Compatibility

HTML 2, 3.2, 4; Netscape 1, 2, 3, 4; Internet Explorer 2, 3, 4; and
Web TV

Notes

- Under the strict HTML 4 specification the **ALIGN** attribute is
  not supported. Alignment of text can be accomplished using
  style sheets.

- The closing tag for the **<P>** element is optional.

- As a logical element, empty paragraphs are ignored by
  browsers, so do not try to use multiple **<P>** elements in a row
  like **<P><P><P><P>** to add blank lines to a Web page. This
  will not work; use the **
** element instead.

- The HTML 3.2 specification supports only the **ALIGN** attribute
  with values of **CENTER**, **LEFT**, and **RIGHT**.

- The HTML 2 specification supports no attributes for the
  <P> element.

<PARAM> (Object Parameter)

This element specifies a parameter to pass to an embedded object
using the **<OBJECT>** or **<APPLET>** element. This element should
occur only within the scope of one of these elements.

Syntax

```
<PARAM
     ID="unique alphanumeric identifier"
     NAME="parameter name"
     TYPE="MIME Type"
     VALUE="parameter value"
     VALUETYPE="DATA | OBJECT | REF">

</PARAM>
```

Attributes Defined by Internet Explorer 4

```
DATAFLD="column name"
DATAFORMATAS="HTML | TEXT"
DATASRC="data source ID"
```

Attributes

DATAFLD   This Internet Explorer–specific attribute is used to indicate the column name in the data source that is bound to the **<PARAM>** element's value.

DATAFORMATAS   This Internet Explorer–specific attribute indicates if the bound data is plain text (**TEXT**) or HTML (**HTML**).

DATASRC   The value of this attribute is set to an identifier indicating the data source to pull data from. Bound data is used to set the value of the parameters passed to the object or applet with which this **<PARAM>** element is associated.

ID   See "Core Attributes Reference," earlier in this chapter.

NAME   This attribute contains the parameter's name. The name of the parameter depends on the particular object being inserted into the page, and it is assumed that the object knows how to handle the passed data. Do not confuse the **NAME** attribute with the **NAME** attribute used for form elements. In the latter case, the **NAME** attribute does not have a similar meaning as **ID**, but rather specifies the name of the data to be passed to an enclosing **<OBJECT>** element.

TYPE   When the **VALUETYPE** attribute is set to **REF**, the **TYPE** attribute can be used to indicate the type of the information to be retrieved. Legal values for this attribute are in the form of MIME types such as **text/html**.

VALUE   This attribute contains the parameter's value. The actual contents of this attribute depend on the object and the particular parameter being passed in, as determined by the **NAME** attribute.

VALUETYPE   This HTML 4–specific attribute specifies the type of the **VALUE** attribute being passed in. Possible values for this attribute include **DATA**, **OBJECT**, and **REF**. A value of **DATA** specifies that the information passed in through the **VALUE** parameter should be treated just as data. A value of **REF** indicates that the information being passed in is a URL that indicates where the data to use is located. The information is not retrieved, but the

URL is passed to the object, which may then retrieve the information if necessary. The last value of **OBJECT** indicates that the value being passed in is the name of an object as set by its **ID** attribute. In practice, the **DATA** attribute is used by default.

Attribute and Event Support

NETSCAPE 4   NAME and VALUE. (ID may be implied.)

INTERNET EXPLORER 4   NAME, DATAFLD, DATAFORMATAS, DATASRC, and VALUE.

Event Handlers
None.

Examples

```
<APPLET CODE="plot.class">
    <PARAM NAME="min" VALUE="5">
    <PARAM NAME="max" VALUE="30">
    <PARAM NAME="ticks" VALUE=".5">
    <PARAM NAME="line-style" VALUE="dotted">
</APPLET>

<OBJECT CLASSID="clsid:D27CDB6E-AE6D-11cf-96B8-444553540000"
        CODEBASE="swflash.cab#version=2,0,0,0"
        HEIGHT="100" WIDTH="100">
    <PARAM ID="param1" NAME="Movie" VALUE="SplashLogo.swf">
    <PARAM ID="param2" NAME="Play" Value="True">
</OBJECT>
```

Compatibility
HTML 3.2, 4; Netscape 2, 3, 4; and Internet Explorer 3, 4

Notes

- The closing tag for this element is forbidden.
- The HTML 3.2 specification supports only the **NAME** and **VALUE** attributes for this element.

<PLAINTEXT>   (Plain Text)

This depreciated element from the HTML 2 specification renders the enclosed text as plain text and forces the browser to ignore any enclosed HTML. Typically, information affected by the

<PLAINTEXT> element is rendered in monospaced font. This element is no longer part of the HTML standard.

Syntax (HTML 2; Depreciated Under HTML 4)

```
<PLAINTEXT>
```

Attributes and Events Defined by Internet Explorer 4

```
CLASS="class name(s)"
ID="unique alphanumeric identifier"
LANG="language code"
LANGUAGE="JAVASCRIPT | JSCRIPT | VBS | VBSCRIPT"
STYLE="style information"
TITLE="advisory text"
onclick="script"
ondblclick="script"
ondragstart="script"
onhelp="script"
onkeydown="script"
onkeypress="script"
onkeyup="script"
onmousedown="script"
onmousemove="script"
onmouseout="script"
onmouseover="script"
onmouseup="script"
onselectstart="script"
```

Attributes

CLASS   See "Core Attributes Reference," earlier in this chapter.

ID   See "Core Attributes Reference," earlier in this chapter.

LANG   See "Language Reference," earlier in this chapter.

LANGUAGE   In the Microsoft implementation, this attribute specifies the scripting language to be used with an associated script bound to the element, typically through an event handler attribute. Possible values may include **JAVASCRIPT**, **JSCRIPT**, **VBS**, and **VBSCRIPT**. Other values that include the version of the language used, such as **JavaScript1.1**, may also be possible.

STYLE   See "Core Attributes Reference," earlier in this chapter.

TITLE   See "Core Attributes Reference," earlier in this chapter.

2

Attribute and Event Support

NETSCAPE 4   **CLASS, ID, LANG,** and **STYLE** are implied.

INTERNET EXPLORER 4   All attributes and events.

Event Handlers

See "Events Reference," earlier in this chapter.

Example

```
<HTML>
<HEAD><TITLE>Plaintext Example</TITLE></HEAD>
<BODY>
The rest of this file is in plain text.
<PLAINTEXT>
Even though this is supposed to be <B>bold</B>, the tags
still show.  There is no way to turn plain text off once
it is on. </PLAINTEXT> does nothing to help. Even </BODY>
and </HTML> will show up.
```

Compatibility

HTML 2; Netscape 1, 2, 3, 4; and Internet Explorer 2, 3, 4

Notes

- No closing tag for this element is necessary, since the browser will ignore all tags after the starting tag.

- This element should not be used. Plain text information can be indicated by a file type, and information can be inserted in a preformatted fashion using the **<PRE>** element.

<PRE>   (Preformatted Text)

This element is used to indicate that the enclosed text is preformatted, meaning that spaces, returns, tabs, and other formatting characters are preserved. Browsers will, however, acknowledge most HTML elements that are found with the **<PRE>** element. Preformatted text will generally be rendered by the browsers in a monospaced font.

Syntax

```
<PRE
    CLASS="class name(s)"
```

```
DIR="LTR | RTL"
ID="unique alphanumeric value"
LANG="language code"
STYLE="style information"
TITLE="advisory text"
WIDTH="number" (transitional)
onclick="script"
ondblclick="script"
onkeydown="script"
onkeypress="script"
onkeyup="script"
onmousedown="script"
onmousemove="script"
onmouseout="script"
onmouseover="script"
onmouseup="script">
```

```
</PRE>
```

Attributes and Events Defined by Internet Explorer 4

```
LANGUAGE="JAVASCRIPT | JSCRIPT | VBS | VBSCRIPT"
ondragstart="script"
onhelp="script"
onselectstart="script"
```

Attributes and Events Defined by Netscape 4

```
COL="columns"
WRAP
```

Attributes

CLASS   See "Core Attributes Reference," earlier in this chapter.

DIR   See "Language Reference," earlier in this chapter.

ID   See "Core Attributes Reference," earlier in this chapter.

LANG   See "Language Reference," earlier in this chapter.

LANGUAGE   In the Microsoft implementation, this attribute specifies the scripting language to be used with an associated script bound to the element, typically through an event handler attribute. Possible values may include **JAVASCRIPT**, **JSCRIPT**, **VBS**, and **VBSCRIPT**. Other values that include the version of the language used, such as **JavaScript1.1**, may also be possible.

STYLE   See "Core Attributes Reference," earlier in this chapter.

TITLE   See "Core Attributes Reference," earlier in this chapter.

WIDTH   This attribute should be set to the **WIDTH** of the preformatted region. The value of the attribute should be the number of characters to display. In practice, this attribute is not supported and is dropped under the strict HTML 4 specification.

Attribute and Event Support

NETSCAPE 4   CLASS, COLS, ID, LANG, STYLE, and WRAP.

INTERNET EXPLORER 4   All attributes and events except **DIR** and **WIDTH**.

Event Handlers

See "Events Reference," earlier in this chapter.

Example

```
<PRE>
Within PREFORMATTED text      A L L      formatting
  IS      PRESERVED
    NO       m    a    t    t    e    r
how wild it is. Remember that some
<B>HTML</B> markup is allowed within the &lt;PRE&gt;
element.
</PRE>
```

Compatibility

HTML 2, 3.2, 4; Netscape 1, 2, 3, 4; Internet Explorer 2, 3, 4; and WebTV

Notes

- The HTML 4 transitional specification states that the **<APPLET>**, **<BASEFONT>**, **<BIG>**, **<FONT>**, **<IMG>**, **<OBJECT>**, **<SMALL>**, **<SUB>**, and **<SUP>** elements should not be used within the **<PRE>** element. The strict HTML 4 specification states that only the **<BIG>**, **<IMG>**, **<OBJECT>**, **<SMALL>**, **<SUB>**, and **<SUP>** elements should not be used within the **<PRE>** element. The other excluded elements are missing, as they are depreciated from the strict specification. While these attributes should not be used, it appears that the two most popular browsers will render them anyway.

- The strict HTML 4 specification drops support for the **WIDTH** attribute, which was not generally supported anyway.

- The HTML 2 and 3.2 specifications support only the **WIDTH** attribute for **<PRE>**.

<Q> (Quote)

This element indicates that the enclosed text is a short inline quotation.

Syntax

```
<Q
    CITE="URL of source"
    CLASS="class name(s)"
    DIR="LTR | RTL"
    ID="unique alphanumeric string"
    LANG="language code"
    STYLE="style information"
    TITLE="advisory text"
    onclick="script"
    ondblclick="script"
    onkeydown="script"
    onkeypress="script"
    onkeyup="script"
    onmousedown="script"
    onmousemove="script"
    onmouseout="script"
    onmouseover="script"
    onmouseup="script">

</Q>
```

Attributes and Events Defined by Internet Explorer 4

```
    LANGUAGE="JAVASCRIPT | JSCRIPT | VBS | VBSCRIPT"
    ondragstart="script"
    onhelp="script"
    onselectstart="script"
```

Attributes

CITE   The value of this attribute is a URL that designates a source document or message for the information quoted. This attribute is

2

intended to point to information explaining the context or the reference for the quote.

CLASS   See "Core Attributes Reference," earlier in this chapter.

DIR   See "Language Reference," earlier in this chapter.

ID   See "Core Attributes Reference," earlier in this chapter.

LANG   See "Language Reference," earlier in this chapter.

LANGUAGE   In the Microsoft implementation, this attribute specifies the scripting language to be used with an associated script bound to the element, typically through an event handler attribute. Possible values may include **JAVASCRIPT**, **JSCRIPT**, **VBS**, and **VBSCRIPT**. Other values that include the version of the language used, such as **JavaScript1.1**, may also be possible.

STYLE   See "Core Attributes Reference," earlier in this chapter.

TITLE   See "Core Attributes Reference," earlier in this chapter.

Attribute and Event Support

INTERNET EXPLORER 4   All attributes and events except **CITE** and **DIR**.

Event Handlers
See "Events Reference," earlier in this chapter.

Example
```
<Q STYLE="color: green">"A few green balls and a rainbow bar
will give you an exciting Web page Christmas Tree!"</Q>
```

Compatibility
HTML 4; Internet Explorer 4

Notes

- This element is intended for short quotations that don't require paragraph breaks, as compared to text that would be contained within **<BLOCKQUOTE>**. Microsoft documentation continues to indicate this is a block element, when it is not.

- Internet Explorer does not make any sort of style change for quotations, but it is possible to apply a style rule.

<S>   (Strikethrough)

This element renders the enclosed text with a line drawn through it.

Syntax (Transitional Only)

```
<S
    CLASS="class name(s)"
    DIR="LTR | RTL"
    ID="unique alphanumeric identifier"
    LANG="language code"
    STYLE="style information"
    TITLE="advisory text"
    onclick="script"
    ondblclick="script"
    onkeydown="script"
    onkeypress="script"
    onkeyup="script"
    onmousedown="script"
    onmousemove="script"
    onmouseout="script"
    onmouseover="script"
    onmouseup="script">

</S>
```

Attributes and Events Defined by Internet Explorer 4

```
    LANGUAGE="JAVASCRIPT | JSCRIPT | VBS | VBSCRIPT"
    ondragstart="script"
    onhelp="script"
    onselectstart="script"
```

Attributes

CLASS   See "Core Attributes Reference," earlier in this chapter.

DIR   See "Language Reference," earlier in this chapter.

ID   See "Core Attributes Reference," earlier in this chapter.

LANG   See "Language Reference," earlier in this chapter.

LANGUAGE   In the Microsoft implementation, this attribute specifies the scripting language to be used with an associated script bound to the element, typically through an event handler attribute. Possible values may include **JAVASCRIPT**, **JSCRIPT**, **VBS**, and **VBSCRIPT**. Other values that include the version of the language used, such as **JavaScript1.1**, may also be possible.

STYLE   See "Core Attributes Reference," earlier in this chapter.

TITLE   See "Core Attributes Reference," earlier in this chapter.

Attribute and Event Support

NETSCAPE 4   **CLASS**, **ID**, **LANG**, and **STYLE** are implied.

INTERNET EXPLORER 4   All attributes and events except **DIR**.

Event Handlers

See "Events Reference," earlier in this chapter.

Examples

```
This line contains a <S>misstake</S>.

<S ID="strike1" onmouseover="this.style.color='red'"
    onmouseout="this.style.color='black'">Fastball</S>
```

Compatibility

HTML 4 (transitional); Netscape 3; Internet Explorer 2, 3, 4; and WebTV

Notes

- This element should act the same as the **<STRIKE>** element.

- This HTML 3 element was eventually adopted by Netscape and Microsoft and was later incorporated into the HTML 4 transitional specification.

- The strict HTML 4 specification does not include the **<S>** element or the **<STRIKE>** element. It is possible to indicate strikethrough text using a style sheet.

<SAMP>   (Sample Text)

This element is used to indicate sample text. Enclosed text is generally rendered in a monospaced font.

Syntax

```
<SAMP
    CLASS="class name(s)"
    DIR="LTR | RTL"
    ID="unique alphanumeric string"
    LANG="language code"
    STYLE="style information"
    TITLE="advisory text"
    onclick="script"
    ondblclick="script"
    onkeydown="script"
    onkeypress="script"
    onkeyup="script"
    onmousedown="script"
    onmousemove="script"
    onmouseout="script"
    onmouseover="script"
    onmouseup="script">

</SAMP>
```

Attributes and Events Defined by Internet Explorer 4

```
    LANGUAGE="JAVASCRIPT | JSCRIPT | VBS | VBSCRIPT"
    ondragstart="script"
    onhelp="script"
    onselectstart="script"
```

Attributes

CLASS   See "Core Attributes Reference," earlier in this chapter.

DIR   See "Language Reference," earlier in this chapter.

ID   See "Core Attributes Reference," earlier in this chapter.

LANG   See "Language Reference," earlier in this chapter.

LANGUAGE   In the Microsoft implementation, this attribute specifies the scripting language to be used with an associated script bound to the element, typically through an event handler attribute. Possible values may include **JAVASCRIPT**, **JSCRIPT**, **VBS**, and **VBSCRIPT**. Other values that include the version of the language used, such as **JavaScript1.1**, may also be possible.

STYLE   See "Core Attributes Reference," earlier in this chapter.

TITLE   See "Core Attributes Reference," earlier in this chapter.

Attribute and Event Support

INTERNET EXPLORER 4   All attributes and events except **DIR**.

Event Handlers

See "Events Reference," earlier in this chapter.

Example

Use the following salutation in all e-mail messages to the boss:

<SAMP>Please excuse the interruption, oh exalted manager.**</SAMP>**

Compatibility

HTML 2, 3.2, 4; Netscape 1, 2, 3, 4; Internet Explorer 2, 3, 4; and WebTV

Notes

- As a logical element, **<SAMP>** is useful to bind style rules to.
- The HTML 2 and 3.2 specifications supported no attributes for this element.

<SCRIPT>   (Scripting)

This element encloses statements in a scripting language for client-side processing. Scripting statements can either be included inline or loaded from an external file and may be commented out to avoid execution by non-scripting-aware browsers.

Syntax

```
<SCRIPT
    CHARSET="character set"
    DEFER
    EVENT="event name" (reserved)
    FOR="element ID" (reserved)
    LANGUAGE="scripting language name"
    SRC="URL of script code"
    TYPE="MIME type">

</SCRIPT>
```

Attributes Defined by Internet Explorer 4

```
CLASS="class name(s)"
ID="unique alphanumeric identifier"
TITLE="advisory text"
```

Attributes

CHARSET This attribute defines the character encoding of the script. The value is a space- and/or comma-delimited list of character sets as defined in RFC 2045. The default value is **ISO-8859-1**.

CLASS This Microsoft-defined attribute does not make much sense given that scripting code would not be bound by style sheet rules. Its meaning as defined in the "Core Attributes Reference" in this chapter is unclear within the context of the <**SCRIPT**> element.

DEFER Presence of this attribute indicates that the browser may defer execution of the script enclosed by the <**SCRIPT**> element. In practice, deferring code may be more up to the position of the <**SCRIPT**> element or the contents. This attribute was added very late to the HTML 4 specification and its support is currently minimal.

EVENT This Microsoft attribute is used to define a particular event that the script should react to. It must be used in conjunction with the **FOR** attribute. Event names are the same as event handler attributes, for example, **onclick**, **ondblclick**, and so on.

FOR The **FOR** attribute is used to define the name or ID of the element to which an event defined by the **EVENT** attribute is related. For example, <**SCRIPT EVENT="onclick" FOR="button1" LANGUAGE="VBSCRIPT"**> defines a VBScript that will execute when a click event is issued for an element named "button1."

ID See "Core Attributes Reference," earlier in this chapter.

LANGUAGE This attribute specifies the scripting language being used. The Netscape implementation supports JavaScript. The Microsoft implementation supports JScript (a JavaScript clone) as well as VBScript, which can be indicated by either **VBS** or **VBSCRIPT**. Other values that include the version of the language used, such as **JavaScript1.1** and **JavaScript1.2**, may also be possible and are useful to exclude browsers from executing script code that is not supported.

SRC   This attribute specifies the URL of a file containing scripting code. Typically, files containing JavaScript code will have a .js extension, and a server will attach the appropriate MIME type; if not, the **TYPE** attribute may be used to explicitly set the content type of the external script file. The **LANGUAGE** attribute may also be helpful in determining this.

TITLE   See "Core Attributes Reference," earlier in this chapter.

TYPE   This attribute should be set to the MIME type corresponding to the scripting language used. For JavaScript, for example, this would be **text/javascript**. In practice, the **LANGUAGE** attribute is the more common way to indicate which scripting language is in effect.

Attribute and Event Support

NETSCAPE 4   **LANGUAGE** and **SRC**.

INTERNET EXPLORER 4   All attributes and events except **CHARSET** and **DEFER**.

WEBTV   **LANGUAGE** and **SRC**.

Event Handlers

There are no events directly associated with the **<SCRIPT>** element. However, the Microsoft implementation does allow the **EVENT** attribute to be used to indicate what event a particular script may be associated with.

Examples

```
<SCRIPT LANGUAGE="JavaScript">
<!-- alert("Hello World !!!"); // -->
</SCRIPT>

<!-- code in external file -->
<SCRIPT LANGUAGE="JavaScript1.2" SRC="superrollover.js">
</SCRIPT>

<SCRIPT FOR="myButton" EVENT="onclick"
        LANGUAGE="JavaScript">
<!-- alert("I've been clicked!"); // -->
</SCRIPT>
<FORM>
<INPUT TYPE="BUTTON" NAME="myButton" VALUE="Click me">
</FORM>
```

Compatibility

HTML 4; Netscape 2, 3, 4; and Internet Explorer 3, 4

Notes

- It is common practice to "comment out" statements enclosed by the **<SCRIPT>** element. Without commenting, scripts are displayed as page content by browsers that do not support scripting. The particular comment style may be dependent on the language being used. For example, in JavaScript use

```
<SCRIPT LANGUAGE="JavaScript">
<!-- JavaScript code here // -->
</SCRIPT>
```

and in VBScript use

```
<SCRIPT LANGUAGE="VBSCRIPT">
<!-- VBScript code here // -->
</SCRIPT>
```

- The HTML 3.2 specification defined a placeholder **<SCRIPT>** element, but otherwise the element is new to HTML 4.

- Refer to the **<NOSCRIPT>** element reference in this chapter to see how content may be identified for non-scripting-aware browsers.

<SELECT>   (Selection List)

This element defines a selection list within a form. Depending on the form of the selection list, the control allows the user to select one or more list options.

Syntax

```
<SELECT
    CLASS="class name(s)"
    DIR="LTR | RTL"
    DISABLED
    ID="unique alphanumeric identifier"
    LANG="language code"
    MULTIPLE
    NAME="unique alphanumeric name"
    SIZE="number"
```

```
STYLE="style information"
TABINDEX="number"
TITLE="advisory text"
onblur="script"
onchange="script"
onclick="script"
ondblclick="script"
onfocus="script"
onkeydown="script"
onkeypress="script"
onkeyup="script"
onmousedown="script"
onmousemove="script"
onmouseout="script"
onmouseover="script"
onmouseup="script">
```

<OPTION> elements

`</SELECT>`

Attributes and Events Defined by Internet Explorer 4

```
ACCESSKEY="character"
ALIGN="ABSBOTTOM | ABSMIDDLE | BASELINE | BOTTOM |
       LEFT | MIDDLE | RIGHT | TEXTTOP | TOP"
DATAFLD="column name"
DATASRC="data source ID"
LANGUAGE="JAVASCRIPT | JSCRIPT | VBS | VBSCRIPT"
onafterupdate="script"
onbeforeupdate="script"
ondragstart="script"
onhelp="script"
onresize="script"
onrowenter="script"
onrowexit="script"
onselectstart="script"
```

Attributes Defined by WebTV

```
AUTOACTIVATE
BGCOLOR="color name | #RRGGBB"
EXCLUSIVE
SELCOLOR="color name | #RRGGBB"
TEXT="color name | #RRGGBB"
USESTYLE
```

Attributes

ACCESSKEY This Microsoft attribute specifies a keyboard navigation accelerator for the element. Pressing ALT or a similar key in association with the specified character selects the form control correlated with that key sequence. Page designers are forewarned to avoid key sequences already bound to browsers.

ALIGN This Microsoft-specific attribute controls the alignment of the image with respect to the content on the page. The default value is **LEFT**, but other values like **ABSBOTTOM, ABSMIDDLE, BASELINE, BOTTOM, MIDDLE, RIGHT, TEXTTOP,** and **TOP** may also be supported. The meaning of these values should be similar to inserted objects such as images.

AUTOACTIVATE In the WebTV implementation, this attribute causes the selection list control to immediately activate when the user selects it, allowing the user to quickly use the arrow keys to move up and down. Without this attribute, the process is a two-step procedure to select the control and then move around.

BGCOLOR In the WebTV implementation, this attribute specifies the background color of the selection list. The value for this attribute can be either a named color, such as **red**, or a color specified in the hexadecimal *#RRGGBB* format, such as **#FF0000**.

CLASS See "Core Attributes Reference," earlier in this chapter.

DATAFLD This attribute is used to indicate the column name in the data source that is bound to the options in the **<SELECT>** element.

DATASRC The value of this attribute is set to an identifier indicating the data source to pull data from.

DIR See "Language Reference," earlier in this chapter.

DISABLED This attribute is used to turn off a form control. Elements will not be submitted nor may they receive any focus from the keyboard or mouse. Disabled form controls will not be part of the tabbing order. The browser may also gray out the form that is disabled, in order to indicate to the user that the form control is inactive. This attribute requires no value.

EXCLUSIVE In the WebTV implementation, this attribute prevents duplicate entries in the selection list. The attribute requires no value.

ID   See "Core Attributes Reference," earlier in this chapter.

LANG   See "Language Reference," earlier in this chapter.

LANGUAGE   In the Microsoft implementation, this attribute specifies the scripting language to be used with an associated script bound to the element, typically through an event handler attribute. Possible values may include **JAVASCRIPT**, **JSCRIPT**, **VBS**, and **VBSCRIPT**. Other values that include the version of the language used, such as **JavaScript1.1**, may also be possible.

MULTIPLE   This attribute allows the selection of multiple items in the selection list. The default is single-item selection.

NAME   This attribute allows a form control to be assigned a name so that it can be referenced by a scripting language. **NAME** is supported by older browsers such as Netscape 2–generation browsers, but the W3C encourages the use of the **ID** attribute. For compatibility purposes both may have to be used.

SELCOLOR   In the WebTV implementation, this attribute specifies the background color for selected items. Its value can be either a named color, such as **green**, or a color specified in the hexadecimal *#RRGGBB* format, such as **#00FF00**. The default for this attribute in WebTV is **#EAEAEA**.

SIZE   This attribute sets the number of visible items in the selection list. When the **MULTIPLE** attribute is not present, only one entry should show; however, when **MULTIPLE** is present, this attribute is useful to set the size of the scrolling list box.

STYLE   See "Core Attributes Reference," earlier in this chapter.

TABINDEX   This attribute takes a numeric value indicating the position of the form control in the tabbing index for the form. Tabbing proceeds from the lowest positive **TABINDEX** value to the highest. Negative values for **TABINDEX** will leave the form control out of the tabbing order. When tabbing is not explicitly set, the browser may tab through items in the order they are encountered. Form controls that are disabled due to the presence of the **DISABLED** attribute will not be part of the tabbing index, though read-only controls will be.

TEXT   In the WebTV implementation, this attribute specifies the text color for items in the list. Its value can be either a named color, such as **blue**, or a color specified in the hexadecimal *#RRGGBB* format, such as **#0000FF**.

TITLE   See "Core Attributes Reference," earlier in this chapter.

USESTYLE   This WebTV-specific attribute causes text to be rendered in the style in effect for the page. The attribute requires no value.

Attribute and Event Support

NETSCAPE 4   MULTIPLE, NAME, SIZE, onblur, onchange, and onfocus. (CLASS, ID, LANG, and STYLE are implied.)

INTERNET EXPLORER 4   All W3C-defined attributes and events except **DIR** and **TITLE**, and all attributes and events defined by Internet Explorer 4.

WEBTV   AUTOACTIVATE, BGCOLOR, MULTIPLE, NAME, SELCOLOR, SIZE, TEXT, USESTYLE, onblur, onchange, onfocus, and onclick.

Event Handlers

See "Events Reference," earlier in this chapter.

Examples

```
Choose your favorite colors
<SELECT MULTIPLE SIZE="2">
    <OPTION>Red
    <OPTION>Blue
    <OPTION>Green
    <OPTION>Yellow
</SELECT>

Taco choices
<SELECT NAME="tacomenu">
    <OPTION VALUE="SuperChicken">Chicken
    <OPTION VALUE="Baja">Fish
    <OPTION VALUE="RX-Needed">Carnitas
</SELECT>
```

Compatibility

HTML 2, 3.2, 4; Netscape 1, 2, 3, 4; Internet Explorer 2, 3, 4; and WebTV

Notes

- The HTML 4 specification reserves the attributes **DATAFLD** and **DATASRC** for future use.

- The HTML 2 and 3.2 specifications define only **MULTIPLE**, **NAME**, and **SIZE** attributes.

<SMALL> (Small Text)

This element renders the enclosed text one font size smaller than a document's base font size unless it is already set to the smallest size.

Syntax

```
<SMALL
    CLASS="class name(s)"
    DIR="LTR | RTL"
    ID="unique alphanumeric string"
    LANG="language code"
    STYLE="style information"
    TITLE="advisory text"
    onclick="script"
    ondblclick="script"
    onkeydown="script"
    onkeypress="script"
    onkeyup="script"
    onmousedown="script"
    onmousemove="script"
    onmouseout="script"
    onmouseover="script"
    onmouseup="script">

</SMALL>
```

Attributes and Events Defined by Internet Explorer 4

```
    LANGUAGE="JAVASCRIPT | JSCRIPT | VBS | VBSCRIPT"
    ondragstart="script"
    onhelp="script"
    onselectstart="script"
```

Attributes

CLASS   See "Core Attributes Reference," earlier in this chapter.

DIR   See "Language Reference," earlier in this chapter.

ID   See "Core Attributes Reference," earlier in this chapter.

LANG   See "Language Reference," earlier in this chapter.

LANGUAGE   In the Microsoft implementation, this attribute specifies the scripting language to be used with an associated script bound to the element, typically through an event handler attribute. Possible values may include **JAVASCRIPT**, **JSCRIPT**, **VBS**, and **VBSCRIPT**. Other values that include the version of the language used, such as **JavaScript1.1**, may also be possible.

STYLE   See "Core Attributes Reference," earlier in this chapter.

TITLE   See "Core Attributes Reference," earlier in this chapter.

Attribute and Event Support

NETSCAPE 4   **CLASS**, **ID**, **LANG**, and **STYLE** are implied.

INTERNET EXPLORER 4   All attributes and events except **DIR**.

Event Handlers
See "Events Reference," earlier in this chapter.

Examples
Here is some **<SMALL>**small text.**</SMALL>**

This element can be applied **<SMALL><SMALL><SMALL>**multiple times**</SMALL></SMALL></SMALL>** to make things even smaller.

Compatibility
HTML 3.2, 4; Netscape 2, 3, 4; Internet Explorer 2, 3, 4; and WebTV

Notes

- The **<SMALL>** element can be used multiple times to decrease the size of text to a greater degree. Using more than six **<SMALL>** elements together doesn't make sense, since browsers currently only support relative font sizes from 1 to 7. As style sheets become more common, this element may fall out of favor.

- The default base font size for a document is typically **3**, though it can be changed with the **<BASEFONT>** element.

<SPACER>   (Extra Space)

This proprietary element specifies an invisible region for pushing content around a page.

Syntax (Defined by Netscape 3)

```
<SPACER
      ALIGN="ABSMIDDLE | ABSBOTTOM | BASELINE | BOTTOM |
             LEFT | MIDDLE | RIGHT | TEXTTOP | TOP"
      HEIGHT="pixels"
      SIZE="pixels"
      TYPE="BLOCK | HORIZONTAL | VERTICAL"
      WIDTH="pixels">
```

Attributes

ALIGN   This attribute specifies the alignment of the spacer with respect to surrounding text. It is only used with spacers with **TYPE="BLOCK"**. The default value for the **ALIGN** attribute is **BOTTOM**. The meanings of the **ALIGN** values are similar to those used with the **<IMG>** element.

HEIGHT   This attribute specifies the height of the invisible region in pixels. It is only used with spacers with **TYPE="BLOCK"**.

SIZE   Used with **TYPE="BLOCK"** and **TYPE="HORIZONTAL"** spacers, this attribute sets the spacer's width in pixels. Used with a **TYPE="VERTICAL"** spacer, this attribute is used to set the spacer's height.

TYPE   This attribute indicates the type of invisible region. A **HORIZONTAL** spacer adds horizontal space between words and objects. A **VERTICAL** spacer is used to add space between lines. A **BLOCK** spacer defines a general-purpose positioning rectangle like an invisible image that text may flow around.

WIDTH   This attribute is used only with the **TYPE="BLOCK"** spacer and is used to set the width of the region in pixels.

Attribute and Event Support

NETSCAPE 4   All attributes.

WEBTV   All attributes.

Examples

A line of text with two**<SPACER TYPE="HORIZONTAL"**
SIZE="20">words separated by 20 pixels. Here is a
line of text.**
**
<SPACER TYPE="VERTICAL" SIZE="50">

Here is another line of text with a large space between
the two lines.**<SPACER ALIGN="LEFT" TYPE="BLOCK"**
HEIGHT="100" WIDTH="100"> This is a bunch of text that
flows around an invisible block region. You could have
easily performed this layout with a table.

Compatibility

Netscape 3, 4; WebTV

Notes

- This element should not be used. If the effect of this element is
  required and style sheets cannot be used, an invisible pixel
  trick may be a more appropriate choice. The invisible pixel
  trick requires a transparent image, which is then resized with
  the **HEIGHT** and **WIDTH** attributes of the **<IMG>** element:

  <IMG SRC="pixel.gif" HEIGHT="100" WIDTH="100">

- This is an empty element; no closing tag is allowed.

<SPAN>   (Text Span)

This element is used to group inline text, typically so scripting or
style rules can be applied to the content. As it has no preset or
rendering meaning, this is the most useful inline element for
associating style and script with content.

Syntax

```
<SPAN
    CLASS="class name(s)"
    DATAFLD="column name" (reserved)
```

```
DATAFORMATAS="HTML | TEXT" (reserved)
DATASRC="data source ID" (reserved)
DIR="LTR | RTL"
ID="unique alphanumeric string"
LANG="language code"
STYLE="style information"
TITLE="advisory text"
onclick="script"
ondblclick="script"
onkeydown="script"
onkeypress="script"
onkeyup="script"
onmousedown="script"
onmousemove="script"
onmouseout="script"
onmouseover="script"
onmouseup="script">
```

```
</SPAN>
```

Attributes and Events Defined by Internet Explorer 4

```
LANGUAGE="JAVASCRIPT | JSCRIPT | VBS | VBSCRIPT"
ondragstart="script"
onhelp="script"
onselectstart="script"
```

Attributes

CLASS   See "Core Attributes Reference," earlier in this chapter.

DATAFLD   This attribute is used to indicate the column name in the data source that is bound to the contents of the **<SPAN>** element.

DATAFORMATAS   This attribute indicates if the bound data is plain text (**TEXT**) or HTML (**HTML**). The data bound with **<SPAN>** should be used to set the content of the element and may include HTML markup.

DATASRC   The value of this attribute is set to an identifier indicating the data source to pull data from.

DIR   See "Language Reference," earlier in this chapter.

ID   See "Core Attributes Reference," earlier in this chapter.

LANG   See "Language Reference," earlier in this chapter.

LANGUAGE   In the Microsoft implementation, this attribute specifies the scripting language to be used with an associated script bound to the element, typically through an event handler attribute. Possible values may include **JAVASCRIPT**, **JSCRIPT**, **VBS**, and **VBSCRIPT**. Other values that include the version of the language used, such as **JavaScript1.1**, may also be possible.

STYLE   See "Core Attributes Reference," earlier in this chapter.

TITLE   See "Core Attributes Reference," earlier in this chapter.

Attribute and Event Support

NETSCAPE 4   **CLASS**, **ID**, **LANG**, and **STYLE**.

INTERNET EXPLORER 4   All attributes and events except **DIR**.

Event Handlers
See "Events Reference," earlier in this chapter.

Examples
```
Here is some<SPAN STYLE="font: 14pt; color: purple">
very strange</SPAN>text.

<SPAN ID="toggletext" onclick="this.style.color='red'"
     ondblclick="this.style.color='black'">
Click and Double Click Me
</SPAN>
```

Compatibility
HTML 4; Netscape 4; and Internet Explorer 3, 4

Notes

- The HTML 4 specification reserves the **DATAFLD**, **DATAFORMATAS**, and **DATASRC** attributes for future use. Internet Explorer 4 supports them.

- Unlike <DIV>, as an inline element <SPAN> does not cause any line breaks.

<STRIKE> (Strikeout Text)

This element is used to indicate strikethrough text, namely, text
with a line drawn through it. The **<S>** element provides shorthand
notation for this element.

Syntax (Transitional Only)

```
<STRIKE
    CLASS="class name(s)"
    DIR="LTR | RTL"
    ID="unique alphanumeric string"
    LANG="language code"
    STYLE="style information"
    TITLE="advisory text"
    onclick="script"
    ondblclick="script"
    onkeydown="script"
    onkeypress="script"
    onkeyup="script"
    onmousedown="script"
    onmousemove="script"
    onmouseout="script"
    onmouseover="script"
    onmouseup="script">

</STRIKE>
```

Attributes and Events Defined by Internet Explorer 4

```
    LANGUAGE="JAVASCRIPT | JSCRIPT | VBS | VBSCRIPT"
    ondragstart="script"
    onhelp="script"
    onselectstart="script"
```

Attributes

CLASS   See "Core Attributes Reference," earlier in this chapter.

DIR   See "Language Reference," earlier in this chapter.

ID   See "Core Attributes Reference," earlier in this chapter.

LANG   See "Language Reference," earlier in this chapter.

LANGUAGE   In the Microsoft implementation, this attribute specifies the scripting language to be used with an associated script bound to the element, typically through an event handler attribute. Possible values may include **JAVASCRIPT**, **JSCRIPT**, **VBS**, and **VBSCRIPT**. Other values that include the version of the language used, such as **JavaScript1.1**, may also be possible.

STYLE   See "Core Attributes Reference," earlier in this chapter.

TITLE   See "Core Attributes Reference," earlier in this chapter.

Attribute and Event Support

NETSCAPE 4   CLASS, ID, **LANG**, and **STYLE** are implied.

INTERNET EXPLORER 4   All attributes and events except **DIR**.

Event Handlers
See "Events Reference," earlier in this chapter.

Example
```
This line contains a spelling <STRIKE>misstake</STRIKE>
mistake.
```

Compatibility
HTML 3.2, 4 (transitional); Netscape 3; Internet Explorer 2, 3, 4; and WebTV

Notes

- This element should act the same as the <S> element.

- The strict HTML 4 specification does not include the <STRIKE> element nor the <S> element. It is possible to indicate strikethrough text using a style sheet.

<STRONG>   (Strong Emphasis)

This element indicates strongly emphasized text. It is usually rendered in a bold typeface, but is a logical element rather than a physical one.

Syntax

```
<STRONG
      CLASS="class name(s)"
      DIR="LTR | RTL"
      ID="unique alphanumeric string"
      LANG="language code"
      STYLE="style information"
      TITLE="advisory text"
      onclick="script"
      ondblclick="script"
      onkeydown="script"
      onkeypress="script"
      onkeyup="script"
      onmousedown="script"
      onmousemove="script"
      onmouseout="script"
      onmouseover="script"
      onmouseup="script">

</STRONG>
```

Attributes and Events Defined by Internet Explorer 4

```
      LANGUAGE="JAVASCRIPT | JSCRIPT | VBS | VBSCRIPT"
      ondragstart="script"
      onhelp="script"
      onselectstart="script"
```

Attributes

CLASS   See "Core Attributes Reference," earlier in this chapter.

DIR   See "Language Reference," earlier in this chapter.

ID   See "Core Attributes Reference," earlier in this chapter.

LANG   See "Language Reference," earlier in this chapter.

LANGUAGE   In the Microsoft implementation, this attribute specifies the scripting language to be used with an associated script bound to the element, typically through an event handler attribute. Possible values may include **JAVASCRIPT**, **JSCRIPT**, **VBS**, and **VBSCRIPT**. Other values that include the version of the language used, such as **JavaScript1.1**, may also be possible.

STYLE   See "Core Attributes Reference," earlier in this chapter.

TITLE   See "Core Attributes Reference," earlier in this chapter.

Attribute and Event Support

NETSCAPE 4   **CLASS, ID, LANG,** and **STYLE** are implied.

INTERNET EXPLORER 4   All attributes and events except **DIR.**

Event Handlers

See "Events Reference," earlier in this chapter.

Examples

```
It is really <STRONG>important</STRONG> to pay attention.

<STRONG STYLE="font-family: impact; font-size: 28pt">
Important Info
</STRONG>
```

Compatibility

HTML 2, 3.2, 4; Netscape 1, 2, 3, 4; Internet Explorer 2, 3, 4; and WebTV

Notes

- This element generally renders as bold text. As a logical element, however, **<STRONG>** is useful to bind style rules to.

- As compared to **<B>**, this element does have meaning and voice browsers may state **<STRONG>** enclosed text in a different voice than text that is enclosed by **<B>**.

<STYLE>   (Style Information)

This element is used to surround style sheet rules for a document. This element should be found only in the **<HEAD>** of a document. Style rules within a document's **<BODY>** element should be set with the style attribute for a particular element.

Syntax

```
<STYLE
     DIR="LTR | RTL"
     LANG="language code"
```

```
MEDIA="ALL | PRINT | SCREEN | others"
TITLE="advisory text"
TYPE="MIME Type">
```

```
</STYLE>
```

2

Attributes Defined by Internet Explorer 4

DISABLED

Attributes

DIR   This attribute is used to set the text direction of the title for the style sheet, either left to right (**LTR**) or right to left (**RTL**).

DISABLED   This Microsoft-defined attribute is used to disable a style sheet. The presence of the attribute is all that is required to disable the style sheet. In conjunction with scripting, this attribute could be used to turn on and off various style sheets in a document.

LANG   The value of this attribute is a language code, like all other **LANG** attributes; however, this attribute defines the language of the **TITLE** attribute rather than the content of the element.

MEDIA   This attribute specifies the destination medium for the style information. The value of the attribute may be a single media descriptor like **SCREEN** or a comma-separated list. Possible values for this attribute include **ALL**, **AURAL**, **BRAILLE**, **PRINT**, **PROJECTION**, and **SCREEN**. Other values may also be defined, depending on the browser. Internet Explorer supports **ALL**, **PRINT**, and **SCREEN** as values for this attribute.

TITLE   This attribute associates an informational title with the style sheet.

TYPE   This attribute is used to define the type of style sheet. The value of the attribute should be the MIME type of the style sheet language used. The most common current value for this attribute is **text/css**, which indicates a Cascading Style Sheet format.

Attribute and Event Support

NETSCAPE 4   TYPE.

INTERNET EXPLORER 4   DISABLED, MEDIA (ALL | PRINT | SCREEN), TITLE, and TYPE.

Event Handlers

None.

Example

```
<HTML>
<HEAD>
<TITLE>Style Sheet Example</TITLE>
<STYLE TYPE="text/css">
<!--
    BODY {background: black; color: white;
    font: 12pt Helvetica}
    H1 {color: red; font: 14pt Impact}
-->
</STYLE>
</HEAD>
<BODY>
<H1>A 14 point red Impact heading on a black
background.</H1>
Regular body text, which is 12-point white Helvetica.
</BODY>
</HTML>
```

Compatibility

HTML 4; Netscape 4; and Internet Explorer 3, 4

Notes

- Style information can also be specified in external style sheets as defined by the **<LINK>** element.
- Style information can also be associated with a particular element using the **STYLE** attribute.
- Style rules are generally commented out within the **<STYLE>** element to avoid interpretation by nonconforming browsers.

<SUB> (Subscript)

This element renders its content as subscripted text.

Syntax

```
<SUB
    CLASS="class name(s)"
```

```
DIR="LTR | RTL"
ID="unique alphanumeric string"
LANG="language code"
STYLE="style information"
TITLE="advisory text"
onclick="script"
ondblclick="script"
onkeydown="script"
onkeypress="script"
onkeyup="script"
onmousedown="script"
onmousemove="script"
onmouseout="script"
onmouseover="script"
onmouseup="script">
```

</SUB>

Attributes and Events Defined by Internet Explorer 4

```
LANGUAGE="JAVASCRIPT | JSCRIPT | VBS | VBSCRIPT"
ondragstart="script"
onhelp="script"
onselectstart="script"
```

Attributes

CLASS   See "Core Attributes Reference," earlier in this chapter.

DIR   See "Language Reference," earlier in this chapter.

ID   See "Core Attributes Reference," earlier in this chapter.

LANG   See "Language Reference," earlier in this chapter.

LANGUAGE   In the Microsoft implementation, this attribute specifies the scripting language to be used with an associated script bound to the element, typically through an event handler attribute. Possible values may include **JAVASCRIPT**, **JSCRIPT**, **VBS**, and **VBSCRIPT**. Other values that include the version of the language used, such as **JavaScript1.1**, may also be possible.

STYLE   See "Core Attributes Reference," earlier in this chapter.

TITLE   See "Core Attributes Reference," earlier in this chapter.

Attribute and Event Support

NETSCAPE 4   **CLASS**, **ID**, **LANG**, and **STYLE** are implied.

INTERNET EXPLORER 4   All attributes and events except **DIR**.

Event Handlers

See "Events Reference," earlier in this chapter.

Example

```
Here is some <SUB>subscripted</SUB> text.
```

Compatibility

HTML 3.2, 4; Netscape 2, 3, 4; Internet Explorer 2, 3, 4; and
WebTV

Notes

The HTML 3.2 specification supports no attributes for the
<**SUP**> element.

<SUP>   (Superscript)

This element renders its content as superscripted text.

Syntax

```
<SUP
      CLASS="class name(s)"
      DIR="LTR | RTL"
      ID="unique alphanumeric string"
      LANG="language code"
      STYLE="style information"
      TITLE="advisory text"
      onclick="script"
      ondblclick="script"
      onkeydown="script"
      onkeypress="script"
      onkeyup="script"
      onmousedown="script"
      onmousemove="script"
      onmouseout="script"
      onmouseover="script"
      onmouseup="script">

</SUP>
```

Attributes and Events Defined by Internet Explorer 4

```
LANGUAGE="JAVASCRIPT | JSCRIPT | VBS | VBSCRIPT"
ondragstart="script"
onhelp="script"
onselectstart="script"
```

2

Attributes

CLASS   See "Core Attributes Reference," earlier in this chapter.

DIR   See "Language Reference," earlier in this chapter.

ID   See "Core Attributes Reference," earlier in this chapter.

LANG   See "Language Reference," earlier in this chapter.

LANGUAGE   In the Microsoft implementation, this attribute specifies the scripting language to be used with an associated script bound to the element, typically through an event handler attribute. Possible values may include **JAVASCRIPT**, **JSCRIPT**, **VBS**, and **VBSCRIPT**. Other values that include the version of the language used, such as **JavaScript1.1**, may also be possible.

STYLE   See "Core Attributes Reference," earlier in this chapter.

TITLE   See "Core Attributes Reference," earlier in this chapter.

Attribute and Event Support

NETSCAPE 4   **CLASS**, **ID**, **LANG**, and **STYLE** are implied.

INTERNET EXPLORER 4   All attributes and events except **DIR**.

Event Handlers
See "Events Reference," earlier in this chapter.

Example
```
Here is some <SUP>superscripted</SUP> text.
```

Compatibility
HTML 3.2, 4; Netscape 2, 3, 4; Internet Explorer 2, 3, 4; and WebTV

Notes
The HTML 3.2 specification defines no attributes for this element.

<TABLE> (Table)

This element is used to define a table. Tables are used to organize data as well as to provide structure for laying out pages.

Syntax

```
<TABLE
    ALIGN="CENTER | LEFT | RIGHT" (transitional)
    BGCOLOR="color name | #RRGGBB" (transitional)
    BORDER="pixels"
    CELLPADDING="pixels"
    CELLSPACING="pixels"
    CLASS="class name(s)"
    DATAPAGESIZE="number of records to display"
    DIR="LTR | RTL"
    FRAME="ABOVE | BELOW | BORDER | BOX | HSIDES |
           LHS | RHS | VOID | VSIDES"
    ID="unique alphanumeric identifier"
    LANG="language code"
    RULES="ALL | COLS | GROUPS | NONE | ROWS"
    STYLE="style information"
    SUMMARY="summary information"
    TITLE="advisory text"
    WIDTH="percentage | pixels"
    onclick="script"
    ondblclick="script"
    onkeydown="script"
    onkeypress="script"
    onkeyup="script"
    onmousedown="script"
    onmousemove="script"
    onmouseout="script"
    onmouseover="script"
    onmouseup="script">

</TABLE>
```

Attributes and Events Defined by Internet Explorer 4

```
    BACKGROUND="URL"
    BORDERCOLOR="color name | #RRGGBB"
    BORDERCOLORDARK="color name | #RRGGBB"
    BORDERCOLORLIGHT="color name | #RRGGBB"
    COLS="number"
    DATASRC="data source ID"
```

```
HEIGHT="percentage | pixels"
LANGUAGE="JAVASCRIPT | JSCRIPT | VBS | VBSCRIPT"
onafterupdate="script"
onbeforeupdate="script"
onblur="script"
ondragstart="script"
onfocus="script"
onhelp="script"
onresize="script"
onrowenter="script"
onrowexit="script"
onselectstart="script"
```

Attributes Defined by Netscape 4

```
BACKGROUND="URL of image" file
BORDERCOLOR="color name | #RRGGBB"
COLS="number of columns"
HEIGHT="pixels"
HSPACE="pixels"
VSPACE="pixels"
```

Attributes Defined by WebTV

```
ALIGN="BLEEDLEFT | BLEEDRIGHT | JUSTIFY"
BACKGROUND="URL of image file"
CELLBORDER="pixels"
GRADANGLE="gradient angle"
GRADCOLOR="color value"
HREF="URL"
HSPACE="pixels"
NAME="string"
NOWRAP
TRANSPARENCY="number (0-100)"
VSPACE="pixels"
```

Attributes

ALIGN   This attribute specifies the alignment of the table with respect to surrounding text. The HTML 4 specification defines **CENTER**, **LEFT**, and **RIGHT**. WebTV also defines **BLEEDLEFT** and **BLEEDRIGHT**, which cause the table to bleed over the right and left margins of the page, and **JUSTIFY**, which is used to justify the table within the browser window. Some browsers may also support alignment values, such as **ABSMIDDLE**, that are common to block objects.

BACKGROUND This nonstandard attribute, which is supported by Internet Explorer, Netscape, and WebTV, specifies the URL of a background image for the table. The image is tiled if it is smaller than the table dimensions. Netscape displays the background image in each table cell, rather than behind the complete table like Internet Explorer.

BGCOLOR This attribute specifies a background color for a table. Its value can be either a named color, such as **red**, or a color specified in the hexadecimal *#RRGGBB* format, such as **#FF0000**.

BORDER This attribute specifies in pixels the width of a table's borders. A value of **0** makes a borderless table, which is useful for graphic layout.

BORDERCOLOR This attribute, supported by Internet Explorer 4 and Netscape 4, is used to set the border color for a table. The attribute should only be used with a positive value for the **BORDER** attribute. The value of the attribute can be either a named color, such as **green**, or a color specified in the hexadecimal *#RRGGBB* format, such as **#00FF00**. Internet Explorer colors the entire table border, including cell borders; Netscape only colors the outer border of the table.

BORDERCOLORDARK This Internet Explorer–specific attribute specifies the darker of two border colors used to create a three-dimensional effect for cell borders. It must be used with the **BORDER** attribute set to a positive value. The attribute value can be either a named color, such as **blue**, or a color specified in the hexadecimal *#RRGGBB* format, such as **#00FF00**.

BORDERCOLORLIGHT This Internet Explorer–specific attribute specifies the lighter of two border colors used to create a three-dimensional effect for cell borders. It must be used with the **BORDER** attribute set to a positive value. The attribute value can be either a named color, such as **red**, or a color specified in the hexadecimal *#RRGGBB* format, such as **#FF0000**.

CELLBORDER In the WebTV implementation, this attribute sets the width in pixels of the border between table cells. If this value is not present, the default border as specified by the **BORDER** attribute is used.

CELLPADDING This attribute sets the width in pixels between the edge of a cell and its content.

<TABLE> (Table) **251**

CELLSPACING   This attribute sets the width in pixels between individual cells.

CLASS   See "Core Attributes Reference," earlier in this chapter.

COLS   This attribute specifies the number of columns in the table and is used to help quickly calculate the size of the table. This attribute was part of the preliminary specification of HTML 4, but was later dropped. A few browsers, notably Netscape 4, already support it.

DATAPAGESIZE   The value of this Microsoft-specific attribute is the number of records that can be displayed in the table when data binding is used.

DATASRC   The value of this Microsoft-specific attribute is an identifier indicating the data source to pull data from.

DIR   See "Language Reference," earlier in this chapter.

FRAME   This attribute specifies which edges of a table are to display a border frame. A value of **ABOVE** indicates only the top edge; **BELOW** indicates only the bottom edge; and **BORDER** and **BOX** indicate all edges, which is the default when the **BORDER** attribute is a positive integer. A value of **HSIDES** indicates only the top and bottom edges should be displayed; **LHS** indicates the left-hand edge should be displayed; **RHS** indicates the right-hand edge should be displayed; **VSIDES** indicates the left and right edges should both be displayed; and **VOID** indicates no border should be displayed.

GRADANGLE   This WebTV-specific attribute defines the gradient angle for a table, ranging from 90 to –90 degrees. **GRADANGLE="0"** yields a left-to-right gradient, while **GRADANGLE="90"** yields a top-to-bottom gradient. The beginning color of the gradient is defined by the **BGCOLOR** attribute, and the ending color is defined by the **GRADCOLOR** attribute.

GRADCOLOR   This WebTV-specific attribute defines the end color of a table's background gradient, in conjunction with the gradient angle defined by the **GRADANGLE** attribute and the starting color defined by the **BGCOLOR** attribute.

HEIGHT   For Netscape 4, this attribute allows the author to specify the height of the table in pixels. Internet Explorer 4 allows both pixels and percentages.

HREF   This WebTV-specific attribute is used to make the entire table function as a hyperlink anchor to the specified URL.

HSPACE   This Netscape-specified attribute indicates the horizontal space in pixels between the table and surrounding content. This attribute is also supported by WebTV but, oddly, not by Internet Explorer.

ID   See "Core Attributes Reference," earlier in this chapter.

LANG   See "Language Reference," earlier in this chapter.

LANGUAGE   In the Microsoft implementation, this attribute specifies the scripting language to be used with an associated script bound to the element, typically through an event handler attribute. Possible values may include **JAVASCRIPT**, **JSCRIPT**, **VBS**, and **VBSCRIPT**. Other values that include the version of the language used, such as **JavaScript1.1**, may also be possible.

NAME   This WebTV attribute is used to assign the table a unique name. It is synonymous with the **ID** attribute.

NOWRAP   This WebTV-specific attribute keeps table rows from wrapping if they extend beyond the right margin. The attribute requires no value.

RULES   This attribute controls the display of dividing rules within a table. A value of **ALL** specifies dividing rules for rows and columns. A value of **COLS** specifies dividing rules for columns only. A value of **GROUPS** specifies horizontal dividing rules between groups of table cells defined by the <THEAD>, <TBODY>, <TFOOT>, or <COLGROUP> elements. A value of **ROWS** specifies dividing rules for rows only. A value of **NONE** indicates no dividing rules and is the default.

STYLE   See "Core Attributes Reference," earlier in this chapter.

SUMMARY   This attribute is used to provide a text summary of the table's purpose and structure. This element is used for accessibility, and its presence is important for nonvisual user agents.

TITLE   See "Core Attributes Reference," earlier in this chapter.

TRANSPARENCY   This WebTV-specific attribute specifies the degree of transparency of the table. Values range from **0** (totally opaque) to **100** (totally transparent). A value of **50** is optimized for fast rendering.

VSPACE This Netscape attribute indicates the vertical space in pixels between the table and surrounding content. This attribute is also supported by WebTV but, oddly, not by Internet Explorer.

WIDTH This attribute specifies the width of the table either in pixels or as a percentage value of the enclosing window.

Attribute and Event Support

NETSCAPE 4 ALIGN (LEFT | RIGHT), BGCOLOR, BORDER, CELLPADDING, CELLSPACING, COLS, HEIGHT, HSPACE, VSPACE, and WIDTH. (CLASS, ID, LANG, and STYLE are implied.)

INTERNET EXPLORER 4 All W3C-defined attributes and events except DIR and SUMMARY, and all attributes and events defined by Internet Explorer 4.

WEBTV ALIGN (BLEEDLEFT | BLEEDRIGHT | CENTER | LEFT | RIGHT), BACKGROUND, BGCOLOR, BORDER, CELLPADDING, CELLSPACING, GRADANGLE, GRADCOLOR, HSPACE, ID, NOWRAP, TRANSPARENCY, and WIDTH.

Event Handlers

See "Events Reference," earlier in this chapter.

Examples

```
<TABLE BGCOLOR="WHITE" BORDER="2">
    <TR>
        <TD>Cell 1</TD>
        <TD>Cell 2</TD>
        <TD>Cell 3</TD>
        <TD>Cell 4</TD>
    </TR>
    <TR>
        <TD>Cell 5</TD>
        <TD>Cell 6</TD>
    </TR>
</TABLE>

<TABLE RULES="ALL" BGCOLOR="YELLOW">
 <CAPTION>Widgets by Area</CAPTION>
```

```
<THEAD ALIGN="CENTER" BGCOLOR="GREEN" VALIGN="CENTER">
    <TD>This is a Header</TD>
</THEAD>
<TFOOT ALIGN="RIGHT" BGCOLOR="RED" VALIGN="BOTTOM">
    <TD>This is part of the footer.</TD>
    <TD>This is also part of the footer.</TD>
</TFOOT>

<TBODY>
    <TR>
        <TD></TD>
        <TH>Regular Widget</TD>
        <TH>Super Widget</TD>
    </TR>
    <TR>
        <TH>West Coast</TH>
        <TD>10</TD>
        <TD>12</TD>
    </TR>
    <TR>
        <TH>East Coast</TH>
        <TD>1</TD>
        <TD>20</TD>
    </TR>
</TBODY>
</TABLE>
```

Compatibility

HTML 3.2, 4; Netscape 1.1, 2, 3, 4; Internet Explorer 2, 3, 4; and
WebTV

Notes

- In addition to displaying tabular data, tables are used to support graphic layout and design.

- The HTML 4 specification reserves the future use of the **DATAFLD**, **DATAFORMATAS**, and **DATASRC** attributes for the **<TABLE>** element.

- The HTML 3.2 specification defines only the **ALIGN**, **BORDER**, **CELLPADDING**, **CELLSPACING**, and **WIDTH** attributes for the **<TABLE>** element.

- The **COLS** attribute may provide an undesirable result under Netscape, which assumes the size of each column in the table is exactly the same.

<TBODY>   (Table Body)

This element is used to group the rows within the body of a table so that common alignment and style defaults can be set easily for numerous cells.

Syntax

```
<TBODY
        ALIGN="CENTER | CHAR | JUSTIFY | LEFT | RIGHT"
        CHAR="character"
        CHAROFF="offset"
        CLASS="class name(s)"
        DIR="LTR | RTL"
        ID="unique alphanumeric identifier"
        LANG="language code"
        STYLE="style information"
        TITLE="advisory text"
        VALIGN="BASELINE | BOTTOM | MIDDLE | TOP"
        onclick="script"
        ondblclick="script"
        onkeydown="script"
        onkeypress="script"
        onkeyup="script"
        onmousedown="script"
        onmousemove="script"
        onmouseout="script"
        onmouseover="script"
        onmouseup="script">

</TBODY>
```

Attributes and Events Defined by Internet Explorer 4

```
        BGCOLOR="color name | #RRGGBB"
        LANGUAGE="JAVASCRIPT | JSCRIPT | VBS | VBSCRIPT"
        VALIGN="CENTER"
        ondragstart="script"
        onhelp="script"
        onselectstart="script"
```

Attributes

ALIGN   This attribute is used to align the contents of the cells within the <TBODY> element. Common values are **CENTER**, **JUSTIFY**, **LEFT**, and **RIGHT**. The HTML 4 specification also defines a value of **CHAR**. When **ALIGN** is set to **CHAR**, the attribute **CHAR** must be present and set to the character to which cells should be aligned. A common use of this approach would be to set cells to align on a decimal point.

BGCOLOR   This attribute specifies a background color for the cells within the <TBODY> element. Its value can be either a named color, such as **red**, or a color specified in the hexadecimal *#RRGGBB* format, such as **#FF0000**.

CHAR   This attribute is used to define the character to which element contents are aligned when the **ALIGN** attribute is set to the **CHAR** value.

CHAROFF   This attribute contains an offset as a positive or negative integer to align characters as related to the **CHAR** value. A value of **2**, for example, would align characters in a cell two characters to the right of the character defined by the **CHAR** attribute.

CLASS   See "Core Attributes Reference," earlier in this chapter.

DIR   See "Language Reference," earlier in this chapter.

ID   See "Core Attributes Reference," earlier in this chapter.

LANG   See "Language Reference," earlier in this chapter.

LANGUAGE   In the Microsoft implementation, this attribute specifies the scripting language to be used with an associated script bound to the element, typically through an event handler attribute. Possible values may include **JAVASCRIPT**, **JSCRIPT**, **VBS**, and **VBSCRIPT**. Other values that include the version of the language used, such as **JavaScript1.1**, may also be possible.

STYLE   See "Core Attributes Reference," earlier in this chapter.

TITLE   See "Core Attributes Reference," earlier in this chapter.

VALIGN   This attribute is used to set the vertical alignment for the table cells with the <TBODY> element. HTML 4 defines

BASELINE, BOTTOM, MIDDLE, and TOP. Internet Explorer
replaces MIDDLE with CENTER; the effect should be the same.

Attribute and Event Support

INTERNET EXPLORER 4   All W3C-defined attributes and events
except CHAR, CHAROFF, and DIR. (Note: Internet Explorer 4 does
not support the CHAR and JUSTIFY values for ALIGN, nor the
MIDDLE value for VALIGN.)

Event Handlers

See "Events Reference," earlier in this chapter.

Example

```
<TABLE RULES="ALL" BGCOLOR="YELLOW">

   <TBODY ALIGN="CENTER" BGCOLOR="RED" STYLE="bodystyle"
          VALIGN="BASELINE">
     <TR>
      <TD></TD>
      <TH>Regular Widget</TH>
      <TH>Super Widget</TH>
     </TR>
     <TR>
      <TH>West Coast</TH>
      <TD>10</TD>
      <TD>12</TD>
     </TR>
     <TR>
      <TH>East Coast</TH>
      <TD>1</TD>
      <TD>20</TD>
     </TR>
   </TBODY>
</TABLE>
```

Compatibility

HTML 4; Internet Explorer 4

Notes

This element is contained by the <TABLE> element and contains
one or more table rows as indicated by the <TR> element.

<TD> (Table Data)

This element specifies a data cell in a table. The element should occur within a table row as defined by the **<TR>** element.

Syntax

```
<TD
      ABBR="abbreviation"
      ALIGN="CENTER | JUSTIFY | LEFT | RIGHT"
      AXIS="group name"
      BGCOLOR="color name | #RRGGBB" (transitional)
      CHAR="character"
      CHAROFF="offset"
      CLASS="CLASS name"
      COLSPAN="number"
      DIR="LTR | RTL"
      HEADERS="space separated list of associated header
              cell's ID values"
      HEIGHT="pixels" (transitional)
      ID="unique alphanumeric identifier"
      LANG="language code"
      NOWRAP (transitional)
      ROWSPAN="number"
      SCOPE="COL | COLGROUP | ROW | ROWGROUP"
      STYLE="style information"
      TITLE="advisory text"
      VALIGN="BASELINE | BOTTOM | MIDDLE | TOP"
      WIDTH="pixels" (transitional)
      onclick="script"
      ondblclick="script"
      onkeydown="script"
      onkeypress="script"
      onkeyup="script"
      onmousedown="script"
      onmousemove="script"
      onmouseout="script"
      onmouseover="script"
      onmouseup="script">

</TD>
```

Attributes and Events Defined by Internet Explorer 4

```
BACKGROUND="URL of image file"
BORDERCOLOR="color name | #RRGGBB"
BORDERCOLORDARK="color name | #RRGGBB"
BORDERCOLORLIGHT="color name | #RRGGBB"
LANGUAGE="JAVASCRIPT | JSCRIPT | VBS | VBSCRIPT"
VALIGN="CENTER"
onafterupdate="script"
onbeforeupdate="script"
onblur="script"
ondragstart="script"
onfocus="script"
onhelp="script"
onresize="script"
onrowenter="script"
onrowexit="script"
onscroll="script"
onselectstart="script"
```

Attributes Defined by Netscape 4

```
BACKGROUND="URL of image file"
BORDERCOLOR="color name | #RRGGBB"
```

Attributes Defined by WebTV

```
ABSHEIGHT="pixels"
ABSWIDTH="pixels"
BACKGROUND="URL of image file"
GRADANGLE="gradient angle"
GRADCOLOR="color"
MAXLINES="number"
TRANSPARENCY="number (0-100)"
```

Attributes

ABBR   The value of this attribute is an abbreviated name for a header cell. This may be useful when attempting to display large tables on small screens.

ABSHEIGHT   This WebTV-specific attribute sets the absolute height of a cell in pixels. Content that does not fit within this height is clipped.

ABSWIDTH   This WebTV-specific attribute sets the absolute width of a cell in pixels. Content that does not fit within this width is clipped.

ALIGN   This attribute is used to align the contents of the cells within the **<TBODY>** element. Common values are **CENTER**, **JUSTIFY**, **LEFT**, and **RIGHT**.

AXIS   This attribute is used to provide a name for a group of related headers.

BACKGROUND   This nonstandard attribute, which is supported by Internet Explorer, Netscape and WebTV, specifies the URL of a background image for the table cell. The image is tiled if it is smaller than the cell's dimensions.

BGCOLOR   This attribute specifies a background color for a table cell. Its value can be either a named color, such as **red**, or a color specified in the hexadecimal *#RRGGBB* format, such as **#FF0000**. (Netscape Navigator often fails to render a cell with a colored background unless a nonbreaking space, at least, is inserted in the cell.)

BORDERCOLOR   This attribute, supported by Internet Explorer and Netscape, is used to set the border color for a table cell. The attribute should only be used with a positive value for the **BORDER** attribute. The value of the attribute can be either a named color, such as **green**, or a color specified in the hexadecimal *#RRGGBB* format, such as **#00FF00**.

BORDERCOLORDARK   This Internet Explorer–specific attribute specifies the darker of two border colors used to create a three-dimensional effect for a cell's borders. It must be used with the **BORDER** attribute set to a positive value. The attribute value can be either a named color, such as **blue**, or a color specified in the hexadecimal *#RRGGBB* format, such as **#00FF00**.

BORDERCOLORLIGHT   This Internet Explorer–specific attribute specifies the lighter of two border colors used to create a three-dimensional effect for a cell's borders. It must be used with the **BORDER** attribute set to a positive value. The attribute value can be either a named color, such as **red**, or a color specified in the hexadecimal *#RRGGBB* format, such as **#FF0000**.

CHAR   This attribute is used to define the character to which element contents are aligned when the **ALIGN** attribute is set to the **CHAR** value.

CHAROFF   This attribute contains an offset as a positive or negative integer to align characters as related to the **CHAR** value. A value of **2**, for example, would align characters in a cell two characters to the right of the character defined by the **CHAR** attribute.

CLASS   See "Core Attributes Reference," earlier in this chapter.

COLSPAN   This attribute takes a numeric value that indicates how many columns wide a cell should be. This is useful to create tables with cells of different widths.

DIR   See "Language Reference," earlier in this chapter.

GRADANGLE   This WebTV-specific attribute defines the gradient angle for a table cell, ranging from 90 to –90 degrees. **GRADANGLE="0"** yields a left-to-right gradient, while **GRADANGLE="90"** yields a top-to-bottom gradient. The beginning color of the gradient is defined by the **BGCOLOR** attribute, and the ending color is defined by the **GRADCOLOR** attribute.

GRADCOLOR   This WebTV-specific attribute defines the end color of a table cell's background gradient, in conjunction with the gradient angle defined by the **GRADANGLE** attribute and the starting color defined by the **BGCOLOR** attribute.

HEADERS   This attribute takes a space-separated list of **ID** values that correspond to the header cells related to this cell.

HEIGHT   This attribute indicates the height in pixels of the cell.

ID   See "Core Attributes Reference," earlier in this chapter.

LANG   See "Language Reference," earlier in this chapter.

LANGUAGE   In the Microsoft implementation, this attribute specifies the scripting language to be used with an associated script bound to the element, typically through an event handler attribute. Possible values may include **JAVASCRIPT**, **JSCRIPT**, **VBS**, and **VBSCRIPT**. Other values that include the version of the language used, such as **JavaScript1.1**, may also be possible.

MAXLINES   This WebTV-specific attribute takes a numeric argument indicating the maximum number of content lines to display. Content beyond these lines is clipped.

NOWRAP   This attribute keeps the content within a table cell from automatically wrapping.

ROWSPAN   This attribute takes a numeric value that indicates how many rows high a table cell should span. This attribute is useful in defining tables with cells of different heights.

SCOPE   This attribute specifies the table cells that the current cell provides header information for. A value of **COL** indicates that the cell is a header for the rest of the column below it. A value of **COLGROUP** indicates that the cell is a header for its current column group. A value of **ROW** indicates that the cell contains header information for the rest of the row it is in. A value of **ROWGROUP** indicates that the cell is a header for its row group. This attribute may be used in place of the **HEADER** attribute and is useful for rendering assistance by nonvisual browsers. This attribute was added very late to the HTML 4 specification so support for this attribute is minimal.

STYLE   See "Core Attributes Reference," earlier in this chapter.

TITLE   See "Core Attributes Reference," earlier in this chapter.

TRANSPARENCY   This WebTV-specific attribute specifies the degree of transparency of the table cell. Values range from **0** (totally opaque) to **100** (totally transparent). A value of **50** is optimized for fast rendering.

VALIGN   This attribute is used to set the vertical alignment for the table cell. HTML 4 defines **BASELINE**, **BOTTOM**, **MIDDLE**, and **TOP**. Internet Explorer replaces **MIDDLE** with **CENTER**; the effect should be the same.

WIDTH   This attribute specifies the width of a cell in pixels.

Attribute and Event Support

NETSCAPE 4   ALIGN, BACKGROUND, BGCOLOR, BORDERCOLOR, COLSPAN, HEIGHT, NOWRAP, ROWSPAN, VALIGN, and WIDTH. (**CLASS, ID, LANG,** and **STYLE** are implied.)

INTERNET EXPLORER 4   All W3C-defined attributes and events except **ABBR, AXIS, CHAR, CHAROFF, DIR, HEADERS** and

HEIGHT, and all attributes and events defined by Internet Explorer 4. (Note: Internet Explorer 4 does not support the **JUSTIFY** value for **ALIGN**, nor the **MIDDLE** value for **VALIGN**.)

WEBTV   **ALIGN (CENTER | LEFT | RIGHT), BACKGROUND, BGCOLOR, COLSPAN, GRADANGLE, GRADCOLOR, HEIGHT, ROWSPAN, TRANSPARENCY, VALIGN (BASELINE | BOTTOM | MIDDLE | TOP), and WIDTH.**

Event Handlers

See "Events Reference," earlier in this chapter.

Examples

```
<TD ALIGN="LEFT" VALIGN="TOP">
Put me in the top left corner.
</TD>

<TD ALIGN="BOTTOM" BGCOLOR="RED" VALIGN="RIGHT">
Put me in the bottom right corner.
</TD>
<TABLE BORDER="1" WIDTH="80%">
  <TR>
    <TD COLSPAN="3">
    A pretty wide cell
    </TD>
  <TR>
    <TD>Item 2</TD>
    <TD>Item 3</TD>
    <TD>Item 4</TD>
  </TR>
</TABLE>
```

Compatibility

HTML 3.2, 4; Netscape 1.1, 2, 3, 4; Internet Explorer 2, 3, 4; and WebTV

Notes

- The HTML 3.2 specification defines only **ALIGN, COLSPAN, HEIGHT, NOWRAP, ROWSPAN, VALIGN,** and **WIDTH** attributes.
- This element should always be within the **<TR>** element.

\<TEXTAREA\> (Multiline Text Input)

This element specifies a multiline text input field contained within
a form.

Syntax

```
<TEXTAREA
     ACCESSKEY="character"
     CLASS="class name"
     COLS="number"
     DIR="LTR | RTL"
     DISABLED
     ID="unique alphanumeric identifier"
     LANG="language code"
     NAME="unique alphanumeric identifier"
     READONLY
     ROWS="number"
     STYLE="style information"
     TABINDEX="number"
     TITLE="advisory text"
     onblur="script"
     onchange="script"
     onclick="script"
     ondblclick="script"
     onfocus="script"
     onkeydown="script"
     onkeypress="script"
     onkeyup="script"
     onmousedown="script"
     onmousemove="script"
     onmouseout="script"
     onmouseover="script"
     onmouseup="script"
     onselect="script">

</TEXTAREA>
```

Attributes and Events Defined by Internet Explorer 4

```
     ALIGN="ABSBOTTOM | ABSMIDDLE | BASELINE | BOTTOM |
            LEFT | MIDDLE | RIGHT | TEXTTOP | TOP"
     DATAFLD="column name"
     DATASRC="data source ID"
     LANGUAGE="JAVASCRIPT | JSCRIPT | VBS | VBSCRIPT"
     WRAP="OFF | PHYSICAL | VIRTUAL"
```

```
onafterupdate="script"
onbeforeupdate="script"
ondragstart="script"
onhelp="script"
onresize="script"
onrowenter="script"
onrowexit="script"
onscroll="script")
onselectstart="script"
onstart="script"
```

Attributes Defined by Netscape 4

```
WRAP="HARD | OFF | SOFT"
```

Attributes Defined by WebTV

```
ALLCAPS
AUTOACTIVATE
AUTOCAPS
BGCOLOR="color name | #RRGGBB"
CURSOR="color name | #RRGGBB"
GROWABLE
NOHARDBREAKS
NOSOFTBREAKS
NUMBERS
SHOWKEYBOARD
USESTYLE
```

Attributes

ACCESSKEY   This Microsoft-specific attribute specifies a
keyboard navigation accelerator for the element. Pressing ALT or a
similar key in association with the specified character selects the
form control correlated with that key sequence. Page designers are
forewarned to avoid key sequences already bound to browsers.

ALIGN   Microsoft defines alignment values for this element. The
values for this attribute should behave similar to any included
object or image.

ALLCAPS   This WebTV-specific attribute renders all viewer-
entered text in capital letters. This attribute requires no value.

AUTOACTIVATE   This WebTV-specific attribute causes the text
input control to immediately activate. This attribute requires
no value.

AUTOCAPS This WebTV-specific attribute renders the first letter of all viewer-entered words in a capital letter. This attribute requires no value.

BGCOLOR This WebTV-specific attribute specifies the background color for the text input area. Its value can be either a named color, such as **red**, or a color specified in the hexadecimal *#RRGGBB* format, such as **#FF0000**. The default color for the <TEXTAREA> element under WebTV is **#EAEAEA**.

CLASS See "Core Attributes Reference," earlier in this chapter.

COLS This attribute sets the width in characters of the text area. The typical default values for the size of a <TEXTAREA> element when this attribute is not set is **20** characters.

CURSOR This WebTV-specific attribute is used to indicate the cursor color for the text input area. Its value can be either a named color, such as **red**, or a color specified in the hexadecimal *#RRGGBB* format, such as **#FF0000**. The default value for the cursor color in the WebTV browser is **darkblue (#3333AA)**.

DATAFLD This attribute is used to indicate the column name in the data source that is bound to the content enclosed by the <TEXTAREA> element.

DATASRC The value of this attribute is an identifier indicating the data source to pull data from.

DIR See "Language Reference," earlier in this chapter.

DISABLED This attribute is used to turn off a form control. Elements will not be submitted nor may they receive any focus from the keyboard or mouse. Disabled form controls will not be part of the tabbing order. The browser may also gray out the form that is disabled, in order to indicate to the user that the form control is inactive. This attribute requires no value.

GROWABLE This WebTV-specific attribute allows the text input area to expand vertically to accommodate extra text entered by the user. This attribute requires no value.

ID See "Core Attributes Reference," earlier in this chapter.

LANG See "Language Reference," earlier in this chapter.

LANGUAGE   In the Microsoft implementation, this attribute specifies the scripting language to be used with an associated script bound to the element, typically through an event handler attribute. Possible values may include **JAVASCRIPT**, **JSCRIPT**, **VBS**, and **VBSCRIPT**. Other values that include the version of the language used, such as **JavaScript1.1**, may also be possible.

NAME   This attribute allows a form control to be assigned a name so that it can be referenced by a scripting language. **NAME** is supported by older browsers, such as Netscape 2–generation browsers, but the W3C encourages the use of the **ID** attribute. For compatibility purposes, both attributes may have to be used.

NOHARDBREAKS   This WebTV-specific attribute causes a press of the ENTER key to select the next form element rather than causing a line break in the text input area. The attribute requires no value.

NOSOFTBREAKS   This attribute removes breaks automatically inserted into the text by line wrapping when the form is submitted. The attribute requires no value.

NUMBERS   This WebTV-specific attribute causes the number "1" to be selected in the onscreen keyboard in anticipation of the viewer entering a numeric value.

READONLY   This attribute prevents the form control's value from being changed. Form controls with this attribute set may receive focus from the user but may not be modified. Since they receive focus, a **READONLY** form control will be part of the form's tabbing order. Last, the control's value will be sent on form submission. The attribute can only be used with **<INPUT>** when **TYPE** is set to **TEXT** or **PASSWORD**. The attribute is also used with the **<TEXTAREA>** element.

ROWS   This attribute sets the number of rows in the text area. The value of the attribute should be a positive integer.

SHOWKEYBOARD   In the WebTV implementation, this attribute causes the onscreen keyboard to be displayed when the **<TEXTAREA>** element is selected.

STYLE   See "Core Attributes Reference," earlier in this chapter.

TABINDEX   This attribute takes a numeric value indicating the position of the form control in the tabbing index for the form. Tabbing proceeds from the lowest positive **TABINDEX** value to the highest. Negative values for **TABINDEX** will leave the form control out of the tabbing order. When tabbing is not explicitly set, the browser may tab through items in the order they are encountered. Form controls that are disabled due to the presence of the **DISABLED** attribute will not be part of the tabbing index, though read-only controls will be.

TITLE   See "Core Attributes Reference," earlier in this chapter.

USESTYLE   This WebTV-specific attribute causes text to be rendered in the style in effect for the page. The attribute requires no value.

WRAP   In Netscape and Microsoft browsers, this attribute controls word wrap behavior. A value of **OFF** for the attribute forces the <**TEXTAREA**> not to wrap text, so the viewer must manually enter line breaks. A value of **HARD** causes word wrap and includes line breaks in text submitted to the server. A value of **SOFT** causes word wrap but removes line breaks from text submitted to the server. Internet Explorer supports a value of **PHYSICAL**, which is equivalent to Netcape's **HARD** value, and a value of **VIRTUAL**, which is equivalent to Netscape's **SOFT** value. If the **WRAP** attribute is not included, text will still wrap under Internet Explorer, but under Netscape it will scroll horizontally in the text box. It is always a good idea to include the **WRAP** attribute.

Attribute and Event Support

NETSCAPE 4   COLS, NAME, ROWS, WRAP (HARD | OFF | SOFT), onblur, onchange, onfocus, and onselect. (CLASS, ID, LANG, and STYLE are implied.)

INTERNET EXPLORER 4   All W3C-defined events and attributes except **DIR**, and all attributes and events defined by Internet Explorer 4.

WEBTV   BGCOLOR, COLS, CURSOR, NAME, ROWS, USESTYLE, onblur, onchange, and onfocus.

Event Handlers

See "Events Reference," earlier in this chapter.

Examples

```
<TEXTAREA NAME="CommentBox" COLS="40" ROWS="8">
Default text in field
</TEXTAREA>

<TEXTAREA NAME="comment" ROWS="10" COLS="40"
        WRAP="virtual" ALIGN="center"></TEXTAREA>
```

Compatibility

HTML 2, 3.2, 4; Netscape 1, 2, 3, 4; Internet Explorer 2, 3, 4; and WebTV

Notes

- Any text between the **<TEXTAREA>** and **</TEXTAREA>** tags is rendered as the default entry for the form control.
- The HTML 2 and 3.2 specifications define only the **COLS**, **NAME**, and **ROWS** attribute for this element.
- The HTML 4 specification reserves the **DATAFLD** and **DATASRC** attributes for future use with the **<TEXTAREA>** element.

<TFOOT>   (Table Footer)

This element is used to group the rows within the footer of a table so that common alignment and style defaults can be set easily for numerous cells. This element may be particularly useful when setting a common footer for tables that are dynamically generated.

Syntax

```
<TFOOT
     ALIGN="CENTER | CHAR | JUSTIFY | LEFT | RIGHT"
     BGCOLOR="color name | #RRGGBB" (transitional)
     CHAR="character"
     CHAROFF="offset"
     CLASS="class name(s)"
     DIR="LTR | RTL"
     ID="unique alphanumeric identifier"
     LANG="language code"
     STYLE="style information"
     TITLE="advisory text"
     VALIGN="BASELINE | BOTTOM | MIDDLE | TOP"
```

```
onclick="script"
ondblclick="script"
onkeydown="script"
onkeypress="script"
onkeyup="script"
onmousedown="script"
onmousemove="script"
onmouseout="script"
onmouseover="script"
onmouseup="script">
```

```
</TFOOT>
```

Attributes and Events Defined by Internet Explorer 4

```
LANGUAGE="JAVASCRIPT | JSCRIPT | VBS | VBSCRIPT"
VALIGN="CENTER"
ondragstart="script"
onhelp="script"
onselectstart="script"
```

Attributes

ALIGN   This attribute is used to align the contents of the cells within the **<TFOOT>** element. Common values are **CENTER**, **JUSTIFY**, **LEFT**, and **RIGHT**. The HTML 4 specification also defines a value of **CHAR**. When **ALIGN** is set to **CHAR**, the attribute **CHAR** must be present and set to the character to which cells should be aligned. A common use of this approach would be to set cells to align on a decimal point.

BGCOLOR   This attribute specifies a background color for the cells within the **<TFOOT>** element. Its value can be either a named color, such as **red**, or a color specified in the hexadecimal *#RRGGBB* format, such as **#FF0000**.

CHAR   This attribute is used to define the character to which element contents are aligned when the **ALIGN** attribute is set to the **CHAR** value.

CHAROFF   This attribute contains an offset as a positive or negative integer to align characters as related to the **CHAR** value. A value of **2**, for example, would align characters in a cell two characters to the right of the character defined by the **CHAR** attribute.

CLASS   See "Core Attributes Reference," earlier in this chapter.

DIR   See "Language Reference," earlier in this chapter.

ID   See "Core Attributes Reference," earlier in this chapter.

LANG   See "Language Reference," earlier in this chapter.

LANGUAGE   In the Microsoft implementation, this attribute specifies the scripting language to be used with an associated script bound to the element, typically through an event handler attribute. Possible values may include **JAVASCRIPT**, **JSCRIPT**, **VBS**, and **VBSCRIPT**. Other values that include the version of the language used, such as **JavaScript1.1**, may also be possible.

STYLE   See "Core Attributes Reference," earlier in this chapter.

TITLE   See "Core Attributes Reference," earlier in this chapter.

VALIGN   This attribute is used to set the vertical alignment for the table cells with the **<TFOOT>** element. HTML 4 defines **BASELINE**, **BOTTOM**, **MIDDLE**, and **TOP**. Internet Explorer replaces **MIDDLE** with **CENTER**; the effect should be the same.

Attribute and Event Support

INTERNET EXPLORER 4   All events and attributes except **CHAR**, **CHAROFF**, and **DIR**. (Note: Internet Explorer 4 does not support the **JUSTIFY** value for the **ALIGN** attribute.)

Event Handlers
None.

Example

```
<TABLE BORDER="1" BGCOLOR="YELLOW" WIDTH="80%">
   <TBODY CLASS="tablebody">
     <TR>
       <TD>The contents of the table!</TD>
     </TR>
   </TBODY>
     <TFOOT ALIGN="CENTER" BGCOLOR="RED" CLASS="footer"
           VALIGN="BOTTOM">
       <TD>This is part of the footer.</TD>
       <TD>This is also part of the footer.</TD>
     </TFOOT>
</TABLE>
```

Compatibility

HTML 4; Internet Explorer 4

Notes

This element is only contained by the **<TABLE>** element and
contains table rows as delimited by **<TR>** elements.

<TH>   (Table Header)

This element specifies a header cell in a table. The element should
occur within a table row as defined by a **<TR>** element. The main
difference between this element and **<TD>** is that browsers may
render table headers slightly differently.

Syntax

```
<TH
     ABBR="abbreviation"
     ALIGN="CENTER | JUSTIFY | LEFT | RIGHT"
     AXIS="group name"
     BGCOLOR="color name | #RRGGBB" (transitional)
     CHAR="character"
     CHAROFF="offset"
     CLASS="CLASS name"
     COLSPAN="number"
     DIR="LTR | RTL"
     HEADERS="space-separated list of associated header
               cells' ID values"
     HEIGHT="pixels" (transitional)
     ID="unique alphanumeric identifier"
     LANG="language code"
     NOWRAP (transitional)
     ROWSPAN="number"
     SCOPE="COL | COLGROUP | ROW | ROWGROUP"
     STYLE="style information"
     TITLE="advisory text"
     VALIGN="BASELINE | BOTTOM | MIDDLE | TOP"
     WIDTH="pixels" (transitional)
     onclick="script"
     ondblclick="script"
     onkeydown="script"
     onkeypress="script"
     onkeyup="script"
     onmousedown="script"
```

```
onmousemove="script"
onmouseout="script"
onmouseover="script"
onmouseup="script">
```

`</TH>`

Attributes and Events Defined by Internet Explorer 4

```
BACKGROUND="URL of image" file
BORDERCOLOR="color name | #RRGGBB"
BORDERCOLORDARK="color name | #RRGGBB"
BORDERCOLORLIGHT="color name | #RRGGBB"
LANGUAGE="JAVASCRIPT | JSCRIPT | VBS | VBSCRIPT"
VALIGN="CENTER"
ondragstart="script"
onhelp="script"
onscroll="script"
onselectstart="script"
```

Attributes Defined by Netscape 4

```
BACKGROUND="URL of image file"
BORDERCOLOR="color name | #RRGGBB"
```

Attributes Defined by WebTV

```
ABSHEIGHT="pixels"
ABSWIDTH="pixels"
BACKGROUND="URL of image" file
GRADANGLE
GRADCOLOR
MAXLINES="number"
TRANSPARENCY="number (0-100)"
```

Attributes

ABBR   The value of this attribute is an abbreviated name for a header cell. This may be useful when attempting to display large tables on small screens.

ABSHEIGHT   This WebTV-specific attribute sets the absolute height of a cell in pixels. Content that does not fit within this height is clipped.

ABSWIDTH   This WebTV-specific attribute sets the absolute width of a cell in pixels. Content that does not fit within this width is clipped.

ALIGN   This attribute is used to align the contents of the cells within the \<TBODY\> element. Common values are **CENTER, JUSTIFY, LEFT,** and **RIGHT**.

AXIS   This attribute is used to provide a name for a group of related headers.

BACKGROUND   This nonstandard attribute, which is supported by Internet Explorer, Netscape, and WebTV, specifies the URL of a background image for the table cell. The image is tiled if it is smaller than the cell's dimensions.

BGCOLOR   This attribute specifies a background color for a table cell. Its value can be either a named color, such as red, or a color specified in the hexadecimal *#RRGGBB* format, such as **#FF0000**.

BORDERCOLOR   This attribute, supported by Internet Explorer and Netscape, is used to set the border color for a table cell. The attribute should only be used with a positive value for the **BORDER** attribute. The value of the attribute can be either a named color, such as **green**, or a color specified in the hexadecimal *#RRGGBB* format, such as **#00FF00**.

BORDERCOLORDARK   This Internet Explorer–specific attribute specifies the darker of two border colors used to create a three-dimensional effect for a cell's borders. It must be used with the **BORDER** attribute set to a positive value. The attribute value can be either a named color, such as **blue**, or a color specified in the hexadecimal *#RRGGBB* format, such as **#00FF00**).

BORDERCOLORLIGHT   This Internet Explorer–specific attribute specifies the lighter of two border colors used to create a three-dimensional effect for a cell's borders. It must be used with the **BORDER** attribute set to a positive value. The attribute value can be either a named color, such as **red**, or a color specified in the hexadecimal *#RRGGBB* format, such as **#FF0000**.

CHAR   This attribute is used to define the character to which element contents are aligned when the **ALIGN** attribute is set to the **CHAR** value.

CHAROFF   This attribute contains an offset as a positive or negative integer to align characters as related to the **CHAR** value. A value of **2**, for example, would align characters in a cell two characters to the right of the character defined by the **CHAR** attribute.

CLASS   See "Core Attributes Reference," earlier in this chapter.

COLSPAN   This attribute takes a numeric value that indicates how many columns wide a cell should be. This is useful to create tables with cells of different widths.

DIR   See "Language Reference," earlier in this chapter.

GRADANGLE   This WebTV-specific attribute defines the gradient angle for a table header, ranging from 90 to –90 degrees. **GRADANGLE="0"** yields a left-to-right gradient, while **GRADANGLE="90"** yields a top-to-bottom gradient. The beginning color of the gradient is defined by the **BGCOLOR** attribute, and the ending color is defined by the **GRADCOLOR** attribute.

GRADCOLOR   This WebTV-specific attribute defines the end color of a table header's background gradient, in conjunction with the gradient angle defined by the **GRADANGLE** attribute and the starting color defined by the **BGCOLOR** attribute.

HEADERS   This attribute takes a space-separated list of **ID** values that correspond to the header cells related to this cell.

HEIGHT   This attribute indicates the height in pixels of the header cell.

ID   See "Core Attributes Reference," earlier in this chapter.

LANG   See "Language Reference," earlier in this chapter.

LANGUAGE   In the Microsoft implementation, this attribute specifies the scripting language to be used with an associated script bound to the element, typically through an event handler attribute. Possible values may include **JAVASCRIPT**, **JSCRIPT**, **VBS**, and **VBSCRIPT**. Other values that include the version of the language used, such as **JavaScript1.1**, may also be possible.

MAXLINES   This WebTV-specific attribute takes a numeric argument indicating the maximum number of content lines to display. Content beyond these lines is clipped.

NOWRAP   This attribute keeps the content within a table header cell from automatically wrapping.

ROWSPAN This attribute takes a numeric value that indicates how many rows high a table cell should span. This attribute is useful in defining tables with cells of different heights.

SCOPE This attribute specifies the table cells that the current cell provides header information for. A value of **COL** indicates that the cell is a header for the rest of the column below it. A value of **COLGROUP** indicates that the cell is a header for its current column group. A value of **ROW** indicates that the cell contains header information for the rest of the row it is in. A value of **ROWGROUP** indicates that the cell is a header for its row group. This attribute may be used in place of the **HEADER** attribute and is useful for rendering assistance by nonvisual browsers. This attribute was added very late to the HTML 4 specification, so support for this attribute is minimal.

STYLE See "Core Attributes Reference," earlier in this chapter.

TITLE See "Core Attributes Reference," earlier in this chapter.

TRANSPARENCY This WebTV-specific attribute specifies the degree of transparency of the table header. Values range from **0** (totally opaque) to **100** (totally transparent). A value of **50** is optimized for fast rendering.

VALIGN This attribute is used to set the vertical alignment for the table cell. HTML 4 defines **BASELINE, BOTTOM, MIDDLE,** and **TOP**. Internet Explorer further defines **CENTER**, which should act just like **MIDDLE**.

WIDTH This attribute specifies the width of a header cell in pixels.

Attribute and Event Support

NETSCAPE 4 ALIGN, BACKGROUND, BGCOLOR, BORDERCOLOR, COLSPAN, HEIGHT, NOWRAP, ROWSPAN, VALIGN, and WIDTH. (CLASS, ID, LANG, and STYLE are implied.)

INTERNET EXPLORER 4 ALIGN (CENTER | LEFT | RIGHT), BGCOLOR, CLASS, COLSPAN, ID, LANG, NOWRAP, ROWSPAN, STYLE, TITLE, and VALIGN (BASELINE | BOTTOM | TOP), all W3C-defined events, and all attributes and events defined by Internet Explorer 4.

WEBTV ALIGN (CENTER | LEFT | RIGHT), BGCOLOR, COLSPAN, GRADANGLE, GRADCOLOR, NOWRAP, ROWSPAN,

TRANSPARENCY, VALIGN (BASELINE I BOTTOM I MIDDLE I TOP), and **WIDTH**.

Event Handlers

See "Events Reference," earlier in this chapter.

2

Examples

```
<TABLE BORDER="1">
   <TR>
     <TH>Names</TH>
     <TH>Apples</TH>
     <TH>Oranges</TH>
   </TR>
   <TR>
     <TD>Bobby</TD>
     <TD>10</TD>
     <TD>5</TD>
   </TR>
   <TR>
     <TD>Ruby Sue</TD>
     <TD>20</TD>
     <TD>3</TD>
   </TR>
</TABLE>
```

Compatibility

HTML 3.2, 4; Netscape 1.1, 2, 3, 4; Internet Explorer 2, 3, 4; and WebTV

Notes

- The HTML 3.2 specification defines only **ALIGN, COLSPAN, HEIGHT, NOWRAP, ROWSPAN, VALIGN**, and **WIDTH** attributes.

- This element should always be within the **<TR>** element.

<THEAD> (Table Header)

This element is used to group the rows within the header of a table so that common alignment and style defaults can be set easily for numerous cells. This element may be particularly useful when setting a common head for tables that are dynamically generated.

Syntax

```
<THEAD
    ALIGN="CENTER | CHAR | JUSTIFY | LEFT | RIGHT"
    CHAR="character"
    CHAROFF="offset"
    CLASS="class name(s)"
    DIR="LTR | RTL"
    ID="unique alphanumeric identifier"
    LANG="language code"
    STYLE="style information"
    TITLE="advisory text"
    VALIGN="BASELINE | BOTTOM | MIDDLE | TOP"
    onclick="script"
    ondblclick="script"
    onkeydown="script"
    onkeypress="script"
    onkeyup="script"
    onmousedown="script"
    onmousemove="script"
    onmouseout="script"
    onmouseover="script"
    onmouseup="script">

</THEAD>
```

Attributes and Events Defined by Internet Explorer 4

```
    BGCOLOR="color name | #RRGGBB"
    LANGUAGE="JAVASCRIPT | JSCRIPT | VBS | VBSCRIPT"
    VALIGN="CENTER"
    ondragstart="script"
    onhelp="script"
    onselectstart="script"
```

Attributes

ALIGN   This attribute is used to align the contents of the cells within the **<THEAD>** element. Common values are **CENTER**, **JUSTIFY**, **LEFT**, and **RIGHT**. The HTML 4 specification also defines a value of **CHAR**. When **ALIGN** is set to **CHAR**, the attribute **CHAR** must be present and set to the character to which cells should be aligned. A common use of this approach would be to set cells to align on a decimal point.

BGCOLOR   This attribute specifies a background color for the cells within the **\<THEAD\>** element. Its value can be either a named color, such as **red**, or a color specified in the hexadecimal *#RRGGBB* format, such as **#FF0000**.

CHAR   This attribute is used to define the character to which element contents are aligned when the **ALIGN** attribute is set to the **CHAR** value.

CHAROFF   This attribute contains an offset as a positive or negative integer to align characters as related to the **CHAR** value. A value of **2**, for example, would align characters in a cell two characters to the right of character defined by the **CHAR** attribute.

CLASS   See "Core Attributes Reference," earlier in this chapter.

DIR   See "Language Reference," earlier in this chapter.

ID   See "Core Attributes Reference," earlier in this chapter.

LANG   See "Language Reference," earlier in this chapter.

LANGUAGE   In the Microsoft implementation, this attribute specifies the scripting language to be used with an associated script bound to the element, typically through an event handler attribute. Possible values may include **JAVASCRIPT**, **JSCRIPT**, **VBS**, and **VBSCRIPT**. Other values that include the version of the language used, such as **JavaScript1.1**, may also be possible.

STYLE   See "Core Attributes Reference," earlier in this chapter.

TITLE   See "Core Attributes Reference," earlier in this chapter.

VALIGN   This attribute is used to set the vertical alignment for the table cells with the **\<THEAD\>** element. HTML 4 defines **BASELINE**, **BOTTOM**, **MIDDLE**, and **TOP**. Internet Explorer replaces **MIDDLE** with **CENTER**; the effect should be the same.

Attribute and Event Support

INTERNET EXPLORER 4   All attributes and events except **CHAR**, **CHAROFF**, and **DIR**. (Note: Internet Explorer 4 does not support the **JUSTIFY** value for the **ALIGN** attribute.)

Event Handlers

See "Events Reference," earlier in this chapter.

Example

```
<TABLE BORDER="1" BGCOLOR="YELLOW" WIDTH="80%">
    <THEAD ALIGN="CENTER" BGCOLOR="RED" CLASS="footer"
        VALIGN="BOTTOM">
    <TD>This is the Important Table Headline</TD>
    </THEAD>
    <TBODY CLASS="tablebody">
    <TR>
        <TD>The contents of the table!</TD>
    </TR>
    </TBODY>
</TABLE>
```

Compatibility

HTML 4; Internet Explorer 3, 4

Notes

This element is only contained by the **<TABLE>** element and contains table rows as delimited by **<TR>** elements.

<TITLE>   (Document Title)

This element encloses the title of an HTML document. It must occur within a document's **<HEAD>** element and must be present in all valid documents. Meaningful titles are very important since they are used for bookmarking a page and may be used by search engines attempting to index the document.

Syntax

```
<TITLE
    DIR="LTR | RTL"
    LANG="language code">

</TITLE>
```

Attributes Defined by Internet Explorer 4

```
    ID="unique alphanumeric identifier"
    TITLE="advisory text"
```

Attributes

DIR   See "Language Reference," earlier in this chapter.

ID   See "Core Attributes Reference," earlier in this chapter.

LANG   See "Language Reference," earlier in this chapter.

TITLE   See "Core Attributes Reference," earlier in this chapter.

Attribute and Event Support

INTERNET EXPLORER 4   **ID** and **TITLE**.

Event Handlers

None.

Example

```
<HEAD><TITLE>Big Company: Products: Super Widget
</TITLE></HEAD>
```

Compatibility

HTML 2, 3.2, 4; Netscape 1, 2, 3, 4; Internet Explorer 2, 3, 4; and
WebTV

Notes

* Meaningful names should provide description about the
  document. A poor title would be something like "My Home
  Page," while a better title would be "Joe Smith Home."

* Older versions of Netscape allowed for multiple occurrences of
  the **<TITLE>** element. When multiple **<TITLE>** elements were
  encountered, they could be used to simulate an animated title
  bar. This was a bug with the Netscape browser, however, and
  the effect of multiple **<TITLE>** elements no longer works.

* Browsers may be extremely sensitive with the **<TITLE>**
  element. If the title element is malformed or not closed, the
  page may not even render in the browser.

* The HTML 2 and 3.2 specifications define no attributes for the
  <TITLE> element.

<TR>   (Table Row)

This element specifies a row in a table. The individual cells of the
row are defined by the **<TH>** and **<TD>** elements.

Syntax

```
<TR
     ALIGN="CENTER | JUSTIFY | LEFT | RIGHT"
     BGCOLOR="color name | #RRGGBB" (transitional)
     CHAR="character"
     CHAROFF="offset"
     CLASS="class name(s)"
     DIR="LTR | RTL"
     ID="unique alphanumeric identifier"
     LANG="language code"
     STYLE="style information"
     TITLE="advisory text"
     VALIGN="BASELINE | BOTTOM | MIDDLE | TOP"
     onclick="script"
     ondblclick="script"
     onkeydown="script"
     onkeypress="script"
     onkeyup="script"
     onmousedown="script"
     onmousemove="script"
     onmouseout="script"
     onmouseover="script"
     onmouseup="script">

</TR>
```

Attributes and Events Defined by Internet Explorer 4

```
     BORDERCOLOR="color name | #RRGGBB"
     BORDERCOLORDARK="color name | #RRGGBB"
     BORDERCOLORLIGHT="color name | #RRGGBB"
     LANGUAGE="JAVASCRIPT | JSCRIPT | VBS | VBSCRIPT"
     VALIGN="CENTER"
     onafterupdate="script"
     onbeforeupdate="script"
     onblur="script"
     ondragstart="script"
     onfocus="script"
     onhelp="script"
     onresize="script"
     onrowenter="script"
     onrowexit="script"
     onselectstart="script
```

Attributes Defined by WebTV
    NOWRAP
    TRANSPARENCY="number (0-100)"

Attributes

ALIGN   This attribute is used to align the contents of the cells within the **<THEAD>** element. Common values are **CENTER**, **JUSTIFY**, **LEFT**, and **RIGHT**.

BGCOLOR   This attribute specifies a background color for all the cells in a row. Its value can be either a named color, such as **red**, or a color specified in the hexadecimal *#RRGGBB* format, such as **#FF0000**.

BORDERCOLOR   This attribute, supported by Internet Explorer and Netscape, is used to set the border color for table cells in the row. The attribute should only be used with a positive value for the **BORDER** attribute. The value of the attribute can be either a named color, such as **green**, or a color specified in the hexadecimal *#RRGGBB* format, such as **#00FF00**.

BORDERCOLORDARK   This Internet Explorer–specific attribute specifies the darker of two border colors used to create a three-dimensional effect for the cell's borders. It must be used with the **BORDER** attribute set to a positive value. The attribute value can be either a named color, such as **blue**, or a color specified in the hexadecimal *#RRGGBB* format, such as **#00FF00**.

BORDERCOLORLIGHT   This Internet Explorer–specific attribute specifies the lighter of two border colors used to create a three-dimensional effect for a cell's borders. It must be used with the **BORDER** attribute set to a positive value. The attribute value can be either a named color, such as **red**, or a color specified in the hexadecimal *#RRGGBB* format, such as **#FF0000**.

CHAR   This attribute is used to define the character to which element contents are aligned when the **ALIGN** attribute is set to the **CHAR** value.

CHAROFF   This attribute contains an offset as a positive or negative integer to align characters as related to the **CHAR** value. A value of **2**, for example, would align characters in a cell two characters to the right of the character defined by the **CHAR** attribute.

CLASS   See "Core Attributes Reference," earlier in this chapter.

DIR   See "Language Reference," earlier in this chapter.

ID   See "Core Attributes Reference," earlier in this chapter.

LANG   See "Language Reference," earlier in this chapter.

LANGUAGE   In the Microsoft implementation, this attribute specifies the scripting language to be used with an associated script bound to the element, typically through an event handler attribute. Possible values may include **JAVASCRIPT**, **JSCRIPT**, **VBS**, and **VBSCRIPT**. Other values that include the version of the language used, such as **JavaScript1.1**, may also be possible.

NOWRAP   This WebTV-specific attribute keeps table rows from wrapping if they extend beyond the right margin.

STYLE   See "Core Attributes Reference," earlier in this chapter.

TITLE   See "Core Attributes Reference," earlier in this chapter.

TRANSPARENCY   This WebTV-specific attribute specifies the degree of transparency of the table. Values range from **0** (totally opaque) to **100** (totally transparent). A value of **50** is optimized for fast rendering.

VALIGN   This attribute is used to set the vertical alignment for the table cells with the **<TR>** element. HTML 4 defines **BASELINE**, **BOTTOM**, **MIDDLE**, and **TOP**. Internet Explorer replaces **MIDDLE** with **CENTER**; the effect should be the same.

Attribute and Event Support

NETSCAPE 4   ALIGN, BGCOLOR, and **VALIGN**. (**CLASS**, **ID**, **LANG**, and **STYLE** are implied.)

INTERNET EXPLORER 4   ALIGN (CENTER | LEFT | RIGHT), BGCOLOR, ID, LANG, STYLE, TITLE, and **VALIGN (BASELINE | BOTTOM | TOP)**, all W3C-defined events, and all attributes and events defined by Internet Explorer 4.

WEBTV   ALIGN (CENTER | LEFT | RIGHT), BGCOLOR, NOWRAP, TRANSPARENCY, and **VALIGN (BASELINE | BOTTOM | MIDDLE | TOP)**.

Event Handlers

See "Events Reference," earlier in this chapter.

Example

```
<TABLE WIDTH="300" BORDER="1">
    <TR BGCOLOR="RED" ALIGN="CENTER" VALIGN="CENTER">
        <TD>3</TD>
        <TD>5.6</TD>
        <TD>7.9</TD>
    </TR>
</TABLE>
```

Compatibility

HTML 3.2, 4; Netscape 1.1, 2, 3, 4; Internet Explorer 2, 3, 4; and WebTV

Notes

- This element is contained by the **<TABLE>**, **<THEAD>**, **<TBODY>**, and **<TFOOT>** elements. It contains the **<TH>** and **<TD>** elements.

- The HTML 3.2 specification defines only the **ALIGN** and **VALIGN** attributes for this element.

<TT> (Teletype Text)

This element is used to indicate that text should be rendered in a monospaced font similar to teletype text.

Syntax

```
<TT
    CLASS="class name(s)"
    DIR="LTR | RTL"
    ID="unique alphanumeric identifier"
    LANG="language code"
    STYLE="style information"
    TITLE="advisory text"
    onclick="script"
    ondblclick="script"
    onkeydown="script"
```

```
onkeypress="script"
onkeyup="script"
onmousedown="script"
onmousemove="script"
onmouseout="script"
onmouseover="script"
onmouseup="script">
```

```
</TT>
```

Attributes and Events Defined by Internet Explorer 4

```
LANGUAGE="JAVASCRIPT | JSCRIPT | VBS | VBSCRIPT"
ondragstart="script"
onhelp="script"
onselectstart="script"
```

Attributes

CLASS   See "Core Attributes Reference," earlier in this chapter.

DIR   See "Language Reference," earlier in this chapter.

ID   See "Core Attributes Reference," earlier in this chapter.

LANG   See "Language Reference," earlier in this chapter.

LANGUAGE   In the Microsoft implementation, this attribute specifies the scripting language to be used with an associated script bound to the element, typically through an event handler attribute. Possible values may include **JAVASCRIPT**, **JSCRIPT**, **VBS**, and **VBSCRIPT**. Other values that include the version of the language used, such as **JavaScript1.1**, may also be possible.

STYLE   See "Core Attributes Reference," earlier in this chapter.

TITLE   See "Core Attributes Reference," earlier in this chapter.

Attribute and Event Support

NETSCAPE 4   **CLASS**, **ID**, **LANG**, and **STYLE** are implied.

INTERNET EXPLORER 4   All attributes and events except **DIR**.

Event Handlers

See "Events Reference," earlier in this chapter.

Example
Here is some **<TT>**monospaced text.**</TT>**

Compatibility
HTML 2, 3.2, 4; Netscape 1, 2, 3, 4; Internet Explorer 2, 3, 4; and WebTV

<U> (Underline)

This element is used to indicate that the enclosed text should be displayed underlined.

Syntax (Transitional Only)
```
<U
     CLASS="class name(s)"
     DIR="LTR | RTL"
     ID="unique alphanumeric string"
     LANG="language code"
     STYLE="style information"
     TITLE="advisory text"
     onclick="script"
     ondblclick="script"
     onkeydown="script"
     onkeypress="script"
     onkeyup="script"
     onmousedown="script"
     onmousemove="script"
     onmouseout="script"
     onmouseover="script"
     onmouseup="script">

</U>
```

Attributes and Events Defined by Internet Explorer 4
```
     LANGUAGE="JAVASCRIPT | JSCRIPT | VBS | VBSCRIPT"
     ondragstart="script"
     onhelp="script"
     onselectstart="script"
```

Attributes

CLASS   See "Core Attributes Reference," earlier in this chapter.

DIR   See "Language Reference," earlier in this chapter.

ID   See "Core Attributes Reference," earlier in this chapter.

LANG   See "Language Reference," earlier in this chapter.

LANGUAGE   In the Microsoft implementation, this attribute specifies the scripting language to be used with an associated script bound to the element, typically through an event handler attribute. Possible values may include **JAVASCRIPT**, **JSCRIPT**, **VBS**, and **VBSCRIPT**. Other values that include the version of the language used, such as **JavaScript1.1**, may also be possible.

STYLE   See "Core Attributes Reference," earlier in this chapter.

TITLE   See "Core Attributes Reference," earlier in this chapter.

Attribute and Event Support

NETSCAPE 4   **CLASS**, **ID**, **LANG**, and **STYLE** are implied.

INTERNET EXPLORER 4   All attributes and events except **DIR**.

Event Handlers
See "Events Reference," earlier in this chapter.

Examples
Here is some **<U>**underlined text**</U>**.

Be careful with **<U>**underlined text**</U>**; it looks like
<A HREF="http://www.yahoo.com/">links.**</A>**

Compatibility
HTML 3.2, 4 (transitional); Netscape 3, 4; Internet Explorer 2, 3, 4; and WebTV

Notes

- Under the strict HTML 4 specification, the **<U>** element is not defined. The capabilities of this element are possible using style sheets.

- Underlining text can be problematic because it looks similar to a link, especially in a black-and-white environment.

<UL> (Unordered List)

This element is used to indicate an unordered list, namely, a collection of items that do not have a numerical ordering. The individual items in the list are defined by the <LI> element, which is the only allowed element within <UL>.

2

Syntax

```
<UL
        CLASS="class name(s)"
        COMPACT (transitional)
        DIR="LTR | RTL"
        ID="unique alphanumeric identifier"
        LANG="language code"
        STYLE="style information"
        TITLE="advisory text"
        TYPE="CIRCLE | DISC | SQUARE" (transitional)
        onclick="script"
        ondblclick="script"
        onkeydown="script"
        onkeypress="script"
        onkeyup="script"
        onmousedown="script"
        onmousemove="script"
        onmouseout="script"
        onmouseover="script"
        onmouseup="script">

        List items specified by <LI> elements

</UL>
```

Attributes and Events Defined by Internet Explorer 4

```
        LANGUAGE="JAVASCRIPT | JSCRIPT | VBS | VBSCRIPT"
        ondragstart="script"
        onhelp="script"
        onselectstart="script"
```

Attributes

CLASS   See "Core Attributes Reference," earlier in this chapter.

COMPACT   This attribute indicates that the list should be rendered in a compact style. Few browsers actually change the rendering of the list regardless of the presence of this attribute. The **COMPACT** attribute requires no value.

DIR   See "Language Reference," earlier in this chapter.

ID   See "Core Attributes Reference," earlier in this chapter.

LANG   See "Language Reference," earlier in this chapter.

LANGUAGE   In the Microsoft implementation, this attribute specifies the scripting language to be used with an associated script bound to the element, typically through an event handler attribute. Possible values may include **JAVASCRIPT**, **JSCRIPT**, **VBS**, and **VBSCRIPT**. Other values that include the version of the language used, such as **JavaScript1.1**, may also be possible.

STYLE   See "Core Attributes Reference," earlier in this chapter.

TITLE   See "Core Attributes Reference," earlier in this chapter.

TYPE   The **TYPE** attribute is used to set bullet style for the list. The values defined under HTML 3.2 and the transitional version of HTML 4 are **CIRCLE**, **DISC**, and **SQUARE**. A user agent may decide to use a different bullet depending on the nesting level of the list unless the **TYPE** attribute is used. The WebTV interface also supports a **TRIANGLE** bullet. The **TYPE** attribute is dropped under the strict version of HTML 4, since style sheets can provide richer bullet control.

Attribute and Event Support

NETSCAPE 4   CLASS, ID, LANG, STYLE, and TYPE.

INTERNET EXPLORER 4   All attributes and events except COMPACT and DIR.

WEBTV   TYPE.

Event Handlers

See "Events Reference," earlier in this chapter.

Examples

```
<UL COMPACT TITLE="Sushi Short List" TYPE="CIRCLE">
    <LI>Maguro
```

```
    <LI>Ebi
    <LI>Hamachi
</UL>

<!-- Common but bad example -->
<UL>
Indenting using lists should not be used, though it
is common. Many Web editors generate code laden with
nonbreaking spaces and unordered lists.
</UL>
```

2

Compatibility

HTML 2, 3.2, 4; Netscape 1, 2, 3, 4; Internet Explorer 2, 3, 4; and
WebTV

Notes

- HTML 2 supports only the **COMPACT** attribute.

- The HTML 3.2 specification supports **COMPACT** and **TYPE**.

- Under the strict HTML 4 specification, the **<UL>** element does
  not support the **COMPACT** attribute or the **TYPE** attribute.
  Both of these attributes can be safely replaced with style rules.

- Many Web page designers and page development tools use
  the **<UL>** element to indent text. Be aware that the only
  element that should occur within a **<UL>** element is **<LI>**,
  according to HTML standards, so such HTML markup does not
  conform to standards. However, this common practice is likely
  to continue.

<VAR> (Variable)

This element is used to indicate a variable. Variables are identifiers
that occur in a programming language or a mathematical
expression. The element is logical, though enclosed text is often
rendered in italics.

Syntax

```
<VAR
    CLASS="class name(s)"
    DIR="LTR | RTL"
    ID="unique alphanumeric value"
    LANG="language code"
```

```
STYLE="style information"
TITLE="advisory text"
onclick="script"
ondblclick="script"
onkeydown="script"
onkeypress="script"
onkeyup="script"
onmousedown="script"
onmousemove="script"
onmouseout="script"
onmouseover="script"
onmouseup="script">
```

```
</VAR>
```

Attributes and Events Defined by Internet Explorer 4

```
LANGUAGE="JAVASCRIPT | JSCRIPT | VBS | VBSCRIPT"
ondragstart="script"
onhelp="script"
onselectstart="script"
```

Attributes

CLASS   See "Core Attributes Reference," earlier in this chapter.

DIR   See "Language Reference," earlier in this chapter.

ID   See "Core Attributes Reference," earlier in this chapter.

LANG   See "Language Reference," earlier in this chapter.

LANGUAGE   In the Microsoft implementation, this attribute specifies the scripting language to be used with an associated script bound to the element, typically through an event handler attribute. Possible values may include **JAVASCRIPT**, **JSCRIPT**, **VBS**, and **VBSCRIPT**. Other values that include the version of the language used, such as **JavaScript1.1**, may also be possible.

STYLE   See "Core Attributes Reference," earlier in this chapter.

TITLE   See "Core Attributes Reference," earlier in this chapter.

Attribute and Event Support

NETSCAPE 4   **CLASS**, **ID**, **LANG**, and **STYLE** are implied.

INTERNET EXPLORER 4   All attributes and events except **DIR**.

Event Handlers
See "Events Reference," earlier in this chapter.

Example
Assign the value 5 to the variable **<VAR>**x**</VAR>**.

Compatibility
HTML 2, 3.2, 4; Netscape 1, 2, 3, 4; Internet Explorer 2, 3, 4; and
WebTV

Notes

- As a logical element, **<VAR>** is a perfect candidate for style
  sheet binding.
- The HTML 2 and 3.2 specifications support no attributes for
  this element.

<WBR>   (Word Break)

This nonstandard element is used to indicate a place where a line
break can occur if necessary. This element is used in conjunction
with the **<NOBR>** element, which is used to keep text from
wrapping. When used this way, **<WBR>** can be thought of as a soft
line break in comparison to the **
** element. This element is
common to both Netscape and Microsoft implementations, though
it is not part of any HTML standard.

Syntax
```
<WBR
     CLASS="class name(s)"
     ID="unique alphanumeric value"
     LANGUAGE="JAVASCRIPT | JSCRIPT | VBS | VBSCRIPT"
     STYLE="style information"
     TITLE="advisory text">
```

Attributes

CLASS   See "Core Attributes Reference," earlier in this chapter.

ID   See "Core Attributes Reference," earlier in this chapter.

LANGUAGE   In the Microsoft implementation, this attribute
specifies the scripting language to be used with an associated
script bound to the element, typically through an event handler

attribute. Possible values may include **JAVASCRIPT**, **JSCRIPT**, **VBS**, and **VBSCRIPT**. Other values that include the version of the language used, such as **JavaScript1.1**, may also be possible.

STYLE   See "Core Attributes Reference," earlier in this chapter.

TITLE   See "Core Attributes Reference," earlier in this chapter.

Attribute and Event Support

NETSCAPE 4   **CLASS**, **ID**, **STYLE**, and **TITLE** are implied.

INTERNET EXPLORER 4   All attributes.

Event Handlers

See "Events Reference," earlier in this chapter.

Example

```
<NOBR>A line break can occur here<WBR>but not
elsewhere, even if the line is really long.</NOBR>
```

Compatibility

Netscape 1.1, 2, 3, 4; Internet Explorer 2, 3, 4

Notes

- This element was introduced in Netscape 1.1.
- This is an empty element, so no closing tag is required.

<XMP>   (Example)

This depreciated element indicates that the enclosed text is an example. Example text is generally rendered in a monospaced font, and the spaces, tabs, and returns are preserved, as with the **<PRE>** element. As the **<XMP>** element is no longer standard, the **<PRE>** or **<SAMP>** elements should be used instead.

Syntax (Defined by HTML 2; Depreciated Under HTML 4)

```
<XMP>
</XMP>
```

<XMP> (Example) **295**

Attributes and Events Defined by Internet Explorer 4

```
CLASS="class name(s)"
ID="unique alphanumeric value"
LANG="language code"
LANGUAGE="JAVASCRIPT | JSCRIPT | VBS | VBSCRIPT"
STYLE="style information"
TITLE="advisory text"
onclick="script"
ondblclick="script"
ondragstart="script"
onhelp="script"
onkeydown="script"
onkeypress="script"
onkeyup="script"
onmousedown="script"
onmousemove="script"
onmouseout="script"
onmouseover="script"
onmouseup="script"
onselectstart="script"
```

Attributes

CLASS   See "Core Attributes Reference," earlier in this chapter.

ID   See "Core Attributes Reference," earlier in this chapter.

LANG   See "Language Reference," earlier in this chapter.

LANGUAGE   In the Microsoft implementation, this attribute specifies the scripting language to be used with an associated script bound to the element, typically through an event handler attribute. Possible values may include **JAVASCRIPT**, **JSCRIPT**, **VBS**, and **VBSCRIPT**. Other values that include the version of the language used, such as **JavaScript1.1**, may also be possible.

STYLE   See "Core Attributes Reference," earlier in this chapter.

TITLE   See "Core Attributes Reference," earlier in this chapter.

Attribute and Event Support

NETSCAPE 4   CLASS, ID, STYLE, and TITLE.

INTERNET EXPLORER 4   All attributes.

Event Handlers

See "Events Reference," earlier in this chapter.

Example

<XMP>This is a large block of text used as an example.
Note that returns as well as   S P A C E S are
preserved.**</XMP>**

Compatibility

HTML 2; Netscape 1, 2, 3, 4; Internet Explorer 2, 3, 4; and WebTV

Notes

This element is very old, though it continues to be documented.
It was first depreciated under HTML 3.2 and continues to be
unsupported under HTML 4. Page designers should not use this
element. Internet Explorer documentation supports this element
but recommends use of **<PRE>** or **<SAMP>** instead.

Chapter 3
Special Characters

This chapter lists the special characters available in standard HTML and HTML 4. Note that browser support of the entities listed is based on testing in the following browser versions: Netscape 1.22, Netscape 2.02, Netscape 3.01, Netscape Communicator 4.02, Microsoft Internet Explorer 3.02, Microsoft Internet Explorer 4.02, and WebTV. In the tables in this chapter, the following abbreviations are used for the different Netscape and Internet Explorer versions:

N1 = Netscape Navigator 1.22
N2 = Netscape Navigator 2.02
N3 = Netscape Navigator 3.01
N4 = Netscape Communicator 4.02
IE3 = Internet Explorer 3.02
IE4 = Internet Explorer 4.01

Standard HTML Character Entities

Web browsers do not read certain characters if they appear in an HTML document. To get around this limitation, codes have been assigned to certain characters. These codes consist of numbered entities, and some, but not all, of these numbered entities have corresponding named entities. For example, the numbered entity Ë produces the character Ë. The named entity **Ë** produces the same character. Note that the named entity suggests the intended rendering of the character, which provides a handy mnemonic device for dedicated HTML codes. While **Ë** is widely supported, not all character entities work in all browsers.

Theoretically, a browser vendor could even create arbitrary interpretations of these codes. For instance, WebTV has assigned its own unique renderings for the entities numbered 128 and 129, since 128 and 129 are not assigned a character under the HTML specifications. The codes numbered 32 through 255 (with some gaps) were assigned standard ASCII keyboard characters. Some of these codes duplicate characters that Web browsers can already interpret. The entity 6 represents the numeral 6, while G represents the letter "G." Character entities become more practical when it is necessary to employ characters used in foreign languages, such as "Œ" or "Å," or special characters such as "¶." Readers may note that the entity numbered 160 (the nonbreaking space as inserted with) is commonly found in pages generated by Web editors. While it is possible to force layout using this character, heavy use is generally frowned upon. The following table lists these standard entities and their intended renderings, and identifies which browsers support each.

Numbered Entity	Named Entity	Browser Support	Intended Rendering	Description
&#32;		N1, N2, N3, N4, IE3, IE4, WebTV		Space
&#33;		N1, N2, N3, N4, IE3, IE4, WebTV	!	Exclamation point
&#34;	&quot;	N1, N2, N3, N4, IE3, IE4, WebTV	"	Double quote
&#35;		N1, N2, N3, N4, IE3, IE4, WebTV	#	Number symbol
&#36;		N1, N2, N3, N4, IE3, IE4, WebTV	$	Dollar symbol
&#37;		N1, N2, N3, N4, IE3, IE4, WebTV	%	Percent symbol
&#38;	&amp;	N1, N2, N3, N4, IE3, IE4, WebTV	&	Ampersand
&#39;		N1, N2, N3, N4, IE3, IE4, WebTV	'	Single quote
&#40;		N1, N2, N3, N4, IE3, IE4, WebTV	(	Opening parenthesis

Numbered Entity	Named Entity	Browser Support	Intended Rendering	Description
&#41;		N1, N2, N3, N4, IE3, IE4, WebTV	)	Closing parenthesis
&#42;		N1, N2, N3, N4, IE3, IE4, WebTV	*	Asterisk
&#43;		N1, N2, N3, N4, IE3, IE4, WebTV	+	Plus sign
&#44;		N1, N2, N3, N4, IE3, IE4, WebTV	,	Comma
&#45;		N1, N2, N3, N4, IE3, IE4, WebTV	–	Minus sign
&#46;		N1, N2, N3, N4, IE3, IE4, WebTV	.	Period
&#47;		N1, N2, N3, N4, IE3, IE4, WebTV	/	Slash/ virgule/bar
&#48;		N1, N2, N3, N4, IE3, IE4, WebTV	0	Zero
&#49;		N1, N2, N3, N4, IE3, IE4, WebTV	1	One
&#50;		N1, N2, N3, N4, IE3, IE4, WebTV	2	Two
&#51;		N1, N2, N3, N4, IE3, IE4, WebTV	3	Three
&#52;		N1, N2, N3, N4, IE3, IE4, WebTV	4	Four

3

Numbered Entity	Named Entity	Browser Support	Intended Rendering	Description
&#53;		N1, N2, N3, N4, IE3, IE4, WebTV	5	Five
&#54;		N1, N2, N3, N4, IE3, IE4, WebTV	6	Six
&#55;		N1, N2, N3, N4, IE3, IE4, WebTV	7	Seven
&#56;		N1, N2, N3, N4, IE3, IE4, WebTV	8	Eight
&#57;		N1, N2, N3, N4, IE3, IE4, WebTV	9	Nine
&#58;		N1, N2, N3, N4, IE3, IE4, WebTV	:	Colon
&#59;		N1, N2, N3, N4, IE3, IE4, WebTV	;	Semicolon
&#60;	&lt;	N1, N2, N3, N4, IE3, IE4, WebTV	<	"Less than" symbol
&#61;		N1, N2, N3, N4, IE3, IE4, WebTV	=	Equal sign
&#62;	&gt;	N1, N2, N3, N4, IE3, IE4, WebTV	>	"Greater than" symbol
&#63;		N1, N2, N3, N4, IE3, IE4, WebTV	?	Question mark
&#64;		N1, N2, N3, N4, IE3, IE4, WebTV	@	"At" symbol

Numbered Entity	Named Entity	Browser Support	Intended Rendering	Description
&#65;		N1, N2, N3, N4, IE3, IE4, WebTV	A	
&#66;		N1, N2, N3, N4, IE3, IE4, WebTV	B	
&#67;		N1, N2, N3, N4, IE3, IE4, WebTV	C	
&#68;		N1, N2, N3, N4, IE3, IE4, WebTV	D	
&#69;		N1, N2, N3, N4, IE3, IE4, WebTV	E	
&#70;		N1, N2, N3, N4, IE3, IE4, WebTV	F	
&#71;		N1, N2, N3, N4, IE3, IE4, WebTV	G	
&#72;		N1, N2, N3, N4, IE3, IE4, WebTV	H	
&#73;		N1, N2, N3, N4, IE3, IE4, WebTV	I	
&#74;		N1, N2, N3, N4, IE3, IE4, WebTV	J	
&#75;		N1, N2, N3, N4, IE3, IE4, WebTV	K	
&#76;		N1, N2, N3, N4, IE3, IE4, WebTV	L	

3

Numbered Entity	Named Entity	Browser Support	Intended Rendering	Description
&#77;		N1, N2, N3, N4, IE3, IE4, WebTV	M	
&#78;		N1, N2, N3, N4, IE3, IE4, WebTV	N	
&#79;		N1, N2, N3, N4, IE3, IE4, WebTV	O	
&#80;		N1, N2, N3, N4, IE3, IE4, WebTV	P	
&#81;		N1, N2, N3, N4, IE3, IE4, WebTV	Q	
&#82;		N1, N2, N3, N4, IE3, IE4, WebTV	R	
&#83;		N1, N2, N3, N4, IE3, IE4, WebTV	S	
&#84;		N1, N2, N3, N4, IE3, IE4, WebTV	T	
&#85;		N1, N2, N3, N4, IE3, IE4, WebTV	U	
&#86;		N1, N2, N3, N4, IE3, IE4, WebTV	V	
&#87;		N1, N2, N3, N4, IE3, IE4, WebTV	W	
&#88;		N1, N2, N3, N4, IE3, IE4, WebTV	X	
&#89;		N1, N2, N3, N4, IE3, IE4, WebTV	Y	

Numbered Entity	Named Entity	Browser Support	Intended Rendering	Description
&#90;		N1, N2, N3, N4, IE3, IE4, WebTV	Z	
&#91;		N1, N2, N3, N4, IE3, IE4, WebTV	[	Opening bracket
&#92;		N1, N2, N3, N4, IE3, IE4, WebTV	\	Backslash
&#93;		N1, N2, N3, N4, IE3, IE4, WebTV	]	Closing bracket
&#94;		N1, N2, N3, N4, IE3, IE4, WebTV	^	Caret
&#95;		N1, N2, N3, N4, IE3, IE4, WebTV	_	Underscore
&#96;		N1, N2, N3, N4, IE3, IE4, WebTV	`	Grave accent, no letter
&#97;		N1, N2, N3, N4, IE3, IE4, WebTV	a	
&#98;		N1, N2, N3, N4, IE3, IE4, WebTV	b	
&#99;		N1, N2, N3, N4, IE3, IE4, WebTV	c	
&#100;		N1, N2, N3, N4, IE3, IE4, WebTV	d	
&#101;		N1, N2, N3, N4, IE3, IE4, WebTV	e	
&#102;		N1, N2, N3, N4, IE3, IE4, WebTV	f	

3

Numbered Entity	Named Entity	Browser Support	Intended Rendering	Description
&#103;		N1, N2, N3, N4, IE3, IE4, WebTV	g	
&#104;		N1, N2, N3, N4, IE3, IE4, WebTV	h	
&#105;		N1, N2, N3, N4, IE3, IE4, WebTV	i	
&#106;		N1, N2, N3, N4, IE3, IE4, WebTV	j	
&#107;		N1, N2, N3, N4, IE3, IE4, WebTV	k	
&#108;		N1, N2, N3, N4, IE3, IE4, WebTV	l	
&#109;		N1, N2, N3, N4, IE3, IE4, WebTV	m	
&#110;		N1, N2, N3, N4, IE3, IE4, WebTV	n	
&#111;		N1, N2, N3, N4, IE3, IE4, WebTV	o	
&#112;		N1, N2, N3, N4, IE3, IE4, WebTV	p	
&#113;		N1, N2, N3, N4, IE3, IE4, WebTV	q	
&#114;		N1, N2, N3, N4, IE3, IE4, WebTV	r	

Numbered Entity	Named Entity	Browser Support	Intended Rendering	Description
&#115;		N1, N2, N3, N4, IE3, IE4, WebTV	s	
&#116;		N1, N2, N3, N4, IE3, IE4, WebTV	t	
&#117;		N1, N2, N3, N4, IE3, IE4, WebTV	u	
&#118;		N1, N2, N3, N4, IE3, IE4, WebTV	v	
&#119;		N1, N2, N3, N4, IE3, IE4, WebTV	w	
&#120;		N1, N2, N3, N4, IE3, IE4, WebTV	x	
&#121;		N1, N2, N3, N4, IE3, IE4, WebTV	y	
&#122;		N1, N2, N3, N4, IE3, IE4, WebTV	z	
&#123;		N1, N2, N3, N4, IE3, IE4, WebTV	{	Opening brace
|		N1, N2, N3, N4, IE3, IE4, WebTV	|	Vertical bar
&#125;		N1, N2, N3, N4, IE3, IE4, WebTV	}	Closing brace
&#126;		N1, N2, N3, N4, IE3, IE4, WebTV	~	Equivalency symbol (tilde)

Numbered Entity	Named Entity	Browser Support	Intended Rendering	Description

NOTE: In the standard, the values from 127 to 159 are not assigned. Authors are advised not to use them. Many of them only work under Windows, or produce different characters on other operating systems or with different default font sets.

Numbered Entity	Named Entity	Browser Support	Intended Rendering	Description
&#127;		N/A		No character
&#128;		WebTV (nonstandard)		No character defined

NOTE: WebTV renders **€** as a right-pointing arrowhead.

Numbered Entity	Named Entity	Browser Support	Intended Rendering	Description
&#129;	&trade;	— WebTV (nonstandard) ™— IE3, IE4	™	Trademark symbol (Nonstandard numeric value—use ™ or ™ instead)

NOTE: WebTV renders **** as a left-pointing arrowhead.

Numbered Entity	Named Entity	Browser Support	Intended Rendering	Description
&#130;		N2, N3, N4, IE3, IE4, WebTV	,	Low-9 quote (nonstandard)
&#131;		N3, N4, IE3, IE4, WebTV	ƒ	Small "f" with hook (nonstandard)
&#132;		N2, N3, N4, IE3, IE4, WebTV	„	Low-9 double quote (nonstandard)
&#133;		N2, N3, N4, IE3, IE4, WebTV	...	Ellipsis (nonstandard)
&#134;		N2, N3, N4, IE3, IE4, WebTV	†	Dagger (nonstandard)

Numbered Entity	Named Entity	Browser Support	Intended Rendering	Description
&#135;		N2, N3, N4, IE3, IE4, WebTV	‡	Double dagger (nonstandard)
&#136;		N3, N4, IE3, IE4, WebTV	ˆ	Circumflex accent, no letter (nonstandard)
&#137;		N2, N3, N4, IE3, IE4, WebTV	‰	Per thousand (nonstandard)
&#138;		N3, N4, IE3, IE4, WebTV	Š	"S" with caron (nonstandard)
&#139;		N2, N3, N4, IE3, IE4, WebTV	‹	Opening single angle quote (nonstandard)
&#140;		N3, N4, IE3, IE4, WebTV	Œ	"OE" ligature (nonstandard)
&#141;		None	Ÿ	"Y" with umlaut (nonstandard)
&#142;		N/A		No character
&#143;		N/A		No character
&#144;		N/A		No character
&#145;		N1, N2, N3, N4, IE3, IE4, WebTV	'	Opening "smart" single quote (nonstandard)
&#146;		N1, N2, N3, N4, IE3, IE4, WebTV	'	Closing "smart" single quote (nonstandard)

3

Numbered Entity	Named Entity	Browser Support	Intended Rendering	Description
&#147;		N2, N3, N4, IE3, IE4, WebTV	"	Opening "smart" double quote (nonstandard)
&#148;		N2, N3, N4, IE3, IE4, WebTV	"	Closing "smart" double quote (nonstandard)
&#149;		N2, N3, N4, IE3, IE4, WebTV	•	Bullet (nonstandard)
&#150;		N2, N3, N4, IE3, IE4, WebTV	–	En dash (nonstandard)
&#151;		N2, N3, N4, IE3, IE4, WebTV	—	Em dash (nonstandard)
&#152;		N3, N4, IE3, IE4, WebTV	~	Tilde (nonstandard)
&#153;	&trade;	™— N2, N3, N4, IE3, IE4, WebTV ™— IE3, IE4	™	Trademark symbol
&#154;		N3, N4, IE3, IE4, WebTV	š	"s" with caron (nonstandard)
&#155;		N2, N3, N4, IE3, IE4, WebTV	›	Closing single angle quote (nonstandard)
&#156;		N3, N4, IE3, IE4, WebTV	œ	"oe" ligature (nonstandard)
&#157;		N/A		No character
&#158;		N/A		No character
&#159;		N3, N4, IE3	Ÿ	"Y" with umlaut (nonstandard)

Numbered Entity	Named Entity	Browser Support	Intended Rendering	Description
		— N1, N2, N3, N4, IE3, IE4		Nonbreaking space
		— N1, N3, N4, IE3		
&#161;	&iexcl;	¡— N1, N3, N4, IE3, IE4, WebTV	¡	Inverted exclamation point
		¡— N3, N4, IE3, IE4, WebTV		
&#162;	&cent;	¢— N1, N3, N4, IE3, IE4, WebTV	¢	Cent symbol
		¢— N3, N4, IE3, IE4, WebTV		
&#163;	&pound;	£— N1, N3, N4, IE3, IE4, WebTV	£	Pound sterling symbol
		£— N3, N4, IE3, IE4, WebTV		
&#164;	&curren;	¤— N1, N2, N3, N4, IE3, IE4, WebTV	¤	Currency symbol
		¤— N3, N4, IE3, IE4, WebTV		

3

Numbered Entity	Named Entity	Browser Support	Intended Rendering	Description
&#165;	&yen;	¥— N1, N3, N4, IE3, IE4, WebTV	¥	Japanese Yen symbol
		¥— N3, N4, IE3, IE4, WebTV		
&#166;	&brvbar;	¦— N2, N3, N4, IE3, IE4, WebTV	¦	Broken vertical bar
		¦— N3, N4, IE3, IE4, WebTV		
&#167;	&sect;	§— N1, N2, N3, N4, IE3, IE4, WebTV	§	Section symbol
		§— N3, N4, IE3, IE4, WebTV		
&#168;	&uml;	¨— N1, N3, N4, IE3, IE4, WebTV	¨	Umlaut, no letter
		¨— N3, N4, IE3, IE4, WebTV		
&#169;	&copy;	N1, N2, N3, N4, IE3, IE4, WebTV	©	Copyright symbol

Numbered Entity	Named Entity	Browser Support	Intended Rendering	Description
&#170;	&ordf;	ª— N1, N3, N4, IE3, IE4, WebTV	ª	Feminine ordinal indicator
		ª— N3, N4, IE3, IE4, WebTV		
&#171;	&laquo;	«— N1, N2, N3, N4, IE3, IE4, WebTV	«	Opening double angle quote
		«— N3, N4, IE3, IE4, WebTV		
&#172;	&not;	¬— N1, N2, N3, N4, IE3, IE4, WebTV	¬	Logical "not" symbol
		¬— N3, N4, IE3, IE4, WebTV		
&#173;	&shy;	­— N1, N2, N3, N4, IE3, IE4, WebTV	–	Soft hyphen
		­— N3, N4, IE3, IE4, WebTV		
&#174;	&reg;	N1, N2, N3, N4, IE3, IE4, WebTV	®	Registration mark

Numbered Entity	Named Entity	Browser Support	Intended Rendering	Description
&#175;	&macr;	¯— N1, N3, N4, IE3, IE4, WebTV	‾	Macron
		¯— N3, N4, IE3, IE4, WebTV		
&#176;	&deg;	°— N1, N2, N3, N4, IE3, IE4, WebTV	°	Degree symbol
		°— N3, N4, IE3, IE4, WebTV		
&#177;	&plusmn;	±— N1, N2, N3, N4, IE3, IE4, WebTV	±	Plus or minus symbol
		±— N3, N4, IE3, IE4, WebTV		
&#178;	&sup2;	²— N1, N3, N4, IE3, IE4, WebTV	^{2}	Superscript 2
		²— N3, N4, IE3, IE4, WebTV		
&#179;	&sup3;	³— N1, N3, N4, IE3, IE4, WebTV	^{3}	Superscript 3
		³— N3, N4, IE3, IE4, WebTV		

Numbered Entity	Named Entity	Browser Support	Intended Rendering	Description
&#180;	&acute;	´— N1, N3, N4, IE3, IE4, WebTV	´	Acute accent, no letter
		´— N3, N4, IE3, IE4, WebTV		
&#181;	&micro;	µ— N1, N2, N3, N4, IE3, IE4, WebTV	µ	Micron
		µ— N3, N4, IE3, IE4, WebTV		
&#182;	&para;	¶— N1, N2, N3, N4, IE3, IE4, WebTV	¶	Paragraph symbol
		¶— N3, N4, IE3, IE4, WebTV		
&#183;	&middot;	·— N1, N3, N4, IE3, IE4, WebTV	·	Middle dot
		·— N3, N4, IE3, IE4, WebTV		
&#184;	&cedil;	¸— N1, N3, N4, IE3, IE4, WebTV	¸	Cedilla
		¸— N3, N4, IE3, IE4, WebTV		

3

Numbered Entity	Named Entity	Browser Support	Intended Rendering	Description
&#185;	&sup1;	¹— N1, N3, N4, IE3, IE4, WebTV	1	Superscript 1
		¹— N3, N4, IE3, IE4, WebTV		
&#186;	&ordm;	º— N1, N3, N4, IE3, IE4, WebTV	º	Masculine ordinal indicator
		º— N3, N4, IE3, IE4, WebTV		
&#187;	&raquo;	»— N1, N2, N3, N4, IE3, IE4, WebTV	»	Closing double angle quote
		»— N3, N4, IE3, IE4, WebTV		
&#188;	&frac14;	¼— N1, N3, N4, IE3, IE4, WebTV	¼	One-fourth fraction
		¼— N3, N4, IE3, IE4, WebTV		
&#189;	&frac12;	½— N1, N3, N4, IE3, IE4, WebTV	½	One-half fraction
		½— N3, N4, IE3, IE4, WebTV		

Numbered Entity	Named Entity	Browser Support	Intended Rendering	Description
&#190;	&frac34;	¾— N1, N3, N4, IE3, IE4, WebTV ¾— N3, N4, IE3, IE4, WebTV	¾	Three-fourths fraction
&#191;	&iquest;	¿— N1, N3, N4, IE3, IE4, WebTV ¿— N3, N4, IE3, IE4, WebTV	¿	Inverted question mark
&#192;	&Agrave;	N1, N3, N4, IE3, IE4, WebTV	À	"A" with grave accent
&#193;	&Aacute;	N1, N3, N4, IE3, IE4, WebTV	Á	"A" with acute accent
&#194;	&Acirc;	N1, N3, N4, IE3, IE4, WebTV	Â	"A" with circumflex accent
&#195;	&Atilde;	N1, N3, N4, IE3, IE4, WebTV	Ã	"A" with tilde
&#196;	&Auml;	N1, N3, N4, IE3, IE4, WebTV	Ä	"A" with umlaut
&#197;	&Aring;	N1, N3, N4, IE3, IE4, WebTV	Å	"A" with ring
&#198;	&AElig;	N1, N3, N4, IE3, IE4, WebTV	Æ	"AE" ligature
&#199;	&Ccedil;	N1, N3, N4, IE3, IE4, WebTV	Ç	"C" with cedilla

Numbered Entity	Named Entity	Browser Support	Intended Rendering	Description
&#200;	&Egrave;	N1, N3, N4, IE3, IE4, WebTV	È	"E" with grave accent
&#201;	&Eacute;	N1, N3, N4, IE3, IE4, WebTV	É	"E" with acute accent
&#202;	&Ecirc;	N1, N3, N4, IE3, IE4, WebTV	Ê	"E" with circumflex accent
&#203;	&Euml;	N1, N3, N4, IE3, IE4, WebTV	Ë	"E" with umlaut
&#204;	&Igrave;	N1, N3, N4, IE3, IE4, WebTV	Ì	"I" with grave accent
&#205;	&Iacute;	N1, N3, N4, IE3, IE4, WebTV	Í	"I" with acute accent
&#206;	&Icirc;	N1, N3, N4, IE3, IE4, WebTV	Î	"I" with circumflex accent
&#207;	&Iuml;	N1, N3, N4, IE3, IE4, WebTV	Ï	"I" with umlaut
&#208;	&ETH;	N1, N3, N4, IE3, IE4, WebTV	Ð	Uppercase eth
&#209;	&Ntilde;	N1, N3, N4, IE3, IE4, WebTV	Ñ	"N" with tilde
&#210;	&Ograve;	N1, N3, N4, IE3, IE4, WebTV	Ò	"O" with grave accent
&#211;	&Oacute;	N1, N3, N4, IE3, IE4, WebTV	Ó	"O" with acute accent
&#212;	&Ocirc;	N1, N3, N4, IE3, IE4, WebTV	Ô	"O" with circumflex accent

Numbered Entity	Named Entity	Browser Support	Intended Rendering	Description
&#213;	&Otilde;	N1, N3, N4, IE3, IE4, WebTV	Õ	"O" with tilde
&#214;	&Ouml;	N1, N3, N4, IE3, IE4, WebTV	Ö	"O" with umlaut
&#215;	&times;	×— N1, N3, N4, IE3, IE4, WebTV	×	Multiplication symbol
		×— N3, N4, IE3, IE4, WebTV		
&#216;	&Oslash;	N1, N3, N4, IE3, IE4, WebTV	Ø	"O" with slash
&#217;	&Ugrave;	N1, N3, N4, IE3, IE4, WebTV	Ù	"U" with grave accent
&#218;	&Uacute;	N1, N3, N4, IE3, IE4, WebTV	Ú	"U" with acute accent
&#219;	&Ucirc;	N1, N3, N4, IE3, IE4, WebTV	Û	"U" with circumflex accent
&#220;	&Uuml;	N1, N3, N4, IE3, IE4, WebTV	Ü	"U" with umlaut
&#221;	&Yacute;	N1, N3, N4, IE3, IE4, WebTV	Ý	"Y" with acute accent
&#222;	&THORN;	N1, N3, N4, IE3, IE4, WebTV	Þ	Uppercase thorn
&#223;	&szlig;	N1, N3, N4, IE3, IE4, WebTV	ß	"SZ" ligature

3

Numbered Entity	Named Entity	Browser Support	Intended Rendering	Description
&#224;	&agrave;	N1, N3, N4, IE3, IE4, WebTV	à	"a" with grave accent
&#225;	&aacute;	N1, N3, N4, IE3, IE4, WebTV	á	"a" with acute accent
&#226;	&acirc;	N1, N3, N4, IE3, IE4, WebTV	â	"a" with circumflex accent
&#227;	&atilde;	N1, N3, N4, IE3, IE4, WebTV	ã	"a" with tilde
&#228;	&auml;	N1, N3, N4, IE3, IE4, WebTV	ä	"a" with umlaut
&#229;	&aring;	N1, N3, N4, IE3, IE4, WebTV	å	"a" with ring
&#230;	&aelig;	N1, N3, N4, IE3, IE4, WebTV	æ	"ae" ligature
&#231;	&ccedil;	N1, N3, N4, IE3, IE4, WebTV	ç	"c" with cedilla
&#232;	&egrave;	N1, N3, N4, IE3, IE4, WebTV	è	"e" with grave accent
&#233;	&eacute;	N1, N3, N4, IE3, IE4, WebTV	é	"e" with acute accent
&#234;	&ecirc;	N1, N3, N4, IE3, IE4, WebTV	ê	"e" with circumflex accent
&#235;	&euml;	N1, N3, N4, IE3, IE4, WebTV	ë	"e" with umlaut
&#236;	&igrave;	N1, N3, N4, IE3, IE4, WebTV	ì	"i" with grave accent

Numbered Entity	Named Entity	Browser Support	Intended Rendering	Description
&#237;	&iacute;	N1, N3, N4, IE3, IE4, WebTV	í	"i" with acute accent
&#238;	&icirc;	N1, N3, N4, IE3, IE4, WebTV	î	"i" with circumflex accent
&#239;	&iuml;	N1, N3, N4, IE3, IE4, WebTV	ï	"i" with umlaut
&#240;	&eth;	N1, N3, N4, IE3, IE4, WebTV	ð	Lowercase eth
&#241;	&ntilde;	N1, N3, N4, IE3, IE4, WebTV	ñ	"n" with tilde
&#242;	&ograve;	N1, N3, N4, IE3, IE4, WebTV	ò	"o" with grave accent
&#243;	&oacute;	N1, N3, N4, IE3, IE4, WebTV	ó	"o" with acute accent
&#244;	&ocirc;	N1, N3, N4, IE3, IE4, WebTV	ô	"o" with circumflex accent
&#245;	&otilde;	N1, N3, N4, IE3, IE4, WebTV	õ	"o" with tilde
&#246;	&ouml;	N1, N3, N4, IE3, IE4, WebTV	ö	"o" with umlaut
&#247;	&divide;	÷— N1, N3, N4, IE3, IE4, WebTV ÷— N3, N4, IE3, IE4, WebTV	÷	Division symbol

3

Numbered Entity	Named Entity	Browser Support	Intended Rendering	Description
&#248;	&oslash;	N1, N3, N4, IE3, IE4, WebTV	ø	"o" with slash
&#249;	&ugrave;	N1, N3, N4, IE3, IE4, WebTV	ù	"u" with grave accent
&#250;	&uacute;	N1, N3, N4, IE3, IE4, WebTV	ú	"u" with acute accent
&#251;	&ucirc;	N1, N3, N4, IE3, IE4, WebTV	û	"u" with circumflex accent
&#252;	&uuml;	N1, N3, N4, IE3, IE4, WebTV	ü	"u" with umlaut
&#253;	&yacute;	N1, N3, N4, IE3, IE4, WebTV	ý	"y" with acute accent
&#254;	&thorn;	N1, N3, N4, IE3, IE4, WebTV	þ	Lowercase thorn
&#255;	&yuml;	N1, N3, N4, IE3, IE4, WebTV	ÿ	"y" with umlaut

HTML 4 Character Entities

The HTML 4 specification introduces a wide array of new character entities, including additional Latin characters, the Greek alphabet, special spacing characters, arrows, technical symbols, and various shapes. Some of these entities have yet to be supported by browser vendors. Netscape 4 only supports a few of the extended Latin characters and some entities that duplicate characters already available in the preceding standard list (34 through 255). Microsoft Internet Explorer 4 supports many of these entities, including the Greek alphabet and mathematical symbols.

Latin Extended-A

Numbered Entity	Named Entity	Browser Support	Intended Rendering	Description
&#338;	&Oelig;	Œ— N4, IE4 &Oelig;— IE4	Œ	"OE" ligature
&#339;	&oelig;	œ— N4, IE4 œ— IE4	œ	"oe" ligature
&#352;	&Scaron;	Š— N4, IE4 Š— IE4	Š	"S" with caron
&#353;	&scaron;	š— N4, IE4 š— IE4	š	"s" with caron
&#376;	&Yuml;	Ÿ— N4, IE4 Ÿ— IE4	Ÿ	"Y" with umlaut

Latin Extended-B

Numbered Entity	Named Entity	Browser Support	Intended Rendering	Description
&#402;	&fnof;	ƒ— N4, IE4 ƒ— IE4	ƒ	Small "f" with hook

Spacing Modifier Letters

Numbered Entity	Named Entity	Browser Support	Intended Rendering	Description
&#710;	&circ;	ˆ— N4, IE4	ˆ	Circumflex accent
		ˆ— IE4		
&#732;	&tilde;	˜— N4, IE4	˜	Small tilde
		˜— IE4		

General Punctuation

NOTE: In the remaining tables in this chapter, characters marked IE4* display in Internet Explorer 4 on a Windows NT platform. They do not display in Internet Explorer 4 running under a standard Windows 95 installation. To display these characters under Windows 95, download Pan-European language support from the Product Updates page listed under the Help menu in Internet Explorer. Internet Explorer for the Macintosh does not support these characters.

Numbered Entity	Named Entity	Browser Support	Intended Rendering	Description
		None		En space
		None		Em space
		None		Thin space
&#8204;	&zwnj;	IE4*			Zero width nonjoiner
&#8205;	&zwj;	IE4*	⅄	Zero width joiner
&#8206;	&lrm;	None	Unknown	Left-to-right mark
&#8207;	&rlm;	None	Unknown	Right-to-left mark
&#8211;	&ndash;	–— N4, IE4	–	En dash
		–— IE4		

Numbered Entity	Named Entity	Browser Support	Intended Rendering	Description
&#8212;	&mdash;	—— N4, IE4	—	Em dash
		—— IE4		
&#8216;	&lsquo;	‘— N4, IE4	'	Left single quote
		‘— IE4		
&#8217;	&rsquo;	’— N4, IE4	'	Right single quote
		’— IE4		
&#8218;	&sbquo;	‚— N4, IE4	,	Single low-9 quote
		‚— IE4		
&#8220;	&ldquo;	“— N4, IE4	"	Left double quote
		“— IE4		
&#8221;	&rdquo;	”— N4, IE4	"	Right double quote
		”— IE4		
&#8222;	&bdquo;	„— N4, IE4	„	Double low-9 quote
		„— IE4		
&#8224;	&dagger;	†— N4, IE4	†	Dagger
		†— IE4		

Numbered Entity	Named Entity	Browser Support	Intended Rendering	Description
&#8225;	&Dagger;	‡— N4, IE4	‡	Double dagger
		‡— IE4		
&#8226;	&bull;	•— N4, IE4	•	Bullet
		•— IE4		
&#8230;	&hellip;	…— N4, IE4	…	Horizontal ellipsis
		…— IE4		
&#8240;	&permil;	‰— N4, IE4	‰	Per thousand sign
		‰— IE4		
&#8242;	&prime;	IE4*	′	Prime, minutes, or feet
&#8243;	&Prime;	IE4*	″	Double prime, seconds, or inches
&#8249;	&lsaquo;	‹— N4, IE4	‹	Opening single angle quote
		‹— IE4		
&#8250;	&rsaquo;	›— N4, IE4	›	Closing single angle quote
		›— IE4		
&#8254;	&oline;	IE4*	‾	Overline
&#8260;	&frasl;	IE4*	⁄	Slash

Greek

Numbered Entity	Named Entity	Browser Support	Intended Rendering	Description
&#913;	&Alpha;	IE4*	Α	Uppercase alpha
&#914;	&Beta;	IE4*	Β	Uppercase beta
&#915;	&Gamma;	IE4*	Γ	Uppercase gamma
&#916;	&Delta;	IE4*	Δ	Uppercase delta
&#917;	&Epsilon;	IE4*	E	Uppercase epsilon
&#918;	&Zeta;	IE4*	Z	Uppercase zeta
&#919;	&Eta;	IE4*	H	Uppercase eta
&#920;	&Theta;	IE4*	Θ	Uppercase theta
&#921;	&Iota;	IE4*	I	Uppercase iota
&#922;	&Kappa;	IE4*	K	Uppercase kappa
&#923;	&Lambda;	IE4*	Λ	Uppercase lambda
&#924;	&Mu;	IE4*	M	Uppercase mu
&#925;	&Nu;	IE4*	N	Uppercase nu
&#926;	&Xi;	IE4*	Ξ	Uppercase xi
&#927;	&Omicron;	IE4*	O	Uppercase omicron
&#928;	&Pi;	IE4*	Π	Uppercase pi
&#929;	&Rho;	IE4*	P	Uppercase rho
&#931;	&Sigma;	IE4*	Σ	Uppercase sigma
&#932;	&Tau;	IE4*	T	Uppercase tau

Numbered Entity	Named Entity	Browser Support	Intended Rendering	Description
&#933;	&Upsilon;	IE4*	Υ	Uppercase upsilon
&#934;	&Phi;	IE4*	Φ	Uppercase phi
&#935;	&Chi;	IE4*	X	Uppercase chi
&#936;	&Psi;	IE4*	Ψ	Uppercase psi
&#937;	&Omega;	IE4*	Ω	Uppercase omega
&#945;	&alpha;	IE4*	α	Lowercase alpha
&#946;	&beta;	IE4*	β	Lowercase beta
&#947;	&gamma;	IE4*	γ	Lowercase gamma
&#948;	&delta;	IE4*	δ	Lowercase delta
&#949;	&epsilon;	IE4*	ε	Lowercase epsilon
&#950;	&zeta;	IE4*	ζ	Lowercase zeta
&#951;	&eta;	IE4*	η	Lowercase eta
&#952;	&theta;	IE4*	θ	Lowercase theta
&#953;	&iota;	IE4*	ι	Lowercase iota
&#954;	&kappa;	IE4*	κ	Lowercase kappa
&#955;	&lambda;	IE4*	λ	Lowercase lambda
&#956;	&mu;	IE4*	μ	Lowercase mu
&#957;	&nu;	IE4*	ν	Lowercase nu
&#958;	&xi;	IE4*	ξ	Lowercase xi
&#959;	&omicron;	IE4*	o	Lowercase omicron

Numbered Entity	Named Entity	Browser Support	Intended Rendering	Description
&#960;	&pi;	IE4*	π	Lowercase pi
&#961;	&rho;	IE4*	ρ	Lowercase rho
&#962;	&sigmaf;	IE4*	ς	Lowercase final sigma
&#963;	&sigma;	IE4*	σ	Lowercase sigma
&#964;	&tau;	IE4*	τ	Lowercase tau
&#965;	&upsilon;	IE4*	υ	Lowercase upsilon
&#966;	&phi;	IE4*	φ	Lowercase phi
&#967;	&chi;	IE4*	χ	Lowercase chi
&#968;	&psi;	IE4*	ψ	Lowercase psi
&#969;	&omega;	IE4*	ω	Lowercase omega
&#977;	&thetasym;	None	θ	Theta symbol
&#978;	&upsih;	None	Not available	Upsilon with hook symbol
&#982;	&piv	None	Π	Pi symbol

Letter-Like Symbols

Numbered Entity	Named Entity	Browser Support	Intended Rendering	Description
&#8472;	&weierp;	None	℘	Uppercase script P, power set
&#8465;	&image;	None	ℑ	Uppercase blackletter I, or imaginary part symbol

Numbered Entity	Named Entity	Browser Support	Intended Rendering	Description
&#8476;	&real;	None	ℜ	Uppercase blackletter R, or real part symbol
&#8482;	&trade;	™— N4, IE4	™	Trademark symbol
		™— IE3, IE4		
&#8501;	&alefsym;	None	ℵ	Alef symbol, or first transfinite cardinal

Arrows

Numbered Entity	Named Entity	Browser Support	Intended Rendering	Description
&#8592;	&larr;	IE4*	←	Leftward arrow
&#8593;	&uarr;	IE4*	↑	Upward arrow
&#8594;	&rarr;	IE4*	→	Rightward arrow
&#8595;	&darr;	IE4*	↓	Downward arrow
&#8596;	&harr;	IE4*	↔	Left-right arrow
&#8629;	&crarr;	None	↵	Downward arrow with corner leftward
&#8656;	&lArr;	None	⇐	Leftward double arrow
&#8657;	&uArr;	None	⇑	Upward double arrow
&#8658;	&rArr;	IE4*	⇒	Rightward double arrow

Numbered Entity	Named Entity	Browser Support	Intended Rendering	Description
&#8659;	&dArr;	None	⇓	Downward double arrow
&#8660;	&hArr;	IE4*	⇔	Left-right double arrow

Mathematical Operators

Numbered Entity	Named Entity	Browser Support	Intended Rendering	Description
&#8704;	&forall;	IE4*	∀	For all
&#8706;	&part;	IE4*	∂	Partial differential
&#8707;	&exist;	IE4*	∃	There exists
&#8709;	&empty;	None	∅	Empty set, null set, diameter
&#8711;	&nabla;	IE4*	∇	Nabla, or backward difference
&#8712;	&isin;	IE4*	∈	Element of
&#8713;	&notin;	None	∉	Not an element of
&#8715;	&ni;	IE4*	∋	Contains as member
&#8719;	&prod;	IE4*	∏	N-ary product, or product sign
&#8721;	&sum;	IE4*	∑	N-ary summation
&#8722;	&minus;	IE4*	−	Minus sign
&#8727;	&lowast;	None	∗	Asterisk operator
&#8730;	&radic;	IE4*	√	Square root, radical sign
&#8733;	&prop;	IE4*	∼	Proportional to
&#8734;	&infin;	IE4*	∞	Infinity

Numbered Entity	Named Entity	Browser Support	Intended Rendering	Description
&#8736;	&ang;	IE4*	∠	Angle
&#8869;	&and;	IE4*	∧	Logical "and"
&#8870;	&or;	⊦— None ∨— IE4*	∨	Logical "or"
&#8745;	&cap;	IE4*	∩	Intersection, cap
&#8746;	&cup;	IE4*	∪	Union, cup
&#8747;	&int;	IE4*	∫	Integral
&#8756;	&there4;	IE4*	∴	Therefore
&#8764;	&sim;	None	~	Tilde operator
&#8773;	&cong;	None	≅	Approximately equal to
&#8776;	&asymp;	IE4*	~	Almost equal to, asymptotic to
&#8800;	&ne;	IE4*	≠	Not equal to
&#8801;	&equiv;	IE4*	≡	Identical to
&#8804;	&le;	IE4*	≤	Less than or equal to
&#8805;	&ge;	IE4*	≥	Greater than or equal to
&#8834;	&sub;	IE4*	⊂	Subset of
&#8835;	&sup;	IE4*	⊃	Superset of
&#8836;	&nsub;	None	⊄	Not a subset of
&#8838;	&sube;	IE4*	⊆	Subset of or equal to
&#8839;	&supe;	IE4*	⊇	Superset of or equal to

Numbered Entity	Named Entity	Browser Support	Intended Rendering	Description
&#8853;	&oplus;	None	⊕	Circled plus symbol, direct sum
&#8855;	&otimes;	None	⊗	Circled multiplication symbol, vector product
&#8869;	&perp;	IE4*	⊥	Perpendicular
&#8901;	&sdot;	None	⋅	Dot operator

Technical Symbols

Numbered Entity	Named Entity	Browser Support	Intended Rendering	Description
&#8968;	&lceil;	None	⌈	Left ceiling, apl upstile
&#8969;	&rceil;	None	⌉	Right ceiling
&#8970;	&lfloor;	None	⌊	Left floor, apl downstile
&#8971;	&rfloor;	None	⌋	Right floor
&#9001;	&lang;	None	<	Left-pointing angle bracket
&#9002;	&rang;	None	>	Right-pointing angle bracket

Geometric Shapes

Numbered Entity	Named Entity	Browser Support	Intended Rendering	Description
&#9674;	&loz;	IE4*	◊	Lozenge

Miscellaneous Symbols

Numbered Entity	Named Entity	Browser Support	Intended Rendering	Description
&#9824;	&spades;	IE4*	♠	Black spade suit
&#9827;	&clubs;	IE4*	♣	Black club suit
&#9829;	&hearts;	IE4*	♥	Black heart suit
&#9830;	&diams;	IE4*	♦	Black diamond suit

Chapter 4
Color Reference

This chapter lists all the color names commonly supported by the major browsers (Netscape 3 and above, Internet Explorer 3 and above, and WebTV). Sixteen colors (aqua, black, blue, fuchsia, gray, green, lime, maroon, navy, olive, purple, red, silver, teal, white, and yellow) were introduced by Microsoft; the rest were introduced by Netscape. The color reference table in this chapter shows each color along with its corresponding hexadecimal code. Thus, the code **<BODY BGCOLOR="cadetblue">** produces the same result as **<BODY BGCOLOR="#5F9EA0">** under any browser that supports these color names.

When using numbers, it is important to include the pound symbol (#) before the number. Color names are easier to remember than numerical codes but may cause trouble when viewed under old or uncommon browsers. Furthermore, be careful about inventing new color names. A browser will generally map any text entered for the **BGCOLOR** attribute into some color, but it may not render the same across browsers. Interested readers should try setting the **BGCOLOR** attribute to a value such as **"Corn Dog Brown"** or **"My favorite color in the whole wide world"** and noting what is produced.

Given the numerous color charts that exist with errors, browser inconsistencies, and made-up color names, it is generally safer to stick with the hexadecimal approach to colors. WebTV supports the color names but displays several colors differently (as noted in the following table). General WebTV color support also may vary due to the differences between computer monitors and television screens. The "RGB Equivalent" column provides the RGB equivalent of each color, allowing easy reference for Web authors trying to match colors in Photoshop or in other graphics programs.

Color Name	Hexadecimal Code	RGB Equivalent	Notes
aliceblue	F0F8FF	240,248,255	The name "aliceblue" is not supported by Netscape.
antiquewhite	FAEBD7	250,235,215	
aqua	00FFFF	0,255,255	
aquamarine	7FFFD4	127,255,212	
azure	F0FFFF	240,255,255	
beige	F5F5DC	245,245,220	
bisque	FFE4C4	255,228,196	
black	000000	0,0,0	
blanched-almond	FFEBCD	255,235,205	
blue	0000FF	0,0,255	
blueviolet	8A2BE2	138,43,226	WebTV displays "blueviolet" the same as "blue" (0000EE)
brown	A52A2A	165,42,42	
burlywood	DEB887	222,184,135	
cadetblue	5F9EA0	95,158,160	
chartreuse	7FFF00	127,255,0	
chocolate	D2691E	210,105,30	
coral	FF7F50	255,127,80	
cornflowerblue	6495ED	100,149,237	
cornsilk	FFF8DC	255,248,220	
crimson	DC143C	220,20,60	
cyan	00FFFF	0,255,255	
darkblue	00008B	0,0,139	
darkcyan	008B8B	0,139,139	
darkgoldenrod	B8860B	184,134,11	
darkgray	A9A9A9	169,169,169	
darkgreen	006400	0,100,0	
darkkhaki	BDB76B	189,183,107	
darkmagenta	8B008B	139,0,139	
darkolivegreen	556B2F	85,107,47	

Color Name	Hexadecimal Code	RGB Equivalent	Notes
darkorange	FF8C00	255,140,0	
darkorchid	9932CC	153,50,204	
darkred	8B0000	139,0,0	
darksalmon	E9967A	233,150,122	
darkseagreen	8FBC8F	143,188,143	
darkslateblue	483D8B	72,61,139	
darkslategray	2F4F4F	47,79,79	
darkturquoise	00CED1	0,206,209	
darkviolet	9400D3	148,0,211	
deeppink	FF1493	255,20,147	
deepskyblue	00BFFF	0,191,255	
dimgray	696969	105,105,105	
dodgerblue	1E90FF	30,144,255	
firebrick	B22222	178,34,34	
floralwhite	FFFAF0	255,250,240	
forestgreen	228B22	34,139,34	
fuchsia	FF00FF	255,0,255	
gainsboro	DCDCDC	220,220,220	
ghostwhite	F8F8FF	248,248,255	
gold	FFD700	255,215,0	
goldenrod	DAA520	218,165,32	WebTV displays "goldenrod" the same as "gold" (FFD700)
gray	808080	127,127,127	
green	008000	0,128,0	
greenyellow	ADFF2F	173,255,47	WebTV displays "greenyellow" the same as "green" (008000)
honeydew	F0FFF0	240,255,240	
hotpink	FF69B4	255,105,180	
indianred	CD5C5C	205,92,92	
indigo	4B0082	75,0,130	

4

Color Name	Hexadecimal Code	RGB Equivalent	Notes
ivory	FFFFF0	255,255,240	
khaki	F0E68C	240,230,140	
lavender	E6E6FA	230,230,250	
lavenderblush	FFF0F5	255,240,245	
lawngreen	7CFC00	124,252,0	
lemonchiffon	FFFACD	255,250,205	
lightblue	ADD8E6	173,216,230	
lightcoral	F08080	240,128,128	
lightcyan	E0FFFF	224,255,255	
lightgoldenrod-yellow	FAFAD2	250,250,210	
lightgreen	90EE90	144,238,144	
lightgrey	D3D3D3	211,211,211	
lightpink	FFB6C1	255,182,193	
lightsalmon	FFA07A	255,160,122	
lightseagreen	20B2AA	32,178,170	
lightskyblue	87CEFA	135,206,250	
lightslategray	778899	119,136,153	
lightsteelblue	B0C4DE	176,196,222	
lightyellow	FFFFE0	255,255,224	
lime	00FF00	0,255,0	
limegreen	32CD32	50,205,50	WebTV displays "limegreen" the same as "lime" (00FF00)
linen	FAF0E6	250,240,230	
magenta	FF00FF	255,0,255	
maroon	800000	128,0,0	
medium-aquamarine	66CDAA	102,205,170	
mediumblue	0000CD	0,0,205	
mediumorchid	BA55D3	186,85,211	
mediumpurple	9370DB	147,112,219	
medium-seagreen	3CB371	60,179,113	

Color Name	Hexadecimal Code	RGB Equivalent	Notes
medium-slateblue	7B68EE	123,104,238	
medium-springgreen	00FA9A	0,250,154	According to the WebTV spec, WebTV supports "mediumspring green," but the name display does not match the numerical code display.
medium-turquoise	48D1CC	72,209,204	
medium-violetred	C71585	199,21,133	
midnightblue	191970	25,25,112	
mintcream	F5FFFA	245,255,250	
mistyrose	FFE4E1	255,228,225	
moccasin	FFE4B5	255,228,181	
navajowhite	FFDEAD	255,222,173	
navy	000080	0,0,128	
navyblue	9FAFDF	159,175,223	WebTV displays "navyblue" the same as "navy" (000080)
oldlace	FDF5E6	253,245,230	
olive	808000	128,128,0	
olivedrab	6B8E23	107,142,35	WebTV displays "olivedrab" the same as "olive" (808000)
orange	FFA500	255,165,0	

4

Color Name	Hexadecimal Code	RGB Equivalent	Notes
orangered	FF4500	255,69,0	WebTV displays "orangered" the same as "orange" (FFA500)
orchid	DA70D6	218,112,214	
palegoldenrod	EEE8AA	238,232,170	
palegreen	98FB98	152,251,152	
paleturquoise	AFEEEE	175,238,238	
palevioletred	DB7093	219,112,147	
papayawhip	FFEFD5	255,239,213	
peachpuff	FFDAB9	255,218,185	
peru	CD853F	205,133,63	
pink	FFC0CB	255,192,203	
plum	DDA0DD	221,160,221	
powderblue	B0E0E6	176,224,230	
purple	800080	128,0,128	
red	FF0000	255,0,0	
rosybrown	BC8F8F	188,143,143	
royalblue	4169E1	65,105,225	
saddlebrown	8B4513	139,69,19	
salmon	FA8072	250,128,114	
sandybrown	F4A460	244,164,96	
seagreen	2E8B57	46,139,87	
seashell	FFF5EE	255,245,238	
sienna	A0522D	160,82,45	
silver	C0C0C0	192,192,192	
skyblue	87CEEB	135,206,235	
slateblue	6A5ACD	106,90,205	
slategray	708090	112,128,144	
snow	FFFAFA	255,250,250	
springgreen	00FF7F	0,255,127	
steelblue	4682B4	70,130,180	
tan	D2B48C	210,180,140	
teal	008080	0,128,128	
thistle	D8BFD8	216,191,216	

Color Name	Hexadecimal Code	RGB Equivalent	Notes
tomato	FF6347	255,99,71	
turquoise	40E0D0	64,224,208	
violet	EE82EE	238,130,238	
wheat	F5DEB3	245,222,179	
white	FFFFFF	255,255,255	
whitesmoke	F5F5F5	245,245,245	
yellow	FFFF00	255,255,0	
yellowgreen	9ACD32	139,205,50	WebTV displays "yellowgreen" the same as "yellow" (FFFF00)

4

NOTE: Many online color references claim that further color variations can be introduced by adding the numbers 1 through 4 to color names. If this were correct, cadetblue1, cadetblue2, cadetblue3, and cadetblue4 would display as different shades of the same color, with 1 being the lightest and 4 the darkest. Some of these references also claim that gray supports up to 100 color variations (gray10, gray 50, gray90, and so on). Testing reveals that neither of these claims is true for Netscape, Internet Explorer, or WebTV.

Chapter 5
Reading a Document Type Definition

HTML is defined using SGML (Standard Generalized Markup Language), a complex language used to define other languages. This chapter explains how to read the document type definitions (DTDs) that define HTML as an application of SGML. To read the final DTDs (transitional and strict) for HTML 4, visit the World Wide Web consortium site at http://www.w3.org/TR/REC-html40/.

Element Type Declarations

HTML authors should be familiar with two common types of declarations: element type declarations and attribute list declarations.

An *element type declaration* defines three characteristics:

- The element type's *name,* or *generic identifier*
- *Tag minimization* (whether or not start and end tags are required)
- The element type's *content model* (what content it can enclose)

All element type declarations begin with the keyword **ELEMENT** and take the following form:

```
<!ELEMENT name tag_minimization content_model>
```

This is the declaration for the **
** element originally defined in HTML 2:

```
<!ELEMENT BR - O EMPTY>
```

In this element declaration, the element's name is **BR**.

The next part of this element declaration, tag minimization, consists of two parameters. The first parameter indicates the start tag, while the second indicates the end tag. There are two possible values here: - (hyphen) and **O** (uppercase O). A hyphen indicates that the tag is required. An uppercase **O** indicates that it may be omitted. In this example, **O** indicates that **
** does not require an end tag.

The final part of the element declaration is the content model. The content model here is defined as **EMPTY**, which means that the **
** element contains no content.

In some cases, a closing tag value of **O** indicates that the closing tag is optional, as is the case with the paragraph element **<P>**. When combined with a content model of **EMPTY**, however, a closing tag value of **O** means that the closing tag is forbidden and should never be used. The element declaration for **
** tells us that there is no such thing as a closing **</BR>** tag.

Unlike **
**, most HTML elements enclose content. The HTML 4 declaration for a selection list option demonstrates this:

```
<!ELEMENT OPTION - O (#PCDATA)*>
```

When a content model other than **EMPTY** is declared, it takes the form of a *model group* enclosed in parentheses. In this case, the model group contains the keyword **#PCDATA**. This stands for *parsed character data*, character content that contains no element markup but that may contain entity symbols for special characters.

Occurrence Indicators

The following example includes an asterisk, called an *occurrence indicator,* appended to the model group. It indicates how many times the element type or model group may occur.

```
<!ELEMENT OPTION - O (#PCDATA)*>
```

There are three occurrence indicators: **?**, *****, and **+**:

- **?** means optional and at most one occurrence (zero or one occurrence).

- * means optional and any number of occurrences (zero or more occurrences).

- \+ means at least one occurrence required (one or more occurrences).

Thus, the content model in the previous declaration says that the <OPTION> element may contain any amount of character content, including none.

Logical Connectors

5

Content models can also contain other elements, as demonstrated by the HTML 2 declaration for a definition list (<DL>):

```
<!ELEMENT DL - - (DT | DL)+>
```

In this example, the model group contains **DT** and **DL**, the names of element types that a <DL> element may enclose. The vertical bar separating **DT** and **DL** is a *logical connector*, which indicates how the content units it connects are related to each other. There are three logical connectors:

- | means "or" (one and only one of the connected content units must occur).

- **&** means "and" (all of the connected content units must occur).

- , means "sequence" (the connected content units must occur in the specified order).

The element declaration for the <DL> element states that the element must contain either a <DT> or <DL> element, but not both, and may contain any additional number of <DT> or <DL> elements.

Model groups can also be nested inside other model groups. Occurrence indicators, logical operators, and nested model groups are often used to define flexible content models, as in the HTML 4 declaration for the <TABLE> element type, shown in the following illustration.

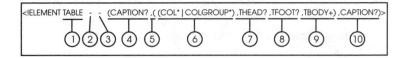

The element type declaration for **<TABLE>** should be read as follows:

1. The element name is **TABLE**.

2. The element requires an opening tag.

3. The element requires a closing tag.

4. Table content begins with zero or one **<CAPTION>** element.

5. This must be followed by another content group (comma indicates sequence; opening parenthesis indicates start of nested content group).

6. The content group must contain zero or more **<COL>** elements *or* zero or more **<COLGROUP>** elements.

7. This must be followed by zero or one **<THEAD>** element.

8. This must be followed by zero or one **<TFOOT>** element.

9. This must be followed by one or more **<TBODY>** elements.

10. The content ends with zero or one **<CAPTION>** element.

Content Exclusion

Some element types cannot contain certain other element types. The excluded tags, or *content exclusion*, follow the model group and are enclosed by parentheses and preceded by a minus sign:

(model group) -*(excluded tags)*

Content Inclusion

Some element types can occur anywhere inside a content model. The included tags, or *content inclusion*, follow the model group and are enclosed by parentheses and preceded by a plus sign.

`(model group) +(included tags)`

The HTML 4 declaration for the **<BODY>** element type illustrates both excluded and included elements:

`<!ELEMENT BODY O O (%block;) -(BODY) +(INS | DEL)>`

In this example, the content exclusion **–(BODY)** says that a **<BODY>** element cannot contain another **<BODY>** element. This is necessary because of the **%block** declaration used in the model group. The leading **%** character identifies this as a *parameter entity*, a macro symbol that refers to a longer character string declared elsewhere in the DTD. Parameter entities, which commonly occur in HTML DTDs, will be discussed shortly (see "Parameter Entities"). The **%block** entity reference is a shorthand way of referring to all block element types, including **<BODY>**. It is simpler to exclude **<BODY>** from the list of block elements than to define a special-purpose declaration.

The content inclusion **+(INS | DEL)** says that the **<INS>** and **<DEL>** elements can occur anywhere in **<BODY>** content. According to specification, **<INS>** and **<DEL>** are used to indicate modifications to **<BODY>** content. They need to be freed from the normal structural constraints imposed on other **<BODY>** elements.

Attribute Declarations

All attribute declarations begin with the keyword **ATTLIST**, followed by the name of the element type they are associated with.

Following this are declarations for one or more individual attributes. Each declaration has three parts:

- The attribute's name
- The attribute's value type
- The attribute's default

The syntax for an attribute declaration is shown here:

```
<!ATTLIST   element-type
      name1     type1     default1
      ...
      nameN     typeN     defaultN
>
```

The HTML 4 **<BDO>** element type shown in Figure 5-1 illustrates a simple attribute declaration.

SGML Keywords

The **<BDO>** example in Figure 5-1 declares that the **lang** attribute has values of type **NAME**, an alphabetic string. **NAME** is one of several SGML keywords, listed here, that are used in HTML declarations to declare an attribute's type:

- **CDATA** Unparsed character data
- **ID** A document-wide unique identifier
- **IDREF** A reference to a document-wide identifier
- **NAME** An alphabetic character string plus a hyphen and a period
- **NMTOKEN** An alphanumeric character string plus a hyphen and a period
- **NUMBER** A character string containing decimal numbers

```
<!ATTLIST   BDO
      lang      NAME         #IMPLIED
      dir       (ltr | rtl)  #REQUIRED
>
```

Figure 5-1.   A simple attribute declaration

The **dir** attribute does not declare its type using a keyword. Instead, the type is specified using an enumerated list containing two possible values, **ltr** and **rtl**.

In the example shown in Figure 5-1, the attribute's default behavior is specified with one of the following keywords. A default value may be specified using a quoted string.

- **#REQUIRED**   This indicates that a value must be supplied for the attribute.

- **#IMPLIED**   This indicates that the attribute is optional.

- **#FIXED**   This indicates that the attribute has a fixed value, which is declared in quotes using an additional parameter. Because the attribute/value pair is assumed to be constant, it does not need to be used in the document instance.

5

Parameter Entities

An entity is basically a macro that allows a short name to be associated with replacement text. Parameter entities define replacement text used in DTD declarations. Syntactically, a parameter entity is distinguished by using the percent (%) symbol. Its general form is shown here:

```
<!ENTITY % name "replacement text">
```

It is used in DTDs as follows:

```
% name;
```

Parameter entities are a convenient way to define commonly occurring pieces of a DTD so that changes only need to be made in one place. HTML 4 uses a parameter entity called **coreattrs** to define the core attributes common to most elements.

```
<!ENTITY % coreattrs
    "id        ID        #IMPLIED
    class      CDATA     #IMPLIED
    style      CDATA     #IMPLIED
    title      CDATA     #IMPLIED"
>
```

These attributes could be added to an attribute list declaration as follows:

```
<!ATTLIST some-element %coreattrs;>
```

In HTML 4, parameter entities can be used inside other parameter entity declarations. In the following example, the **coreattrs** parameter entity is used with the **i18n** and **events** parameter entities to define the expansion text for an aggregate entity called **attrs**:

```
<!ENTITY % attrs "%coreattrs %i18n %events">
```

Here is another example, the HTML 4 declaration for the paragraph element **<P>**:

```
<!ELEMENT P - O (%inline;)* -- paragraph -->
```

In this case, the content model is defined by the parameter entity **inline**. Looking up the definition of this parameter entity in the HTML 4 strict DTD yields the following information:

```
<!-- %inline; covers inline or "text-level" elements -->
<!ENTITY % inline "#PCDATA | %fontstyle; | %phrase; |
                  %special; | %formctrl;">
```

Note that this information is preceded by a comment that clarifies the meaning of the definition. On the second line, **inline** is defined as containing PCDATA (discussed earlier in this chapter in the section "Element Type Declarations") as well as four additional parameter entities. The parameter entity **fontstyle** is shorthand for the font style elements **<TT>**, **<I>**, **<B>**, **<BIG>**, and **<SMALL>**, while **phrase**, **special**, and **formctrl** refer to their own groups of elements.

General Entities

While parameter entities are used to manipulate syntax in DTD declarations, general entities are used to associate symbols with replacement text for use in actual documents. General entities have a versatile syntax. One type, the character entity used for special symbols, is familiar to many HTML authors. For example, HTML authors that need to use the ampersand (&) character use the **&** entity, which is declared as follows:

```
<!ENTITY amp CDATA "&#38;">
```

The **ENTITY** keyword without the % character identifies this as a general entity. The name of the entity is **amp**. The entity type is indicated by the keyword **CDATA**, which stands for *character data*. **CDATA** is followed by the replacement text.

Comments

DTDs contain the type of comments familiar to HTML authors. Comments look like this:

```
<!-- This is a comment. -->
```

Comments may also be embedded inside HTML declarations for explanatory purposes. Embedded comments are delimited by two dashes. A single declaration may contain many embedded comments, as shown here:

```
<!ATTLIST PARAM
name        CDATA                       #REQUIRED   -- property name --
value       CDATA                       #IMPLIED    -- property value --
valuetype   (DATA | REF | OBJECT) DATA              -- How to interpret
                                                       value --
type        CDATA                       #IMPLIED    -- Internet media
                                                       type --
>
```

Marked Section Declaration

Some HTML DTDs use a special SGML construct to allow them to optionally include or exclude certain declarations from a DTD, such as those that support deprecated tags. An SGML *marked section declaration* uses keywords to indicate that the content it encloses should be treated in a special way, as follows:

```
<! [keyword [
affected declarations
]]>
```

HTML DTDs use parameter entities to assign the **INCLUDE** or **IGNORE** keyword to marked section declarations, as shown in the following example. This causes the declarations enclosed by the sections to be included or ignored, respectively.

```
<!ENTITY % HTML.Depreciated "IGNORE">

<! [ %HTML.Deprecated [
affected declarations
]]>
```

In the HTML 4 DTDs, this construct is used when listing elements or attributes reserved for future use, as in the case of the reserved attributes **datasrc**, **datafld**, and **dataformatas**:

```
<!-- Reserved Feature Switch -->
<!ENTITY % HTML.Reserved "IGNORE">
<!-- The following attributes are reserved for possible
     future use. -->
<![ %HTML.Reserved; [
<!ENTITY % reserved
"datasrc %URI; #IMPLIED -- a single or tabular data
                          source --
datafld CDATA #IMPLIED -- the property or column name --
dataformatas (plaintext | html) plaintext -- text or html --"
>
]]>
```

Comments are used liberally to explain this section of the DTD, but the keyword **IGNORE** serves as a strong reminder that these attributes are not yet official parts of the HTML specification (although Microsoft Internet Explorer 4 already supports them).

Examples

Following are a few more examples of how to read portions of a document type definition.

Simple Element and Attribute Definition Example 1

```
<!ELEMENT UL - - (LI)+ -- unordered list -->
<!ATTLIST UL
    %attrs;    -- %coreattrs, %i18n, %events --
>
```

- In the element type definition, the generic identifier **UL** defines the element name.

- In the element type definition, the tag minimization -- states that the element requires both an opening and a closing tag.

- In the element type definition, the content model **(LI)+** states that the element **UL** must contain the element **LI** one or more times. The embedded comment -- **unordered list** -- explains the purpose of the element.

- The attribute declaration states that the element **UL** has the attributes represented by the parameter entity **attrs**. The embedded comment -- **%coreattrs, %i18n, %events** -- lists the three parameter entities contained in the entity **attrs**.

Simple Element and Attribute Definition Example 2

```
<!ELEMENT LI - O (%flow;)* -- list item -->
<!ATTLIST LI
     %attrs;     -- %coreattrs, %i18n, %events --
>
```

- In the element type definition, the generic identifier **LI** defines the element name.

- In the element type definition, the tag minimization - **O** states that the element requires an opening tag but that the closing tag is optional.

- In the element type definition, the content model **(%flow;)*** states that the element **LI** may contain any content defined by the parameter entity **flow** zero or more times. (**%flow** includes all block and inline elements.)

- The attribute declaration states that the element **LI** has the attributes represented by the parameter entity **attrs**. The embedded comment -- **%coreattrs, %i18n, %events** -- lists the three parameter entities contained in the entity **attrs**.

Simple Element and Attribute Definition Example 3

```
<!ELEMENT LINK - O EMPTY -- a media-independent link -->
<!ATTLIST LINK
     %attrs;                    -- %coreattrs,
                                   %i18n, %events --
     charset    %Charset;    #IMPLIED -- char encoding of
                                   linked resource --
```

```
href        %URI;           #IMPLIED -- URI for linked
                                        resource --
hreflang    %LanguageCode;  #IMPLIED -- language code --
type        %ContentType;   #IMPLIED -- advisory
                                        content type --
rel         %LinkTypes;     #IMPLIED -- forward link
                                        types --
rev         %LinkTypes;     #IMPLIED -- reverse link
                                        types --
media       %MediaDesc;     #IMPLIED -- for rendering on
                                        these media --
>
```

- In the element type definition, the generic identifier **LINK** defines the element name.

- In the element type definition, the tag minimization - **O** states that the opening tag is required but the closing tag is not.

- In the element type definition, the content model **EMPTY** states that the element contains no content. Combined with the tag minimization - **O**, this also means that the closing tag is forbidden, not optional.

- The first line of the attribute declaration states that the element **LINK** has the attributes represented by the parameter entity **attrs**. The embedded comment -- **%coreattrs, %i18n, %events** -- lists the three parameter entities contained in the entity **attrs**.

- Subsequent lines of the attribute declaration name other attributes for **LINK**, such as **charset**.

- Attribute names are followed by parameter entities, such as **%Charset**, which define the content allowed in attribute values.

- The SGML keyword **#IMPLIED** states that the associated attribute is optional.

- Embedded comments explain the purpose of the individual attributes.

Content Exclusion Example

```
<!ELEMENT FORM - - (%block; | SCRIPT)+ -(FORM)
-- interactive form -->
```

- In the element type declaration, the generic identifier **FORM** defines the element name.

- The tag minimization - - states that both opening and closing tags are required for this element.

- The content model states that this element may contain block-level elements as defined by the parameter entity **%block** or the element **SCRIPT**, but not both.

- The occurrence indicator **+** that follows the content model states that whichever element is used within the **FORM** element *must* be used one or more times.

- The content exclusion **–(FORM)** states that the **FORM** element may not be repeated within itself.

Content Inclusion Example

```
<!-- %head.misc; defined earlier as "SCRIPT | STYLE | META|
                                      | LINK | OBJECT"-->

<!ENTITY %head.content "TITLE & BASE?">
<!ELEMENT HEAD O O (%head.content;) +(%head.misc;)
-- document head -->
```

- The comment refers to a definition of the parameter entity **%head.misc**, which appeared earlier in the DTD.

- The parameter entity definition for **%head.content** states that both the **TITLE** and **BASE** elements can be used in this context (the **&** means "and") but are optional (the **?** means elements may occur zero or one time).

- In the element type declaration, the generic identifier **HEAD** defines the element name.

- The tag minimization **O O** states that both the opening and closing tags are optional; the **HEAD** element is implied for all HTML documents.

- The content model **(%head.content;)** states that the elements associated with the entity **head.content** may be used inside this element.

- The content inclusion **+(%head.misc;)** states that the elements associated with the entity **head.misc** can occur anywhere within the **HEAD** element.

Appendix A
URL Primer

URLs may be the least understood aspect of the Web. Many accomplished HTML coders have only a vague grasp of how URLs work, and primarily understand how to create HTTP or relative forms. URLs have a much larger role in the Internet; a more complete understanding can help with linking and site development.

What Is a URL?

A *uniform resource locator (URL)* is a standard way to refer to objects on the Internet. (A URL is sometimes called a *universal resource locator*, but that is incorrect.) Even novice users should be familiar with typing a URL, such as http://www.yahoo.com/, in a browser dialog in order to get to a Web site. URLs may also be used to transfer files via FTP or to send electronic mail. HTML authors use URLs in their documents to define hyperlinks to other Web documents.

Despite its potentially confusing collection of slashes and colons, the URL syntax was designed to provide a clear, simple notation that people can easily understand. The designers intended URLs to be useful information that could be included in books, business cards, and magazine advertisements, not just received and linked to via computers. The following is a discussion of the components that make up a URL address.

URL Components

Before you can locate an object on the Internet, you need to locate and access the machine on the Internet (or intranet) where that object resides. Locating the site might be a matter of specifying its domain name or IP address. Accessing the machine might involve providing a user name and password. Once there, where is the file located on that machine? This is generally indicated by the name of the appropriate directory. What is the name of the file, and how will the file be retrieved? What protocol will be used to fetch the information or access the object? A properly formed URL answers these questions by describing where something is and how it will be retrieved. The "how" is specified by the protocol. The "where" is specified by a machine name, directory name, and filename. Slashes and other characters are used to separate the parts of the address into machine-parseable pieces. The basic structure of the URL is shown here:

protocol://site address/directory/filename

Taking a look at the individual pieces of a URL shows that there is significant detail to consider.

Site Address

Any Web document exists on a server computer somewhere on the global Internet or within a private intranet. The first step in finding a document is to identify its server. The most convenient way to do this on a TCP/IP-based network is with a symbolic name, called a *domain name*. On the Internet at large, a fully qualified domain name typically consists of a machine name followed by a domain name. For example, www.microsoft.com specifies a machine named *www* in the microsoft.com domain. Although www is the most common machine name used for Web servers, this is only a convention, not a rule. Local machines can have names like the user's own name (jsmith, bdobbs), that of a favorite cartoon character (like Daffy or Cartman), or even an esoteric machine name (dell-p6-200-a12).

Machine naming conventions are important because they allow users to form URLs without explicitly spelling them out. A user who understands domain names and machine naming conventions should be able to guess that Toyota's Web server is located at http://www.toyota.com/.

The other part of most site addresses, the domain name, is fairly regular. Within the United States, a domain name consists of the actual domain or organization name followed by a period and then a domain type. An example would be sun.com. The domain itself is "sun," which represents Sun Microsystems. The "sun" domain exists within the commercial zone because of Sun's corporate status, so it ends with the domain type of com. In the United States, most domain identifiers currently use a three-character code that indicates the type of organization that owns the server. Common codes include *com* for commercial, *gov* for government, *org* for nonprofit organization, and *edu* for educational institutions. Other common codes are *net* for network, *mil* for military, and *us*, which is used for a variety of organizations and individuals including K–12 education, libraries, and city and county governments.

Domain space beyond the United States is somewhat more complicated. A fully qualified domain name, including a country code, is generally written as follows:

machine name . domain name . domain type . country code

Zone identifiers outside the United States use a two-character code to indicate the country hosting the server. These include *ca* for Canada, *mx* for Mexico, and *jp* for Japan. Within each country, the local naming authorities may create domain types at their own discretion. These may not correspond to American extensions. For example, www.sony.co.jp specifies a Web server for Sony in the *co* zone of Japan. In this case, *co*, rather than *com*, indicates a *commercial* venture. In the United Kingdom, educational domain space has a different name, *ac*. Oxford University's Web server is www.ox.ac.uk, where *ac* indicates *academic*, rather than the U.S. *edu* extension, for *education*. Despite a flattening of geographical name use for large multinational companies like Sony, regional naming differences are very much alive. Web page authors linking to non-native domains are encouraged to understand the naming conventions of those environments. One special top-level domain, *int*, is reserved for organizations established by *international* treaties between governments, such as the European Union (eu.int) and NATO (nato.int). Top-level domains like *com* and *net* should be considered similar to int in that they do not necessarily correspond to a particular geographic area.

While symbolic names make it convenient for people to refer to Internet servers, a server's real address is its Internet Protocol (IP) numeric address. Every accessible server on the Internet has a unique IP address by which it can be located using the TCP/IP protocol. An IP address is a numeric string made up of four numbers between 0 and 255 separated by periods (for example, 213.6.17.34). A server's symbolic name must be translated or resolved into an IP address before it can be used to locate a server. An Internet service known as Domain Name System (DNS) automatically performs this translation. You can use an IP address instead of a symbolic name to specify an Internet server, although doing this gives up mnemonic convenience. In some cases, it may be necessary, because while every server has an IP address, not all have symbolic names.

Domain names are not case sensitive. So, for example, the address for Big Company could be written as www.BigCompany.com or www.BIGCOMPANY.com. A browser should handle both properly. Case is typically changed for marketing or branding purposes. Directory values following the domain name may be case sensitive, depending on the operating system the Web server is running on. For example, UNIX systems are case sensitive, while Windows machines are not. Trouble can arise if casing is used randomly. As a rule of thumb, keep everything in lowercase, or consistently just capitalize the first letters of directories or filenames.

Once the machine has been specified, either by its domain name or its IP address, it may be necessary to specify the particular directory on the machine in question.

A

Directory

Servers may contain thousands of files. Files need to be organized into manageable units analogous to the manila folders traditionally used to organize paper documents. This unit is known as a directory. Once you know what server a document resides on, the next step toward identifying its location is to specify the directory that contains the file. Just as one manila folder can contain other folders, directories can contain other directories.

Directories contain other directories in a nested, hierarchical structure that resembles the branches of a tree. The directory that contains all others is known as the *root directory*. Taken together, all the directories and files form a file tree, or *file system*. A file is located in a file system by specifying its *directory path*. This is the nested list of all directories that contain the file, from the most general, the root directory, to the most specific. Names of directories hosted on Web servers are separated by forward slashes (/), as is done on the UNIX operating system, rather than

backslashes (\), as in DOS. The following illustration shows a
sample file tree for a Web site:

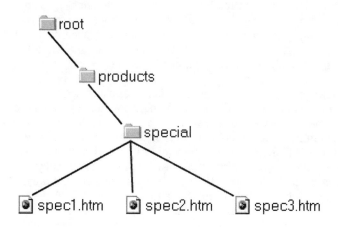

This tree shows how directories are organized within (or above
and below) one another. For example, the directory called "special"
is within the "products" directory, which is within the "root"
directory. The full path should be written as "/products/special/" to
indicate that "special" is an actual directory, not a file in the
"products" directory. When linking to other files, it may be
necessary to refer to a directory above the current directory or the
current directory itself. In the scheme presented, ./ means the
current directory while ../ means one directory up in the hierarchy.
A document in the "special" directory with a link path of ../ will link
up to the "products" directory.

Directory names may follow conventions specific to an operating
system, including being case sensitive. Authors are cautioned to
take a careful look at directory casing. Furthermore, directories may
follow popular usage conventions (for example, "tmp" for a
temporary directory), or they may be arbitrary. Usually they reflect
aspects of media types, subject matter, or access privileges of their
content. For example, a directory called "images" might be used for
a directory containing images.

Filename

Having specified the server and directory path for a document, the next step toward locating it is to specify its filename. This step typically has two parts: a filename followed by a standard file extension. Filenames can be any name that is applicable under the server's operating system. Special characters like spaces, colons, and slashes might play havoc if used in names of Web-available files. A file named test:1.htm would present problems on a Macintosh system, while test/1.htm might be legal on a Macintosh and problematic on a PC or UNIX machine. A dot separates the filename and the extension, which is a code, usually three letters, that identifies the type of information contained in the file. For example, HTML source files have an .htm or .html extension. JPEG images have a .jpg extension. A file's extension is critically important for Web applications because it is usually the only indication of the information type a file contains. A Web server reads a file extension and uses it to determine what headers to attach to a file when delivering it to a browser. If file extensions are omitted or misused, the file may be interpreted incorrectly. When browsers read files directly from disk, they also look at file extensions to determine how to render the file. If the extension is missing or incorrect, a file will not be properly displayed in a Web browser.

While many operating systems support four or more letters for file extensions, using a three-letter extension (.htm) versus a four-letter extension (.html) ensures that cross-platform incompatibilities are minimized. Spaces, uppercase characters, and special characters should also be avoided to provide the greatest flexibility. Authors and users should particularly be aware of case sensitivity in filenames and directory names.

Protocol

Now that a document's server, directory, and filename have been determined, one element remains to be filled in: the protocol. The Internet supports a standard set of resources, each with its own associated protocol. A *protocol* is a structured discussion that computers follow to negotiate resource-specific services. The protocol that makes the Web possible is the Hypertext Transfer Protocol (HTTP). When you click on a hyperlink in a Web document, your browser uses the HTTP protocol to contact a Web server and retrieve the appropriate document. HTTP does not specify how a file is transported from a server to a browser, only how the discussion between the server and browser will take place. The actual transport of files is usually up to a lower-layer network protocol like the Transmission Control Protocol (TCP). This subtle transport misconception is common in the case of the protocol aspect of a URL.

While less frequently used, other protocols are important to HTML authors because they can be invoked by hyperlinks. Here are some examples:

Protocol	Description
file	Enables a hyperlink to access a file on the local file system
File Transfer Protocol (FTP)	Enables a hyperlink to download files from remote systems
Gopher	Enables a hyperlink to access a Gopher server
mailto	Calls SMTP (Simple Mail Transport Protocol), the Internet mail protocol, and enables a hyperlink to send an addressed e-mail message
Network News Transport Protocol (NNTP)	Enables a hyperlink to access a USENET news article
news	Enables a hyperlink to access a USENET newsgroup
telnet	Enables a hyperlink to open a telnet session on a remote host

Beyond the protocol, server address, directory, and filename, URLs often include a user name and password, port number, and sometimes a fragment identifier. Some URLs, such as mailto URLs, might even contain a different form of information altogether—perhaps an e-mail address rather than a server or filename.

User Name and Password

FTP and telnet are protocols for *authenticated services.* Authenticated services may assume access by authorized users, and the protocols may require a user name and password as parameters. A user name and password precedes a server name and looks like this: *username:password@server-address.* The password may be optional or unspecified in the URL, making the form simply *username@server-address.* HTML authors should not include password information in URLs, because the information will be readily viewable in a Web page or within the browser's URL box.

Port Number

While uncommon, it is possible to specify the communication port in a URL. Browsers speaking a particular protocol communicate with servers through entry points, known as *ports*, that are generally identified by numeric addresses. Associated with each protocol is a default port number. For example, an HTTP request defaults to port number 80. A server administrator can configure a server to handle protocol requests at ports other than the default numbers. Usually this occurs for experimental or secure applications. In these cases, the intended port must be explicitly addressed in a URL. To specify a port number, place it after the server address, separated by a colon (for example, site-address:90).

Web administrators are forewarned not to arbitrarily change port numbers. This will confuse users and may result in people having difficulty accessing a site, particularly if access comes from behind a firewall (a security feature) via a proxy server. Such systems may not be set up to allow traffic on nonstandard port numbers.

Fragment Identifier

Another area to discuss is the fragment identifier. After a file has been specified, a user may desire to go directly to a particular point in the file. Because it is possible to set up named links under HTML, there must be a way to link directly to that point. To jump to a particular named link, the URL must include the link name preceded by the pound symbol (#), indicating that the value is a fragment identifier. To specify a point called *contents* in a file called test.htm, use test.htm#contents.

Character Encoding

The components of a URL should be written using only the displayable characters in the US-ASCII character set. Even when using characters within this basic keyboard character range, you will find certain unsafe characters or reserved characters that may have special meaning within the context of a URL or the operating system the resource is found on. If any unsafe, reserved, or nonprintable characters occur in a URL, they must be encoded in a special form. Failure to encode these characters may lead to errors.

The form of encoding consists of a percent sign and two hexadecimal digits corresponding to the value of the character in the ASCII character set. Within many intranet environments, filenames often include user-friendly names like "first quarter earnings 1997.doc." Such names contain unsafe characters. If this file were to live on a departmental Web server, it would have a URL with a file portion of "first%20quarter%20earnings%201997.doc." Notice how the spaces have been mapped to **%20** values—the hex value of the space character in ASCII.

Other characters that are troublesome in URLs include the slash character (/), which encodes as **%2F**; the question mark, which encodes as **%3F**; and the percent sign itself, which encodes as **%25**. Only alphanumeric values and some special characters ($, -, _, ., +, !, *, '), including parentheses, may be used in a URL. Other characters should be encoded. In general, special characters such as accents, spaces, and some punctuation marks have to be encoded. HTML authors are encouraged to name files with encoding in mind so that encoding can be avoided whenever possible. The following table shows the reserved and potentially dangerous characters for URLs:

Character	Encoding
Space	%20
/	%2F
?	%3F
:	%3A
;	%3B
&	%26
@	%40
=	%3D
#	%23
%	%25
>	%3E
<	%3C
{	%7B
}	%7D

Character	Encoding
[	%5B
]	%5D
"	%22
'	%27
`	%60
^	%5E
~	%7E
\	%5C
|	%7C

URL Formulas

All URLs share the same basic syntax: a protocol name, followed by a colon, followed by a protocol-specific resource description:

```
<protocol_name>:<resource_description>
```

Beyond this, enough variation exists between protocol specifics for each to merit a separate discussion.

HTTP URLs

A minimal HTTP URL simply gives a server name. It provides no directory or file information. A minimal HTTP formula commonly occurs for corporate addresses used in advertising.

```
Formula: http://<server>/
Example: http://www.company.com/
```

A minimal HTTP URL implicitly requests the home directory of a Web site. Even when a trailing slash is not used, it is assumed and added either by the user agent or the Web server, so that a URL such as http://www.company.com is reformulated as http://www.company.com/. By default, requesting a directory often results in the server returning a default file from the directory, termed the *index file*. Usually index files are named index.htm or default.htm (or index.html or default.html), depending on the server software being used. This is only convention; Web administrators are free to name default index files whatever they like.

It is interesting to note that many people put special importance on the minimal HTTP URL form, when, like all other file-retrieval URLs, this form simply specifies a particular directory or default index file to return, though this is not always explicitly written out.

Making the HTTP URL example slightly more complex, a formula is presented to retrieve a specific html file assumed to exist in the default directory for the server.

```
Formula: http://<server>/<file>
Example: http://www.company.com/hello.htm
```

An alternative incremental extension adds directory information without specifying a file. While the final slash should be provided, servers will imply its existence if it is omitted and look for an index document in the given directory. In practice, the final slash is optional, but recommended.

```
Formula: http://<server>/<directory>/
Example: http://www.company.com/products/
```

An HTTP URL can specify both a directory and file.

A

```
Formula: http://<server>/<directory>/<file>
Example: http://www.company.com/products/greeting.htm
```

On some systems, there may be special shorthand conventions for directory use. For example, a UNIX-based Web server may support many directories, each owned by a specific user. Rather than spelling out the full path to a user's root directory, the user directory can be abbreviated by using the tilde character (~), followed by the user's account, followed by a slash. Any directory or file information that follows this point is relative to the user's root directory.

```
Formula: http://<server>/~<user>/
Example: http://www.company.com/~jsmith/
```

User directories indicated by the tilde are somewhat similar to the convention used on the UNIX operating system, though other Web servers on different operating systems may provide similar shortcut support.

A URL can refer to a named location inside an HTML document. This can be called a *marker*, or *named link*. How markers are created will be discussed later in the chapter; but for now, to refer

to a document marker, follow the target document's filename with
the pound character (#), then with the marker name.

```
Formula: http://<server>/<directory>/<file>#marker
Example: http://www.company.com/profile.htm#introduction
```

In addition to referring to HTML documents, an HTTP URL can
request any type of file. For example, http://www.company.com/
images/logo.gif would retrieve a GIF image from a server rather
than an HTML file. Authors should be aware that the flexibility of
Web servers and URLs is often overlooked because of the common
belief that all Web-based documents must be in the HTML format
in order to be linked to.

An HTTP URL can even reference and execute a server program.
These server-side programs are typically termed CGI (Common
Gateway Interface) programs, after the interface standard that
describes how to pass data in and out of a program. Quite often,
server-side programs are used to access databases and then
generate HTML documents in response to user-entered queries.
Parameters for such programs can be directly included in a URL by
appending a question mark followed by the actual parameter
string. Because the user may type special characters in a query,
characters normally not allowed within a URL are encoded.
Remember that the formula for special-character encoding is a
percent sign followed by two hex numbers representing the
character's ASCII value. For example, a blank character can be
represented by **%20**.

```
Formula: http://<server>/<directory>/<file>?<parameters>
Example: http://www.company.com/products/
                search.cgi?cost=400.00
```

Forming complex URLs with encoding and query strings seems
very difficult. In reality, this is rarely done manually. Typically, the
browser generates such a string on the fly, based on data provided
via a file form.

Finally, any HTTP request can be directed to a port other than the
default port value of 80 by following the server identification with a
colon and the intended port number.

```
Formula: http://<server>:<port>/<directory>/<file>
Example: http://www.bigcompany.com:8080/products/
                greetings.htm
```

In the preceding example, the URL references a Web server running on port 8080. While any unreserved port number is valid, using nonstandard port numbers on servers is not good practice. To access the address in the example, a user would need to include the port number in the URL. If it is omitted, it will be impossible to access www.bigcompany.com.

There is one case of HTTP that is, in a sense, a different protocol: secured Web transactions using the Secure Sockets Layer (SSL). In this case the protocol is referenced as https, and the port value is assumed to be 443. An example formula for Secure HTTP is shown here; other than the cosmetic difference of the "s" and the different port value, it is identical to other HTTP URLs.

```
Formula: https://server:<port>/<directory>/<file>
Example: https://www.wellsfargo.com/
```

An HTTP URL for a Web page is probably the most common URL, but users may find file or similar types of URLs growing in popularity due to the rise of intranets and serverless-style access.

file URLs

The file protocol specifies a file residing somewhere on a computer or locally accessible computer network. It does not specify an access protocol and has limited value except for one important case. It allows a browser to access files residing on a user's local computer, an important capability for Web page development. In this usage, the server name is omitted or replaced by the keyword **localhost**. Following this is the local directory and file specification. (The third slash is added when referencing a local drive.)

```
Formula: file://<server>/<directory>/<file>
Example: file:///dev/web/testpage.html
```

In some environments, the actual drive name and path to the file is specified. On a Macintosh, a URL might be file:///Macintosh%20HD/ Desktop%20Folder/Bookmarks.html. On a PC, there may be a file URL, such as file://\\pc1\C\Netlog.txt, to access a file on the C drive of a PC on the local network pc1. Depending on browser complexity, file URLs might not be required, as with Internet Explorer 4, where the operating system is tightly coupled with the user agent. It is interesting to note that in the case of intranets, many drives may be mapped or file systems mounted so that no server is required to deliver files. In this "Web serverless" environment, it may be possible to access network drives with a file URL. This idea demonstrates how simple a Web server is. In fact, to some people, a Web server is merely a very inefficient, though open, file server. This realization of file transfer leads us immediately to the idea of the FTP URL.

FTP URLs

The File Transfer Protocol (FTP), which predates the browser-oriented HTTP protocol, transfers files from a server. It is generally not geared toward transferring files to be immediately viewed, but rather to be locally stored. However, a browser may allow such files to be viewed immediately. Today, FTP is most commonly used to download large files, such as complete applications, because of its efficiency. These URLs share with HTTP the formula for indicating a server, port, directory, and file.

Formula: `ftp://<server>:<port>/<directory>/<file>`

A minimal FTP URL specifies a server and then lists the directory: ftp://ftp.company.com. Generally, however, ftp URLs are used to access a particular file in an archive by name and directory, as shown in this formula:

Formula: `ftp://<server>/<directory path>/<file>`
Example: `ftp://ftp.company.com/info/somefile.exe`

The File Transfer Protocol is an authenticated protocol. Every valid FTP request requires a defined user account on the server that is downloading files. In practice, many FTP resources are intended for general access, and it would be impractical to define a unique account for every potential user. An FTP convention known as *anonymous FTP* handles this common situation. The user name "anonymous" or "ftp" allows general access to any public FTP resource supported by a server. As in the previous example, the anonymous user account is implicit in any FTP URL that does not explicitly provide account information.

An FTP URL can specify the name and password for a user account. If included, they precede the server declaration according to the following formula. It is not wise to mention an account password in a public document such as an HTML file. If you omit the password, generally the user agent prompts you to enter one if a password is required.

Formula: `ftp://<user>:<password>@<server>/<directory>/`
          `<file>`
Example: `ftp://jsmith:harmony@ftp.company.com/`
          `products/list`

This formula shows the password embedded within the URL, a dangerous proposition because it is transmitted in plain text and viewable both in the HTML source and browser address bar. Only public passwords should be embedded in any URL for an authenticated service. It is more appropriate to provide a link to the service and require the user name and password to be entered, or to just provide the user ID and have the user agent prompt for the password, as would happen in the next example.

Formula: `ftp://<user>@<server>/<directory>/<file>`
Example: `ftp://jsmith@ftp.company.com/products/sales`

The FTP protocol assumes that a downloaded file contains binary information. You can override this default assumption by appending a type code to an FTP URL. There are three common values: *a*, *i*, and *d*. An *a* code indicates the file is an ASCII text file. The *i* code, which is also the default, indicates the file is an image/binary file. A *d* code causes the URL to return a directory listing of the specified path, instead of a file. An example formula is presented here for completeness.

Formula: `ftp://<server>/<directory>/<file>;type=<code>`
Example: `ftp://ftp.company.com/products;type=d`

In reality, the type codes are rarely encountered, because the binary transfer format generally does not harm text files and the user agent is usually smart enough to handle FTP URLs without type codes. Like many other URLs, the port accessed can be changed to something besides the default port of 21, but this is not recommended.

Gopher URLs

The Gopher system, the first popular document-based technology on the Internet, arose in the early 1990s as a client/server architecture appropriate for campus information systems. It provided a way to hierarchically organize and navigate documents. Gopher servers continue to exist today, but with much of their original purpose overshadowed by the more popular HTML-based Web content. For backward compatibility, you may find it important to link via a Web page to Gopher-based information using a Gopher URL.

A Gopher URL follows the same formula used by other protocols to specify a server and optional port address. However, compared to HTTP or FTP, Gopher URLs differ in the way they specify resources on a server. This specification begins with a single-digit code indicating the resource type referred to. The default code is 1, which indicates a directory list.

Code	Resource Type
0	Text file
1	Directory listing
2	CSO phone book server
3	Error
4	Macintosh binhex file
5	DOS binary file
6	UNIX-uuencoded file
7	Full-text index search
8	telnet session
9	Binary file

Following the code for the resource type is a selector string, which corresponds to a directory and file specification found in other URL formulas. If the resource type supports an appended query, a tab character with an ASCII value of **%09** separates the selector string from the query string.

Formula: gopher://**<server>:<port>/<type><selector>**%09**<query>**
         %09**<gopher+>**

Example: gopher://gopher.company.com/4mac/somefile.hqx

Because of the encoding and the use of the file type numbers, a Gopher URL can look extremely complex. In the preceding example, the 4 indicated a Macintosh binhex file. Normally, users will see 00 or 0 for files and 1 or 11 for directories. The numbers are often repeated because some gopher strings begin with a copy of the content type.

Beyond the file types and encoded characters, Gopher is very similar to other file retrieval URLs. Gopher may also include electronic forms for searching that, like HTTP, add a query string after a question mark. For example,

gopher://mudhoney.micro.umn.edu:4326/7?Mexico

Notice the use of the 7 code to indicate that the type of data is a full-text index search. Also notice in this example that, like many other protocols, Gopher may run on another port than its standard port of 70. This may be specified in the URL. As noted above, this is not recommended.

mailto URLs

Atypically, this protocol does not locate and retrieve an Internet resource. Instead, it opens a window for editing and sending a mail message to a particular user address.

```
Formula: mailto:<user>@<server>
Example: mailto:president@whitehouse.gov
```

This rather simple formula shows standard Internet mail addressing; other more complex addresses may be just as valid. Using mailto URLs is very popular in Web sites for providing a basic feedback mechanism. Note that if a user agent has not been set up properly to send e-mail, this type of URL may produce error messages when used in a link, prompting the user to set up mailing preferences.

A

news URLs

A news URL invokes a news browser that allows access to USENET newsgroups. It can take one of two alternative approaches, each with limitations. In the first approach, a news URL requests a named newsgroup. Like the mailto URL, in this form the URL does not specify which news server to use in order to fulfill the request. A default news server address is usually set as a Web browser preference. Unfortunately, all news servers may not carry the same groups. News archives are large, and tend to be distributed across multiple servers. If the requested news group does not exist on the default news server, it will not be found.

In the second approach, a news URL requests a message on a particular news server using a server-specific message identifier, such as 13c65a7a. Because messages generally have an expiration date, this approach has limited value. In addition, the message identifier obviously varies from server to server, so it is not easily transferable.

```
Formula: news:<newsgroup>
Example: news:microsoft.public
```

```
Formula:  news:<message>@<server>
Example:  news:13c65a7a@news.company.com
```

Both the second form of the news URL and the NNTP URL (to be
discussed next) show the limitations of URLs when dealing with
time-sensitive information. There is no good way to deal with data
that changes as rapidly as USENET news. News URLs are
generally used simply to access a group, rather than a
particular message.

NNTP URLs

The Network News Transport Protocol (NNTP) allows the retrieval
of individual USENET articles qualified by server, newsgroup, and
article number. Like many protocols, an optional port value can be
specified to direct a user agent to a specific server port. The NNTP
URL has a limitation in that a particular article number is
referenced. Article numbers vary from server to server, so this URL
is not transportable. Furthermore, articles generally expire rather
quickly, so fully specified NNTP URLs are of somewhat limited
value.

```
Formula:  nntp://<server>:<port>/<newsgroup>/
                 <article-number>
Example:  nntp://news.company.com/microsoft.public/118
```

The default port value of nntp is 119, but another port value may be
set in the URL. A special version of NNTP that adds security runs
on port 563. The form of the URL is nntps://secnews.company.com/
microsoft.public/118.

In general, the news protocol appears to be used on the Web more
commonly than the NNTP protocol.

telnet URLs

The telnet protocol allows a user to open an interactive terminal
session on a remote host computer. A minimal telnet URL simply
gives the remote system's name. Once a connection is made, the
system prompts for an account name and password.

```
Formula:  telnet://<server>
Example:  telnet://company.com
```

As an authenticated protocol, telnet generally requires a defined
user account on the remote system. When this is unspecified, the

user agent or helper application handling telnet will prompt for such information. Like FTP, a telnet URL can also contain an account name and password as parameters. As with FTP URLs, be careful about including passwords in public access documents like HTML files on the Web. The password is optional in the formula.

```
Formula: telnet://<user>:<password>@<server>
Example: telnet://jsmith:harmony@company.com
Example: telnet://jsmith@company.com
```

Finally, any telnet URL can direct a request to a specific port by appending the port address to the server name.

```
Formula: telnet://<server>:<port>
Example: telnet://company.com:94
```

Some telnet information sources may be configured to run on a particular port besides port 23, the standard telnet port. Consequently, use of the port within a telnet URL is more common than in other URLs.

Other URL Forms

There are a wide variety of other protocols that can be used. However, a browser may not support many of these URL forms. Some protocols, like the WAIS protocol, have historical interest. There is little evidence that people actually use this protocol much on the Web, despite its presence in books only one or two years old. Beyond old protocols like WAIS, there are operating-system-based protocols like finger, and esoteric protocols for things like VEMMI video text services. New protocols are being added all the time. In fact, there are dozens of proposed or even implemented protocols that can be referenced with some form of nonstandard URL. If you are interested in other URL forms, visit http://www.w3.org/pub/WWW/Addressing/schemes or http://www.ics.uci.edu/pub/ietf/uri/ for more information.

Relative URLs

Until now, the discussion has focused on a specific form of URL, typically termed an *absolute URL*. Absolute URLs completely spell out the protocol, host, directory, and filename. Providing such detail can be tedious and unnecessary, though, and this is where a shortened form of a URL, called a *relative URL*, comes in. With relative URLs, the various parts of the address—the site, directory, and protocol—can be inferred by the URL of the current document, or via the **<BASE>** element. The best way to illustrate the idea of relative URLs is by example.

If a Web site has an address of www.bigcompany.com, a user may access the home page with a URL like http://www.bigcompany.com/. A link to this page from an outside system would also contain the address http://www.bigcompany.com/. Once at the site, however, there is no reason to continue spelling out the full address of the site. A fully qualified link from the home page to a staff page in the root directory called staff.html would be http://www.bigcompany.com/staff.html. Starting from the home page, though, the protocol, address, and directory name can be inferred, so all that is needed is the address staff.html. This relative scheme works because http://www.bigcompany.com/ is inferred as the base of all future links, thus allowing for the shorthand relative notation. The relative notation can be used with filenames and directories, as shown in the examples in the following table:

Current Page Address	Destination Address	Relative URL
http://www.bigcompany.com/index.htm	http://www.bigcompany.com/staff.htm	staff.htm
http://www.bigcompany.com/index.htm	http://www.bigcompany.com/products/gadget1.htm	products/gadget1.htm
http://www.bigcompany.com/products/gadget1.htm	http://www.bigcompany.com/index.htm	../index.htm

When relative URLs are used within a Web site, the site becomes transportable. By not spelling out the server name in every link, you can develop a Web site on one server and move it to another. If you used absolute URLs, all links would have to be changed if a server changed names or if the files were moved to another site. Of course, there is a potential downside to relative URLs: they can become confusing in a large site, particularly if there are centralized directories for items such as images. Imagine having URLs like ../../../images/logo.gif in files deep in a site structure. Some users might be tempted to simply copy files to avoid this problem, but then there are issues of updating and caching. One solution is to use the <**BASE**> element. Another would be to use symbolic links on the Web server to reference one copy of the file from multiple locations. However, because HTML is the subject here, let's focus on the former solution.

The <**BASE**> element defines the base for all relative URLs within a document. Setting the **HREF** attribute of this element to a fully qualified URL allows all other relative references to use the defined base. For example, <**BASE HREF="http://www.bigcompany.com/"**> sets all the following anchors that are not fully qualified to prefix http://www.bigcompany.com/ to the destination URL. The <**BASE**> element may occur only once in a document. It is only allowed within the head of an HTML document, so it is impossible to create sections of a document with different base URL values. It is possible to imagine that such a feature might be added to the <**DIV**> element or similar sectioning element, but until then, HTML authors will have to deal with shorthand notation being useful in some places and not in others.

URLS and Beyond

A

In order to link documents together on the Web, a consistent naming scheme must be in place. URLs provide the basic information necessary to locate an object on the Internet by including the host name, directory, filename, and access protocol. URLs are written in a regular format, so it is possible to write an address for any object we might encounter. A common shorthand notation, the relative URL (discussed in the preceding section), is particularly useful when creating links within a Web site. If a document's URL can be determined, whether it is relative or fully spelled out, it can be specified in the <**A**> tag to create an anchor from one document to another. Links within HTML documents can be made with text or with images. A special type of clickable image, called an *image map,* allows an area of an image to be defined as "hot," and different hot sections can be linked to different URLs.

Simply linking documents together is the most basic form of hypertext. It is also possible to add meaning to hypertext links using the <**LINK**> element, as well as the **REL** and **REV** attributes of the anchor tag. Once documents are linked together, providing extra information about the document can be very useful. HTML provides such a facility through the use of the <**META**> tag. But even if Web authors master all aspects of linking, there is a bigger picture to worry about. The Web is a chaotic and changing environment. Navigating among documents and linking documents presents serious challenges to the HTML author. In the future, some of these problems may be solved by URNs (universal resource names), URCs (universal resource characteristics), and improved URLs, which, taken together, make up the uniform resource identifier (URI). *HTML: The Complete Reference*, by Thomas Powell (Osborne/McGraw-Hill, 1998), has a more detailed discussion of these Web addressing forms. Interested readers should also visit the World Wide Web Consortium's Web page on this topic (http://www.w3.org/Addressing).

Appendix B
Useful Links

The number of sites with useful information about HTML and Web development could fill a small book. Here is a short list of 25 links that may prove useful to HTML writers. Many valuable links could be added to this list, but our purpose here is simply to give you a springboard in your online hunt for HTML and Web development information.

World Wide Web Consortium

Home page	http://www.w3.org/
HTML reference	http://www.w3.org/MarkUp/
Style sheets	http://www.w3.org/Style/
Document Object Model	http://www.w3.org/DOM/
Internationalization issues	http://www.w3.org/International/
Web Accessibility Initiative	http://www.w3.org/WAI/
W3C mailing lists	http://www.w3.org/Mail/Lists.html

Microsoft

General Web developer information	http://www.microsoft.com/sitebuilder/
Document authoring information for HTML and DHTML	http://www.microsoft.com/workshop/author/
Style sheet information for Internet Explorer	http://www.microsoft.com/workshop/author/css/css-ie4-f.htm
Internet Explorer Software Development Kit	http://www.microsoft.com/msdn/sdk/inetsdk/
Microsoft typography information including Web typography	http://www.microsoft.com/typography/

B

377

Netscape

General developer information	http://developer.netscape.com
Netscape HTML documentation	http://developer.netscape.com/docs/manuals/dynhtml.html
Netscape HTML tag reference	http://developer.netscape.com/docs/manuals/htmlguid/index.htm

WebTV

General developer information	http://www.webtv.net/primetime/

HTML Validation Services

W3C HTML validation service	http://validator.w3.org/
Web Techs validation service	http://valsvc.webtechs.com/
WebLint	http://www.cre.canon.co.uk/~neilb/weblint/

Other Online HTML and Web Design Resources

HTML: The Complete Reference	http://www.htmlref.com/
HTML Writers Guild	http://www.hwg.org/

WebReference	http://www.webreference.com/
Web Developer's Virtual Library	http://www.stars.com
Builder.com	http://www.builder.com
WebMonkey	http://www.webmonkey.com
Web Review	http://www.webreview.com

B

NOTE: Page numbers in *italics* refer to illustrations or charts.